HURON COUNTY LIBRARY

O9-BRZ-480

3 6492 00416587 1

HURON COUNTY LIBR

Floating the Borders

NEW CONTEXTS IN CANADIAN CRITICISM

edited by

Nurjehan Aziz

TSAR
Toronto

AUG 1 4 2000

HURON COUNTY LIBRARY

We acknowledge the support of the Canada Council for the Arts for our publishing program. We also acknowledge support from the Ontario Arts Council.

© 1999 The Authors

Except for purposes of review, no part of this book may be reproduced in any form without prior permission of the publisher.

Cover art: *Autumn on Lake Erie* (1992), 27" x 27", Chinese ink and watercolour, by Peng Ma.

Canadian Cataloguing in Publication Data

Floating the borders: new contexts in Canadian criticism

Includes bibliographical references and index.
ISBN 0-920661-80-7

1. Canadian literature (English) - Minority authors - History and criticism.*
2. Canadian literature (English) - 20th century - History and criticism.
I. Aziz, Nurjehan

PS8089.5.M55F54 1999   C810.9'8'00904   C99-932829-8
PR9188.2.M55F54 1999

Printed in Canada by Coach House Printing.

TSAR Publications
P. O. Box 6996, Station A
Toronto, Ontario M5W 1X7
Canada

Contents

II. First Engagements (Book Reviews, 1981–1999)

Foreword

What is Canadian Literature? Indeed, what constitutes a Canadian identity? In the past, when it was simpler to do so, several attempts were made to provide an overarching sensibility to define these concepts. One notable attempt was Margaret Atwood's *Survival*. I recall how thrilled I was by its bold comprehensiveness, its panache; and yet it did not take much more thought, beyond this initial reaction, to realize that *Survival*'s formulation seemed to apply to others, not to me or to any group of people I knew intimately. I could not envision myself, or any children I brought up, or anyone I knew who had emigrated from the same place as I did, as having a sensibility or psyche described overwhelmingly by the anxiety of survival. Immigration involves, besides hardships and obstacles, a positive energy, a regenerative and creative outlook. Much has changed in the country since Atwood's formulation, though there are ideologues still, out of that old anxiety of being swallowed up or determined by America or by the new fear of that other perceived monster (actually a bogey-man) "multiculturalism," who yearn for a core Canadian identity, some immutable stuff to display proudly to the world. The problem is, what constitutes that core; and in a demographically changing society doesn't its definition end up being exclusionary and divisive, potentially destructive, and ultimately redundant? I believe that if such an essence exists, or were gradually to develop, it is or will be more subtle than being comprised of a mere response to nature, making a fetish out of low temperatures, or turning away and looking north out of a mule-headed defiance of the south.

Every year between two and three hundred thousand immigrants arrive in this country, which depends on such influxes to stay healthy in a number of ways. No longer do a majority of these newcomers come from Great Britain or Europe. The Bible is not their Great Code, the Mahabharata or the Arabian Nights or the Hadith or the Monkey King inspire them more than Homer, and if they are Westernized it is often through the medium of America. For many immigrants the environment is the bustling city, and the "community" to which they belong; religion and race are immutable factors that make up their identities; their cultural and historical roots lie not in Europe but elsewhere. Can an overarching sensibility embrace these diversities, and in what way?

Temples and mosques are a fact of life; it is not enough, it is false to say that they are simply depositories of fragments of traditions that will in due time wither away. Each way of life, with its stories, histories, traditions, its understanding of the universe and our place in it, that is imported into a country of immigrants such as Canada, evolves, and that evolution leads to transformation. Indeed the thrill, besides the agony, of living in the present age for many is precisely that of observing, living through, and even facilitating these transformations.

And so the title of this anthology, which brings together attempts to study, understand, and explicate the new Canadian literature produced in the past three decades, *Floating the Borders*, is apt; not uprooting and moving boundaries, but simply setting them afloat and free, for an identity, a literature, in the broad sense, to grow, explore, find and define itself; and perhaps keep on defining itself. This broadmindedness, this generously exploratory attitude, is at least one trait of our society that few of us would want to dispute.

—M G Vassanji

I. Con-texts: Locating Spaces (Essays)

Dialogue as a Discursive Strategy in Chinese Canadian Poetry

LIEN CHAO

Poetry is capable not only of serving as a means for the expression of personal identity or even nationalist sentiment. Poetry, as a part of the cultural institutions and historical existence of a people, is itself an arena of struggle. BARBARA HARLOW

Alone and on the edge of their world, far from the centre. This kind of edge in race and family we only half suspect as edge. FRED WAH

Some critics consider poetry a nonpolitical form because of its classic antiquity and economic form. Terry Eagleton's observation supports this critique: "For poetry is of all literary genres the one most apparently sealed from history, the one where 'sensibility' may play in its purest, least socially tainted form" (51). Since poetry usually foregrounds the signifier rather than the context, compared to other literary genres, it has the effect of "pushing communication into the background . . . asserting that language is 'being used for its own sake' " (Easthope 16). However, Easthope also argues that as a certain kind of discourse, poetry is a "means of representation," which "is not a neutral vehicle." As such, poetry "is already 'shaped' for ideology and is therefore itself ideological" (7, 22). Describing resistance poetry, Barbara Harlow points out: "Poetry is capable not only of serving as a means for the expression of personal identity or even nationalist sentiment. Poetry, as a part of the cultural institutions and historical existence of a people, is itself an arena of struggle" (33).

In Canadian literature, poetry is a mainstream genre. George Woodcock remarks in his chapter on Canadian poetry for *Literary History of Canada*: "Nowadays poetry is not merely—in numbers of titles—the most published of all genres in Canada; it sells more reliably than fiction, and poets, recently derived, have become something very near to culture heroes, especially among the young" (286). Many of the founders of Canadian poetry in the 1960s have long since become monumental figures in the literary canon; some are also mainstream critics and educators, teaching Canadian literature in the universities. The economic and career fulfilment for mainstream Canadian poets underlines the potential of poetry which can go beyond the capacity of a literary genre; it is a channel through which social development can be achieved for individuals as well as for communities.

A literary community is a product of the surrounding world. It usually takes several decades for a literary community to develop the quantity and quality of writers and readers, and it can only do so if the overall political and economic timing is right. According to Woodcock, for today's mainstream Canadian poets, who emerged in the 1960s, the establishment of the Canada Council in 1957, which "encouraged and sustained poet-edited magazines and poet-directed presses," made a historical contribution as a financial and political patron (15). Although one cannot underestimate the struggle that the mainstream poets have undergone in the last few decades, these developments have taken place in the politically supportive, culturally and linguistically friendly environment of their mother tongue. The overwhelmingly white Canadian poetry anthologies do not reflect racial and cultural diversities in Canada, not to mention the linguistic diversities other than English and French. Thus through "the Canadian poetic renaissance" (Woodcock 307) led by A J M Smith in the 1940s, to its flourishing in the 1960s and its academic establishment in the 1970s, racial issues were seldom depicted or considered by Canadian poets or critics.

This literary scene began to change in the late 1980s and in the 1990s for several reasons: one, the Native peoples' resistance against five hundred years' European colonization; two, the establishment of large non-white minority communities because of the changes in Canadian immigration patterns; and three, encouragement from the official multicultural policies in the last two decades. Minority writers and poets are currently undergoing a similar journey to that travelled by mainstream Canadian poets in the 1960s. Nevertheless, for the non-white poets, the journey will probably be much longer and more difficult, simply because barriers are everywhere: the overall biases of Canadian history towards these communities, the linguistic barriers for some of them, and the psychological challenge for members from the historically marginalized groups who have never had a voice in Canadian culture. Now that the first-generation writers from these communities are making their appearances in the publishing world, one expects them to establish different, but equally important, components of Canadian poetry, ones that have been missing from the official canon.

This essay examines dialogue as a political and poetic strategy that is widely used by Chinese Canadian poets, such as Jim Wong-Chu, Sean Gunn, Paul Yee, Laiwan, Jam. Ismail, Fred Wah, Lucy Ng, Evelyn Lau, and others. Through dialogue with the dead railway workers, deceased community ancestors, family members, and above all with the reader, these poets are engaged in a continuous process of rereading the community history, relocating the collective values, and redefining the Chinese Canadian identity. Their efforts also include seeking poetic forms and tropes that can best represent their sentiments and lived experience.

Jim Wong-Chu's poetry collection *Chinatown Ghosts* (1986) explores the Chinese Canadian tradition and history as viewed from the interior of Vancouver's Chinatown. The opening poem, "tradition," depicts a certain kind of Chinese food, *zong zhi,* as it is pronounced in Mandarin, which is traditionally served during the memorial festival in spring to commemorate the legendary hero Qu Yuan of the Han Dynasty (206 BC–220 AD). The poem is a dialogue between the reader and "a bundle of rice / wrapped in leaves / forming triangles"; this unknown object, which contains a Chinese ritual and cultural tradition, calls the reader's attention to the signifier as a cultural artifact rather than as merely an arbitrary sign. Using a first-person persona, the poet describes the process of discovering this somewhat exotic food in slow-motion details:

I pull the string
unlocking the tiny knot
releasing the long thin strand
which binds

I tug at the dry green leaves
holding the sweet rice within

peeling it back
I begin to open (11)

The object for the ending verb "open" is actually the title "tradition"; thus the poem reads cyclically, suggesting a symbolic process of discovering and rediscovering a cultural tradition. The closing line, "I begin to open," structurally embeds an implied oxymoron; rhetorically, it suggests an open ending instead of a closure. The reader senses a need to continue reading in order to discover this different tradition. Since this is the first poem of the collection, the "tradition" to be discovered and rediscovered can be related to the title of the book, *Chinatown Ghosts,* a Chinese Canadian history to be reclaimed as a part of the tradition.

Wong-Chu uses dialogue metonymically in his search for the community's history. His poem "old chinese cemetery: kamloops July 1977," which I have discussed in *Beyond Silence* (Chao, 1997), vividly encapsulates the dialogue between a searching poet and the bones of the Gold Mountain men. Another poem, "scenes from the mon sheong home for the aged," describes the lifetime physical and psychological damage that is done to a Chinese road construction worker after he survives an accident caused by a white engineer's mistake. The poet narrates the old man's memory of the accident after many years:

this was a fuller page
of his life

he remembers the road building accident
in 1910

his body among the rubble
blood of dead men ran
thick as pig
so thick
he had to lift his head
to breathe

the *gwai low* engineer
gave wrong instruction
with the dynamite

"I lucky"
the break in his leg
did not pop the skin (28)

The old man is driven mad by his vivid memory of the accident. The few sentences he can speak in English, for example "Where is my china?", indicate his life and the life of his generation as isolation and silence. A similar poem, "fourth uncle," depicts a dialogue between the I-narrator and a Chinese labourer in Victoria, a village relative, whose last dream after a lifetime struggle as a bachelor labourer is to die near the Chinese cemetery:

you said
you travelled and worked
up and down this land
and now you have returned
to die

to be buried
beside the others
in the old chinese cemetery
by the harbour
facing the open sea
facing home (19)

The above dialogues between the poet and the Chinatown ghosts

7

help to recover the silenced lives of the Chinese labourer generation. Dialogue can transform the power relationship between the dominated and the domineering. In his sarcastic narrative poem "equal opportunity," Wong-Chu uses repetition as a rhetoric device to engage the reader in such a practice. By foregrounding economic competition as the main cause of racism in the pioneer days, the poet engages the reader in a dialogue with frontier history:

in early canada
when railways were highways

each stop brought new opportunities

there was a rule

> the chinese could only ride
> the last two cars
> of the trains (14)

Later, underscoring the perverse logic of racism, the poet ridicules the bizarre change in the railway regulations:

until a train derailed
killing all those
in front

(the chinese erected an altar and thanked buddha)

a new rule was made
> the chinese must ride
> the front two cars
> of the trains (14)

The poet repeats the same lines of another accident that "claimed everyone in the back"; so the final offering of "equal opportunity" to all passengers, and the ruling that "the chinese are now allowed / to sit anywhere / on any train," are results of accidents (15). Using repetition to ridicule racism, the poet contests its practice in Canadian history. Centred within Vancouver's Chinatown, Wong-Chu's lyrics, which attest to Chinese Canadian experience, suggest that poetry is not sealed from history. On the contrary, history is inscribed in the poetic discourse.

The investigative and interrogative features of Wong-Chu's poetry are also exemplified in other Chinese Canadian poems, in which various forms of dialogue occur. Sean Gunn's poem, "And Then Something Went" (see my *Beyond Silence*), is a dialogue between poetry and performative media. Laiwan's poem "The Imperialism of Syntax," collected in *Many-Mouthed Birds*, is a linguistic dialogue between English and Chinese since the poem is published in both languages. The poem focuses on the inevitable linguistic assimilation involved in the survival of Chinese immigrants:

> you had travelled long and far to be subject to another's
> language,
> another's *syntax*.
> Right away, those rules of grammar were the forgetting of
> yourself.
> Those letters never pronounced before
> Became the subject of your ridicule.
> The bitterness on your tongue became hidden in need for
> survival
> a proof of assimilation,
> the invisibility of yourself . . .
>
> Now you are here
> do you remember your syntax, your language
> that which would be the remembering of yourself? (58)

The poem underlines the process of cultural assimilation through linguistic assimilation, which occurs daily wherever the official languages are spoken. Through its grammatical rules and syntactic order, English colonizes the mind and the tongue of the non-English speakers; at the same time, it ridicules their willingness to be assimilated. However, Laiwan's poem also exemplifies the resistant nature of postcolonial poetry. By writing about non-white or non-European experience, postcolonial poetry helps dismantle the power of the imperial syntax with its resistant context.

Published in both Chinese and English, the two versions of Laiwan's poem stage a postcolonial irony. While the heritage language is gradually losing its function to the overwhelming mainstream languages, the heritage culture remains a resource of psychological resistance. Since the two versions of Laiwan's poem are printed physically back to back on the two sides of the same page, the linguistic dialogue between them becomes quite a complex experience for different readers. First of all, the poet cannot read Chinese; therefore the Chinese version, which is not exactly a word-by-word translation from English, challenges her as a postcolonial agent whose "dispossession of [her] origin," as footnoted, is hardly reclaimable (57). Secondly, since most English readers cannot read Chinese, the linguistic dialogue between the two versions cannot function equally in the reading. Thus, to a unilingual English reader, who looks at the Chinese print with awe and curiosity, the Chinese version stands as a linguistic barrier. Looking at the English version, a unilingual Chinese reader feels what the poem describes: *"shengyingdi fayin, chengle rang ren xiluodi / xiaoliao"*—"Those letters never pronounced before / became the subject of your ridicule" (57-58; phonetic Mandarin is mine). Therefore, for a unilingual reader in either case, the linguistic dialogue between the two versions of the poem can only converge as an imaginary and intellectual dialogue between the poem and the reader.

A bilingual reader, however, will have a different experience in reading the poem. Comparing the two versions, the reader discovers the English title, "The Imperialism of Syntax," is translated into Chinese as *"zhi min hualedi wenhua"* (phonetic Mandarin is mine), meaning "the colonized culture." In other places, especially in the third stanza, the Chinese syntax is not as clear as the original English lines, because the word-by-word translation is done syntactically rather than semantically, which is how the translator translated the title. Thus the poem debates the level—semantic, syntactic, or phonetic—at which poetry can be properly translated. Regarding translation as a linguistic dialogue between signs and objects/concepts, translation of poetry not only translates words verbally, but also transforms cultural concepts intellectually from one language to another. Overall Laiwan's poem raises important questions for other Chinese Canadian and postcolonial poets.

The agony of a postcolonial subject using the colonizer's language is somehow assuaged in Jam. Ismail's poem *Sacred Texts*. Born in Hong Kong and living in two British colonies, Hong Kong and India, before immigrating to Canada, another postcolonial space, Jam. Ismail writes the resistance of the colonized into her poetry. The excerpt from her volume *Sacred Texts* included in *Many-Mouthed Birds* exemplifies a deconstructive approach to the imperialistic language at all linguistic levels: semantic, syntactic and phonetic. *Sacred Texts*, as it is ironically named, disfigures the traditional formats of poetry or prose by deliberately violating the rules of capitalization, spacing, punctuation, paragraphing, structuring, and typesetting. Phonetically, the group of poems follows the colloquial flow of English in the colonies, contesting the sacred position of the written words in Western culture. Some of Ismail's poems read like casual conversation caught by an eavesdropper, while others sound like episodes of humorous dialogue among friends. Personal names appear in the context; among many participants in the conversation, "bosan" and "dai ji" appear frequently.

Ismail's poems are numbered in itemized paragraphs. In print, they look like a list of things, equally spaced. Some of her paragraphs seem without particular topics, while others depict a slice of life, or a slice of a much bigger phenomenon which reveals an ironic space for postcolonial subjects. For example, the paragraph marked "b.7" offers a glimpse at the unmeasurable space between semantics and the subconscious: "Staring at the typo 'accumiliate' made by a chinese from / zimbabwe, bosan grimmed: yeah, accumulate + / humiliate" (128). The playful combination of "accumulate" and "humiliate" in this specific space questions whether a linguistic signifier is a transparent sign. The poem marked as "c.1" has a confusing subtitle printed deliberately in a box for emphasizing:

11

young ban yen had been thought

ratio quality

italian in kathmandu, filipina in hong
kong, eurasian in kyoto, japanese in anchorage, dismal in
london england, hindu in edmonton, generic oriental in
calgary, western canadian in ottawa, anglophone in
montreal, metis in jasper, eskimo at hudson's bay
department store, vietnamese in chinatown, tibetan in
vancouver, commie at the u.s. border.

on the whole very asian. (128)

The phonetic closeness between "ratio" and "racial," which could be a mispronunciation, satirizes the identity confusion in society. These two paragraphs capture the psychological paranoia in a racist world that is based on face-reading.

Rhetorically and stylistically, *Sacred Texts* challenges the conventional format of prose, especially its rigid concepts of beginning, middle and ending. It also defies the traditional ideal of poetry constituted by versicle stanzas. Rather than following the rigid grammatical rules of English, which help preserve the imperialistic tradition, Ismail distorts the English syntax in order to challenge the ideology of hegemony inscribed within. Her nontraditional syntax indicates liberation and freedom for a postcolonial subject. And her tongue-in-cheek attitude and sometimes sarcastic humour mocks the narrowly conceived identity concept that is traditionally based on race and genealogy.

The subject matter of identity is also explored by Fred Wah as a recurrent topic in his prose poems written over several decades. His Governor General's Literary Award-winning collection, *Waiting for Saskatchewan* (1985), consists of four groups of prose poems under the subtitles of "Breathin' My Name with a Sigh," "Grasp the Sparrow's Tail," "Elite," and "This Dendrite Map: Father/Mother Haibun." Together they form a lengthy dialogue between the speaking subject/the son and the deceased father/the "you." George Bowering observes this depiction in his introduction to Wah's other poetry collection, *Selected Poems: Loki Is Buried at Smoky Creek* (1980): "The death of his father causes the poet to bring to life his memories of earlier life with the no longer breathing Wah" (15). The opening poem of *Waiting For Saskatchewan*, starting with the title line, begins a chain of Wah's frequently-used signifier, foregrounding his mixed origins and family genealogy in this composition:

> Waiting for Saskatchewan
> and the origins grandparents countries places converged
> europe asia railroads carpenters nailed grain elevators
> Swift Current my grandmother in her house
> he built on the street
> and him his cafes namely the "Elite" on Center   (3)

The beginning of the poem also illustrates Wah's poetic style of using fewer punctuation signs and more noun parallels. Wah only uses one set of quotation marks, a few commas, and some capitalization in this poem. He parallels his nouns to each other, such as "origins grandparents countries places" and "europe asia railroads carpenters." Without using verbs regularly to designate the relationship between the nouns as either subject or object, Wah positions the parallelled nouns as equal entities in the line. Thus, rather than creating a traditional syntactic order of subject + verb + object, Wah's parallel nouns and run-on lines produce a nonhierarchical relationship among the words, a paratactic sentence.

Exploring the difference between the hypotactic sentence and the paratactic sentence, Stephen Fredman notes in *Poet's Prose*:

> A hypotactic sentence fulfils our normal plot expectations: . . . there is a logical connection and subordination among the grammatical elements of the sentence plot and an outcome in which the plot reaches a denouement or completion. Like any familiar plot, the hypotactic sentence can be diagrammed hierarchically; it has a logical order. The plot of the paratactic sentence works by a continual sidewise displacement; its wholeness is dependent upon the fraternal bonds of a theoretically endless proliferation of familial resemblances rather than the dynastic bonds of filiation. Thus the conscious sentence writer can subvert, deny, or replace the authority of the hypotactic sentence through the alogical plot and the aural structure

of the paratactic sentence. (30-31)

Wah's use of parallel, unrelated nouns shows that he is a conscious sentence writer. These parallel nouns not only subvert the traditional logical order expected from a hypotactic sentence, but also create a fluid context that allows the reader to generate different meanings.

This fluid context probably indicates a personal sentiment, which might be read as an analogy to Wah's mixed-blood genealogy of Swedish and Chinese immigrant ancestors in Saskatchewan. By mixing the boundaries of prose and poetry to create a prose poetry, Wah finds a metonymic form which helps him explore the duality of his Eurasian identity. He also employs dialogue to engage the reader in a similar quest for meaning(s). A short poem about the impact of his father's death, which triggers the poet's major personal crisis, leads him to search for his mixed identity:

> Father, when you died you left me
> with my own death. Until then I thought
> nothing of it. Now I see it's clear cut
> both genetic "bag" as well as choice. I know now
> I'd better find that double edge . . . (6)

The search for "the double edge" is expressed in a direct dialogue between the poet as the first-person "I" and the father as the addressee "you." Although the "you" never answers, his silence provokes the speaking subject "I" with a consistent presence for many years: "when you die it snows"

> father it is fall
> the leaves turn
> . . . .
> I'm over forty now . . .
> . . . .
> father
> again it is another season,
> . . . .
> your name is my name
> our name is bones

bones alone names (10, 14)

The Eurasian "bones" shared by the father and the son—the father is half Chinese and the son a quarter—binds Wah's poetry with other Chinese Canadian writings by its predominant literary trope of "bones," through which his Chinese genealogy and identity become locatable.

The search for his "genetic 'bag'" as a Eurasian leads the poet to take a physical journey to China. *Grasp the Sparrow's Tail* is a travel diary written during Wah's trip to mainland China via Japan, Taiwan, and Hong Kong in search of his family's "bones." Each journal entry consists of two parts: an italicized prose passage recording the daily travel agenda and a poetic passage printed in normal font. This format itself embeds and embodies different dialogues: dialogues between the fonts, between the travellers (his wife Pauline, pp. 37, 38, 53), between the physical and psychological journeys, and between prose and poetry. While the poet's search for his genealogical roots in Canton is received doubtfully by the Chinese, since a Eurasian is not considered a Chinese, his mental dialogue with his father continues during the trip:

> *So what have I got going besides this "father" list? . . . I've misplaced the family information my mother gave me so I can't check out actual possible connections still here in the Canton region. I mention this to the guides and the others in our tour group, tell them my father was sent here as a child to be raised and educated by his Chinese relatives.*

> You were part Chinese I tell them.
> They look at me. I'm pulling their leg.
> So I'm Chinese too and that's why my name is Wah.
> They don't really believe me. That's o. k.
> When you're not "pure" you just make it up. (43)

The poet's mental dialogues with his father challenge the traditional genealogy based on racial linearity. While his father's meaning is further explored in "Elite," especially in "Elite 9," during the trip the poet sees his father everywhere among the Chinese (Wah 44)—from the rice fields in Canton, to a construction site in Zhengzhou near the Yellow River, the coal-mining town in Taiyuan, a Buddhist temple in Datong in northern China, and to a single window in Huhhot of Inner Mongolia(45, 46, 51). In a direct dialogue, he tells his father "[w]hat always gives you away is your haircut, your walk, or the flash in your eyes" (44). Through the typical Chinese haircut and mannerism, the narrator seems to find kinship with many ordinary Chinese.

However, the more the poet sees his father among the ordinary Chinese, the fewer illusions he has about his dispossessed origin. Wah depicts the cultural dispossession which is happening on a global level; his own disillusionment is revealed near the end of his journey. When his trip ends up in the national capital, the narrator seems to see less and write less. Regional differences are lost in Beijing where images of ancient Utopia are mixed with signs of a modern tourist industry: "Lotus fields everywhere. Look at the hats they wear. Everything happiness and longevity"; "everywhere, the masses, the people from New York airing their teeth" (54-55). Wah's poetic travelogue, Grasp the Sparrow's Tail, named after a movement in *tai chi*, ends magically at the entrance hall to Chairman Mao's mausoleum. Here the poet not only links the huge oil painting of Mount Kun Lun in front of his eyes with the mountains along the Kootenay River in British Columbia in his home town, but also links his search for his father and his family genealogy to the late great Chinese leader Mao Tsedong. The group of poems ends with a simple dialogue between the poet and his father, and with Mao, since the identity of the "you" is not fixed in the context:

Mao, in front of me
the things you cared for too
river, mountain
a town, the whole
blue sky (56)

It is in this simple ending that the poet merges all the noticeable differences between past and present, East and West, China and Canada, Chinese, Caucasian and Eurasian, his father and Mao, into the eternal latitude of poetry, which is probably the only space that is capable of embracing all the differences.

The search for his family genealogy and Eurasian identity is continued in the ten prose poems collected under the subtitle, *Elite*, included in *Waiting for Saskatchewan* and later anthologized in *Many-Mouthed Birds* (169-179). The *Elite* poems begin with an implied oxymoron: "Swift Current Saskatchewan is at the centre" (59), which typifies Wah's style of prose-poetry. It also marks the significance of the prairie town to the poet and his poetry. "Elite" is the name of the Chinese family cafe opened by Wah's grandfather in Swift Current along the CPR. Like other Chinese cafes and restaurants, such as the Disappearing Moon Cafe in Sky Lee's novel, and the tea/boarding house in Winston Christopher Kam's drama, "Elite" is a historical ethnic setting, within which the poet relocates his family history in the history of the Chinese Canadian community. Here "elite" is marked on the title page to be mispronounced as "ee-light" (Wah 57), which ironically foregrounds the linguistic interactions among the settler groups in the prairie, as well as the Chinese immigrants' longing for acceptance.

In *Elite*, the poet continues to use dialogue as a strategy to engage the Eurasian son, the persona "I," and his already deceased Eurasian father, the "You." Speaking the first-person voice, the poet transforms his father's silence into answers to his own questions about their mixed genealogy. "Elite 3" explores the lack of a clearly defined racial identity for Eurasians in either Canadian or Chinese society:

I know when you came back from China you must have felt more Chinese than anything else. But I remember you saying later that the Chinese didn't trust you and the English didn't trust you. You were a half-breed, Eurasian. I remember feeling the possibility of that word "Eurasian" for myself when I first read it in my own troubled adolescence. I don't think you ever felt the relief of that exotic identity though. In North America white is still the standard and you were never white enough. But you weren't pure enough for the Chinese either. You never knew the full comradeship of an ethnic community. So you felt single, outside, though you played the game as we all must . . . I don't think you felt there was anyone else in the world like you. (62)

Delineating his father's double immigration, the poet reclaims his father's silence. At age five, his father is sent from the Canadian prairie to Canton to be educated; and at nineteen, he comes back from Canton to Swift Current, Saskatchewan. His double immigration and twice being made "languageless" are fully recounted in "Elite 9." The poem consists of one unbroken sentence, protesting against the Canadian immigration detention camp at Victoria for jailing returning Asian Canadians before their status in Canada could be clarified. In "Elite 9":

> When you return from China via Victoria on Hong Kong Island and they put you in jail in Victoria on Vancouver Island because your birth certificate had been lost in the Medicine Hat City Hall fire and your parents couldn't prove you were born in Canada until they found your baptism records in the church . . . when you arrived in China in 1916 only four years old unable to speak Chinese and later in the roaring twenties when each time Grandpa gambled away your boat passage so you didn't get back to Canada until 1930 languageless again with anger locked up in the immigration cells on Juan de Fuca strait . . . did you see islands? (69)

The use of one unbroken sentence achieves a totally different dramatic effect from the parallel nouns used earlier in Wah's poems. While the overlapping, nonreflexive parallels disrupt textual and grammatical closures, the one-sentence paragraph without punctuation builds up a syntactic momentum and tension so as to give the reader a metonymic experience of the father's silenced anger, which needs to be discharged.

Besides immigration experience, Wah also depicts the on-going struggle of a Eurasian family in Canadian society. The multiracial Canadian society is mocked by its own miniature at Swift Current: "The ethnicity here feels so direct. I mean the Chinese are still connected to China, the Ukrainians so Ukrainian, in the bar the Icelanders tell stories about Iceland, the Swede still has an accent, the French speak French . . . What is a Metis, anyway?" (62) In this setting, "Elite 4" and "Elite 5" capture the Eurasian family's ongoing endeavour to become mainstream Canadians. "Elite 4" depicts the father taking time off from work in order to go to the church on Sundays with the family:

> You were proud, then, of the fact you were going to church and
> you made a point of telling some of the customers in the restau-
> rant that you had to go to church. That was after you had
> stopped desiring China . . . I think the church thing was white
> responsibility and you did it for that and a sense of our family
> in that community. (63)

In "Elite 5," "that community" of mainstream Canadians, who go
to church on Sundays, shifts to the ice hockey arena, in which the
I-narrator posits his silent father for a place of belonging:

> I think you were the manager or something, you helped out. The
> brim of your hat is turned down, Chicago gangster style . . . I've
> always been "proud" you were part of that team. The Swift
> Current Indians were my first hockey heroes and their move-
> ments over the ice instilled a sense of body and mind-set which
> I have carried with me all my life. Even though you never played
> hockey I know you had the invisible movement of the game
> inside you too. (64-65)

The irony that the father never plays ice hockey except in the son's
imagination expresses the son's growing-up experience as a Eurasian—searching for identifiable mainstream Canadian images, including stereotypes.

"Elite 10," which concludes the series, summarizes the family's
struggle to establish itself in business. Wah depicts the entire family
business history within, again, one unbroken long sentence that runs
for a page and a half without punctuation until its ending. The
family's business experience exemplifies Chinese immigrants' slim
opportunities in Canada after the CPR was completed. The part of the
job market that is open to the Chinese is exclusively self-employment
in the service industry: restaurants, cleaners, cafés, and motels. The
unbroken one-sentence poem provides the reader with a linguistic
opportunity to share the family's persistent search for a better opportunity, which is eventually exhausted as the poem ends with: "finally
the Holmes Motel in Cranbrook in the early sixties where that was the

end of the deals the cafés the houses the driving the building the running right through it, for you, that was it" (71).

The omission of punctuation in both "Elite 9" and "Elite 10" intensifies the resistance of the silent father—"you"—as a partner in the dialogue. Although his silence is displaced by his son's interpretation of that silence, the physical existence of "you" throughout the text still maintains some of its provocative power, and arouses pathos in the reader. In talking to his father, especially by transforming the latter's silence into words and his life into poetry, the I-narrator relocates a Eurasian family history and his personal identity in the collective history of the Chinese Canadians. With this conclusion, a political irony emerges, cutting even more deeply than the I-narrator's childhood preference for his father's participation in mainstream Canadian cultural activities, such as church and hockey. Although a Eurasian descends from a mixed parenthood of a European and an Asian, the I-narrator's eventual association with the Chinese Canadians rather than with the European Canadians denounces the racist attitude of the dominant culture.

The last group of Wah's prose poems in *Waiting for Saskatchewan*, "The Dendrite Map: Father/Mother Haibun," embodies a dialogue between the two poetic forms: *haiku*,[1] and prose poetry. However, the poet replaces the rigid Japanese poetic form of *haiku* with a prose paragraph written with parallel nouns. In addition to exploring a loose *haiku* style, Wah does not attempt to offer "a specific spiritual insight" (Holman 247) when he concludes his poem. Instead his last line suggests a second thought, which is sometimes ironic and other times irrelevant. In this group of poems, besides talking to his deceased father, the poet occasionally talks to his mother. In "Father/Mother Haibun #1," his search for an explanation of his mixed genealogy continues:

> . . . my Grandfather which made my life "racial" not that he actually came to be there but simply him here/there and her, my Grandmother, her Salvation Army Englishness really solid in the middle of his flux but both of them cutting "geo" out of their world thus Maple Creek Moose Jaw North Battleford Medicine Hat somewhere in England and Canton China places in their lives much more than in their world, you, my father, almost too,

thus me . . . (75)

Here the poet underlines the Chinese blood in him and his father, which makes them experience "racial" minority status in Canada. This political statement also explains why he often seeks to talk to his father, instead of to his mother, about the family genealogy. However, as Wah's serious statement is often balanced by his ironic disengagement from a narrowly constrained meaning, the poem ends with a loose, unfinished *haiku* line printed in bold letters: **"Two weeks late I turn the calendar, crave for ripe tomatoes"** (75). The concluding line is totally detached from the main prose passage about his grandparents who made him a Eurasian. It dismisses the reader's expectation of finding the "truth" in conclusion. In "Father/Mother Haibun #11," the narrator talks to his mother about the family genealogy:

> Mother somewhere you flying over me with love and close
> careless caress from Sweden your soft smooth creme skin
> only thoughts from your mother without comparison the
> lightness of your life / blood womaness which is mine . . . (86)

The depiction of his mother's fair European skin continues to underline racially divided Canadian society in which people are defined by their skin colour. Although the poet's family has mixed blood, it is the Chinese blood in him and his father that makes their lives "racial" and binds them to the Chinese Canadian community by the "bones."

A group of new prose poems, "Seasons Greetings from the Diamond Grill," published in *Canadian Literature* in 1994, continues Wah's tireless search for family genealogy and for the place of Chinese Canadian culture in prose poetry. As he usually does, Wah begins his poem with an oxymoron to capture the irony of the visible but slightly off-centre place of Chinatown in Canadian culture:

> On the edge of Centre. Just off Main. Chinatown, at least in most
> cities, is always close to the centre but just on the edge of it,
> because of the cafes. In places like Swift Current, Regina, Cal-
> gary, Vancouver, the Chinese cafes are clumped together in a
> section of town usually within a few blocks of the hub. Not way
> out. Not rural. Downtown. but on the edge of. In smaller towns

like Red Deer, Nelson, Fernie, the cafes are more part of the centre. (8)

The paragraph is an ironic dialogue between the polemic concepts of the centre and the margin. The borderline in between seems to be decided by the size of the city and by the attitude of local white Canadians toward minority groups and their cultural products. As Chinese food has become more and more cosmopolitan these days, Chinese cafes and restaurants are conveniently located at the near-centre scene in Canadian cities. Contrastingly, Chinese stores are located somewhat off the centre, geographically and conceptually. Instead of the cafes or the restaurants, the poet depicts a Chinese store as the focus of his poem, thus discursively transforming the margin into a centre. It is in this marginalized centre that ethnic Chinese culture is not only well preserved but also actively engaging the community. Wah describes the Chinese store as a cultural centre that does not signify marginality to its subjects:

> . . . the Chinese store—a room really, smoky, dark and quiet, clock ticking. Dark brown wood panelling, some porcelain planters on the windowsill, maybe some goldfish. Goldfish for Gold Mountain men. Not so far, then, from the red carp of their childhood ponds. Brown skin stringy salt-and-pepper beard polished bent knuckles and at least one super-long fingernail for picking. Alone and on the edge of their world, far from the centre. This kind of edge in race and family we only half suspect as edge. (*Seasons Greetings from the Diamond Grill*, 8)

The paradox that the margin is also a centre emerges from the rich texture of life in the back of the Chinese store. This time Wah uses a long list of paralleled adjectives, and present and past participles to capture the passionate voices behind the Chinese store:

. . . you can hear, mysteriously amplified through the window, the click-clacking of mah-jong pieces being shuffled over the table tops. The voices from up there or behind the curtain are hot tempered, powerful, challenging, aggressive, bickering, accusatory, demeaning, bravado, superstitious, bluffing, gossipy, serious, goading, letting off steam, ticked off, fed up, hot under the collar, hungry for company, hungry for language, hungry for luck. (*Seasons Greetings from the Diamond Grill* 8–9)

While the margin is depicted as preoccupied as the centre by human desires and emotions, the polemic difference between them is dismissed. Furthermore, the traditional power relationship between them is also conceptually displaced by the new paradigm of similarity.

Wah's recent poems also speak more provocatively against racism in Canadian society. The poet calls the reader's attention to street racism, such as a child's name-calling: "Until she called me a 'Chink' I wasn't one. That was in elementary school." With another similar situation of name-calling, the I-narrator is completely victimized:

The old Chinamen had always just been friends of my dad's. . . I went fishing down by the boat-houses with one of them. . . We were walking back up the hill with our catch of suckers and some kids started chiding Chinky, chinky Chinaman and I figured I'd better not be caught with him any more. (*Seasons Greetings from the Diamond Grill* 10)

Wah captures what racism sometimes does to a victim. As racism undercuts the victim's self-esteem with shame, sometimes the victim adopts a similar discriminatory attitude against other victims:

I became as white as I could, which, considering I'm mostly Scandinavian, was pretty easy for me. Not for my dad and some of my cousins though. They were stuck, I thought, with how they looked. And I not only heard my friends put down the Chinks (and the Japs, and the Wops, and the Spiks, and the Douks) but comic books and movies confirmed that the Chinese are yellow (meaning cowardly), not-to-be-trusted, heathens,

23

devils, slant-eyed, dirty, and talk incomprehensible gobblydee-gook. Thus "gook n. Slang. 1. A dirty, sludgy, or slimy substance. 2. An Oriental. An offensive term used derogatorily." (*Seasons Greetings from the Diamond Grill* 10)

This paragraph maps out a chain reaction of racism starting from probably an innocent child's name-calling in the street. The poet digs into society to reveal the nature of name-calling, which is never as simple as it looks. Like the comic books, the movies, the popular slang, the dictionary, and the language, which are all products of the existing culture, racism is a cultural product.

Wah continues to search for his family genealogy and through it, for a Eurasian identity in the new poems. If in *Grasp the Sparrow's Tail*, the poet's travel diary in China, traditional genealogy based on pure racial lineage is deconstructed, in *Seasons Greetings from the Diamond Grill*, genealogy becomes fictitious between the poet and the reader: "Who am I thought I might say to my friend Charlie Chim Chong Say Wong Liu Chung, the chinese poet. He said he could tell me more about my father than I can imagine" (*Seasons Greetings from the Diamond Grill* 9). The tongue-in-cheek humour continues with the exploration of the narrator's family name:

> Like my name. This chinese doctor I go to for acupuncture always gets it wrong. He calls me Mah. And I say no, it's Wah . . . He says Wah just means overseas Chinese. So I'm just Fred Overseas.
>
> I tell him my dad was really Kuan Wah Soon. He says my family comes from Canton region. Then he smiles. He knows so much. (*Seasons Greetings from the Diamond Grill*, 9)

If the poet's father was called "Kuan Wah Soon," his family name should be "Soon" instead of "Wah," which was part of his father's first name. However, since what really matters to Wah's poetry is not the location of his origin but his search for genealogical connections, this illusive origin remains a resource of his poetry.

Wah's fascination with genealogy produces more poetry when he depicts his relationship with his daughters. As the mixed blood in his family keeps mixing, the poet illustrates how arbitrary and subjective racial stereotyping can be:

Strange to watch your bloods. Like one of those sped-up movies of a cell dividing under a microscope. For just a split second your body'll do something Asian—like poised over a dish of Lo Bok with your chopsticks. There's just a brief Chinese glint in your eyes that flashes some shadow of track across your blond and ruddy Anglo-Swedish dominance . . .

And I've watched you both closely at times to see if I can detect any of that Nordic gloom my grandparents brought over from Sweden. Once in awhile during your teenage years I worried that depressive despair might overwhelm you as it has me from time to time. But what foolish stereotyping, to generalize about an ethnic quality like that. (*Seasons Greetings from the Diamond Grill* 10-11)

Seasons Greetings from the Diamond Grill ends metaphorically with a simple analogy of bread and butter as daily necessities for everyone: here traditional butter is replaced by a mixed, cheaper, and perhaps better product called "oleomargarine," ironically and symbolically, "for the world's starving, the mix of the century" (*Seasons Greetings from the Diamond Grill* 11). By selecting a simple metaphor as a solution for the complex racial issues in society, Wah sends out an unmistakable message to readers of all races in Canada that an understanding of each other is necessary as it is in a family.

The search for a family genealogy is also a subject of Lucy Ng's prose poetry, entitled "The Sullen Shapes of Poems" published in *Many-Mouthed Birds* (Ng 160-168). Similar to *Waiting for Saskatchewan*, Ng's poems are dialogues of a third-generation Chinese Canadian daughter with both her parents about their family's history. They begin with the first-person narrator talking to her father about his visit to mainland China, recognizing the psychological connection with the origin:

Father. . .
. . . .
Sometimes dreaming or reading, I think I know
what you must have felt when you climbed that
Great Wall or wandered through those magnificent

rooms, finger-deep in dust. Did you feel the
pain of recognition—thirty years gone—as
you chanced upon this, the undiscovered country,
its imprint in your heart? (160)

Another poem begins with a dialogue with the narrator's mother,
an immigrant woman, who plays a double role both at home and in
the community:

Mother, I remember the quiet house—you on your
knees, curved over the bathtub scrubbed white
like the back of a beluga whale . . .
. . . I wondered
how you could do it—your back broken
after six hours crouched in the fields
and then the strawberries stolen when you
went to pee. You came home angry hands
stained red. (163)

A third poem touches upon the life of her grandfather—of the first
generation from her family to emigrate from China. Upon his death,
her grandfather left his descendants a few solid pieces of heirloom to
build a family with:

When grandfather died he left: four benches, two
shoe racks, three bookshelves, a cabinet and a
potty chair for the baby (in the hole he'd dropped
the green plastic beach bucket . . .
its handle broken). . .(166)

During his lifetime he expresses his emotional connection with China
by painting his toolshed "vermilion, the colour, too, of the rooftops
he'd /left behind in China" (166).

A fourth poem depicts the family observing the Chinese remem-
brance ritual for the narrator's uncle who is buried in Canada. The
ritual consists of burning paper clothes, paper shoes, paper money,
and serving wine and food for the dead in front of the grave. Ng's
detailed descriptions portray Chinese immigrants' commitment to

Canada, whereas their connection with Chinese culture becomes part of their cultural heritage in Canada.

> Mother says, Don't crumple them, Uncle
> likes his clothes well pressed. I imagine
> him in the other world receiving his new
> suit eagerly, straightening the lapels,
> and pulling the hat over one eye the
> way detectives do in those black and white
> movies. Afterwards I think—I should have
> poured him another whisky. (165)

Ng also depicts the limited opportunities faced by Chinese immigrants in Canada. The group of nine poems ends with a list of service businesses that the family has undertaken: "Chinese cafe, grocery, laundry—skipping rope / rhymes—you want something different for me / Poet? you say. What's that?" (168). This line sounds similar to the experience described in Wah's "Elite 10" in *Waiting for Saskatchewan*. The recurrent depiction of limited opportunity for Chinese immigrants raises a collective voice of protest against the racist labour market in Canadian history. Using the same narrative strategy of engaging the deceased family members in on-going dialogues, both Wah and Ng construct their family genealogy as a part of community history.

In addition to the dialogues between the narrator and her parents, Ng uses the first-person plural pronoun "we" to engage the reader in a discovery of Chinese Canadian cultural practice. By blending Chinese tradition with Canadian customs, Ng's poems weave valuable ornaments from both cultures into a new tapestry of Chinese Canadian culture. The following poem is about the first New Year after the family settled down in Canada, "the second mainland," or "home," as her father calls it "after Hong Kong and Trinidad (mere islands)" (161).

> The first New Year we danced in the kitchen
> scented with the perfume of joss sticks
> till Father said, Stop. And so we lined up in
> front of the table to give thanks: apples

and oranges, a pair of fat fish, a roast
chicken, vermicelli for long life and
steamed brown sugar dough clusters like
shiny grapes, sweet and rubber textured.
All the time the lucky red signs
above our heads like Canadian flags.
Mother said, Bow.

One bow. Two bows. Three. (162)

The rich texture of Ng's prose poem is not only woven with different names of ornaments, but also with different rituals and customs for the New Year. The symbolic meaning of the New Year is employed here as a significant setting to renew Chinese tradition in Canada. Ng's poem speaks positively about the Canadian culture in which ethnic minorities, such as the Chinese, can preserve their heritages and at the same time absorb new elements from mainstream and other minority cultures.

Besides naming the Chinese ornaments and customs in English, Ng also blends the prose with Japanese *haiku* sensibility and concludes with an informal *haiku* line; thus her poetry includes a dialogue of poetic forms. In the short prose part of her poem, her narration is built around a carefully selected event, which describes in detail how the Chinese immigrants rebuilt their homes in Canada. The informal *haiku* line at the concluding position provides her prose with a depth and sometimes with a new dimension. The poem about the Mother's Chinese vegetable garden reminds the reader of the textuality of a water-colour painting:

In the summer there was the garden—rows
and rows of vegetable greens, leafy clumps;
long furred beans and tender-crisp snow
peas, vines laced round the wood stakes you
drove . . . into the earth. Neat crisscrosses x x x x x. This is
a Chinese garden x x x x x. This is
a Chinese garden. The wind tipping your hand,
your straw hat, gently. (164)

The harmonious green vegetable garden tranquillizes the reader's mind, while Mother's hard work to build such a garden in Canada is emphasized with the ten crisscrosses across the lines. The poem ends with an amusing *haiku* line, recommending Mother's Chinese philosophy of natural recycling: "I remember you spraying piss water; life green life" (164).

By cultivating the different experiences of a three-generation Chinese immigrant family, Ng's group of prose poem presents a reality shared by many Chinese Canadian families: migration from mainland China, or from Hong Kong, or from Trinidad, or from Africa, and eventual settlement in Canada. After two generations' struggle for survival, the third generation starts to see some growth, even the birth of a poet, or an artist. The group of poems ends with the image of the ancient Chinese poet Li Po of the Tang Dynasty (618-907 AD) writing "brushstroke of calligraphy on water"; this connection recognizes the literary tradition of Chinese culture as a heritage that all Chinese descendants can inherit whatever their nationalities. The poem concludes with a meditative *haiku* line: "You gave me these: a river, a boat /a bridge. The sullen shapes of poems" (168). Ng's conclusion, which lists three solid nouns, implies a ritual passage that all immigrant groups have to go through before achieving a reterritorialization in a new land. Several generations after the initial settlement, the Chinese Canadian community has seen the birth of its first-generation writers and its community literature in English.

Community history, family genealogy and cultural heritage become significant components in the poetry written by most Chinese Canadian poets. However, these collective characteristics should not be regarded as restrictions to limit what Chinese Canadian poets ought or ought not to write. Born and raised in Canada, writers who belong to the second, third or fourth generations never needed a boat to cross the oceans to Canada, neither did they experience the difficulties of linguistic and cultural dislocations as did the first generation immigrants. Influenced by the dominant Western ideology of individualism, a few might even want to cut ties with their community. Vancouver poet Evelyn Lau did this by running away from home.

Some of Lau's poems first appeared in various magazines, including academic periodicals, such as *Ariel, Michigan Quarterly Review,*

Queen's Quarterly, and *Southern Review*. Later they were published in three collections: *You Are Not Who You Claim* (1990), *Oedipal Dreams* (first published in 1992; republished in 1994), and *In the House of Slaves* (1994). In 1990, with *Oedipal Dreams*, Lau became the youngest writer ever nominated for the Governeror General's Literary Award.

Lau's three poetry collections depict prostitution and sadomaso-chism as does her prose. Despite the subject matter, which distin-guishes Lau from most other Chinese Canadian poets and from Canadian poets in general, her poetry demonstrates the shared poetic strategy of dialogue that is widely employed by many Chinese Cana-dian poets. Unlike other Chinese Canadian poets who use dialogue to investigate racism, or to search for family genealogy and personal identity, the dialogue in Lau's poetry is carried on between a first-per-son female persona and a second-person male addressee. While "I-versus-You" becomes a dominant narrative paradigm, her poetry depicts the experience of a female subject in the sex industry.

You Are Not Who You Claim typifies Lau's poetic paradigm of I-versus-You. The poet uses dialogue to question the sexual relation-ship between a young female would-be poet and various professional adult males. Lau describes the "you" in detail to remind the ad-dressee of the schemes he uses to manipulate an otherwise innocent relationship with the young female subject. The opening poem, enti-tled "Role Models," depicts the "I" already a sexual object and the "you" a manipulator:

> You arrive on my doorstep
> I seem a small thing to sacrifice
> . . . .
> you watch teenage girls cross the road, your eyes
> weave stockings to fit their legs
> they carry their breasts like welcome burdens
> your daughter stands in a doorway and you hunger
> for her, the body she must have stolen
> while your back was turned
> . . . .
> you insist you are my saviour
> how can I help but know the truth
> and love you for your lies (*You Are Not Who You Claim* 5)

As the "role models" (a term that ironically explains the title) eventually become sexual predators of the "I," the collection exposes the masks worn by the respectable "you," who is sometimes a "lawyer," a "literary lion," a "psychiatrist," and at other times a "drugged" addict, or a "john" (7, 8, 11, 13, 23). The social statuses of the sexual exploiters are mapped out in several poems, when "[t]he neons burn holes into the city's fabric / glaring at the man of the streets" (23), and the "you" everywhere corners the "I" and corrupts her. Lau also lists various games played by the "you," such as "promises," "handful of words," "kisses," and "hug[s]," leading the "I" to sexual exploitation:

Now you sprawl, legs open
in a cafe doorway in the west end
shirt deliberately unbuttoned, a showcase
of chest hair gleaming gold (9)

Listening, I feel again your weight on the bed
springs obeying laws of gravity (8)

you unknot the secrets of your silk tie and
I breathe in sloped shoulders
a mountain of belly (11)

The I-versus-You paradigm presents the "I" as a desirable and disposable sexual commodity. Although gender and sexual confrontations are depicted in Lau's poetry, the power relationship between the "You" and the "I" remains unchanged—the "you" consistently overpowering the naïve and vulnerable "I."

Since the "I" and the "you" are bound by the traditional power relationship between the two sexes, there is an accusatory moral tone in Lau's first poetry collection. When the "I" is a junior, almost like "your daughter stands in a doorway," the "I" accuses the "you" of being a manipulator. However, occasionally when the "I" changes to "you," and the "you" changes to "he," the accusatory overtone disappears. When that happens, prostitution and writing ironically merge into one poetic syntax of harmony: "your thighs straddle his shoulders like run-on sentences" (*You Are Not Who You Claim* 45). In this case, the moral paradigm of I-versus-You is undermined by an inclusive and unifying pronoun "we" as exemplified in the title of another poem "What We Do in the Name of Money" (*You Are Not Who You Claim* 45). As Lau's street experience grows, her poetry becomes a callous witness to her life.

Although the I-versus-You paradigm remains the basic poetic structure in Lau's second collection of poetry, *Oedipal Dreams*, the tension between the narrator and the addressee starts to dissolve. The relationship between the "I" and the "you" becomes an equal business partnership:

> you had written me into your appointment book with initials
> that were not my own.
> I counted the hours into my purse and wrote the important names
> into a black book in the bathroom. (*Oedipal Dreams* 14)

Without the I-narrator's accusation of the "You" as in Lau's first poetry collection, the power relationship between the female narrator and the male addressee reaches an equilibrium in *Oedipal Dreams*. In this collection, her depiction of doctors and psychiatrists reading Freud and sexually exploiting the young female patient (14, 18, 20, 25, 46) may astonish the reader; it does not irritate the "I" narrator. An assignation is presented as a social event, with a sense of reunion rather than moral degradation: "your eyes never rest, I watch our complexities /twine like sunburnt arms in their shallows" (20). At the same time, financial reward is accepted as a justification for the trade of body:

> . . . from that day on all my money began to smell of you
> even that hundred dollar bill.
> I struggled to breathe you into me. . .
> (*Oedipal Dreams* 21)

> two days later I snuck back
> to bi-weekly cash instalments
> and expensive tax-deductible gifts
> to hold you in my arms and . . . (*Oedipal Dreams* 28)

In this collection, sometimes the "I" narrator seems even more callous than the "You" and offers the latter a mirror of self-reflection.

For example, an ironic reflection occurs when the narrator enters the house of a married john:

> you do not see the three wedding photos on the dresser
> where his arm holds a woman who looks happy
> even though she is standing in a park by the edge of a cliff
> with a good view (*Oedipal Dreams* 27)

Sometimes when the first-person I-narrator changes to the second-person "You," the self-reflection allows the persona to see her own Oedipal nightmares:

> but before long it seemed that something ended,
> the light rusted, you rose dazed from a year as if
> from a long sleep and dreams of love,
> dreams twisting into nightmares.
> and there was the silver afternoon, the metal plate of the day
> tearing aside the blanket of your Oedipal dreams,
> tearing him away till the day was dull and the room empty
> and the sky unmoved. And you sat in the middle of your bed,
> not a child, with Daddy grey and bent in the bathroom mirror
> looking terribly confused, his fingers tapping ten anxious
>   thoughts,
>
> old as myth. (*Oedipal Dreams* 46)

Early in her work her representations of prostitution are charged with anger, but in her later work the anger is absent.

Lau's latest poetry collection, *In the House of Slaves*, continues the same theme of prostitution with an emphasis on S & M. In this group of poems, the I-versus-You relationship presents the I-narrator as a torturer or a dominatrix, who is physically in control, while the addressee "You" is a passive sex slave, who is financially in control, even though this relationship is not always clarified. Although the "I" narrator is in fact confined inside the houses owned by her "slaves," Lau's poetry is loaded ironically with details of the powerful female dominatrix in S & M role-playing. Thus she generates a self-deceptive image of her temporary power: cuffs are buckled and unbuckled; knots are tied and untied; her slave is punished or set free. Ironically, in the particular male-female relationship based on sex games, the parties are unusually friendly and civilized: "At the door we exchanged Christmas presents, the red packages from you so many they spilled over my arms" (*In the House of Slaves* 21). Set in the private houses which the "I" narrator frequents for business, Lau's latest poetry further develops male and female stereotypes in the sex industry.

Among the few reviewers of Lau's latest poetry collection, John Moore points out that her characters are not individuals but stereotypes: "Poets who go hunting for metaphors and archetypes on such marginal ground run the risk of succumbing to the sensibility of the subculture they try to exploit, as Lau does here. Instead of archetypes, we get stereotypes" (Moore D18). Lau's own explanation also offers a clue to the logic in her writings: "My experience of sexuality has been, for the most part, some form of prostitution" (Inwood B15). Lau's limited experience in life, which matches the restricted subject matters in her writings, emphasizes the connection between life and art, which, in a very different way, is illustrated by the writings of other Chinese Canadian poets who found their topics from community history and family genealogy. Lau must have realized that her writing, which has been entirely about her experience of the sex trade, starts to gain her such a reputation. She tells a reviewer: "I promise this [*In the House of Slaves*] is the last thing I write about S & M" (Andrews D16).

Despite all the differences between Lau's poetry and the poetry written by the community-based Chinese Canadian poets, there is one discursive strategy that they do share; that is, using personal or collective experience, or both, as a resource for poetry composition. When poetry is employed as a medium for collective and individual experiences, its "purest, least socially tainted" "sensibility" is challenged.

In this essay, I have illustrated the discursive strategy of dialogue that is widely adopted by the Chinese Canadian poets to portray different subject matters. Dialogue provides the poets with a narrative space in which they investigate, question, reclaim, and redefine community history, family genealogy, personal identities and experience. Dialogue is usually issued by the first-person narrator, whereas the addressees could be deceased community or family ancestor(s), bones of Chinese railway labourers, or the reader. In most cases, the addressee, "you," remains silent or unable to reply. However, the consistent presence of the "you" provokes the narrator with a desire to transform the former's silence into words. Jim Wong-Chu's lyrics connect the silence of the Chinese labourers with the identity crisis suffered by contemporary Chinese Canadians. *Chinatown Ghosts* re-writes part of the existing Canadian history by recognizing early Chinese immigrants as nation-builders and community ancestors. Fred Wah's prose poems search consistently for a family genealogy in the collective history of the Chinese Canadians. So do Lucy Ng's prose poems. Fred Wah, Laiwan, and Jam. Ismail write resistantly to disengage the syntactic order of the English language and the cultural hegemony signified through its rules. Paul Yee's poems, "Last Words II" and "The Grass Dragon" also involve the reader in a joint effort to reconstruct the forgotten Chinese Canadian community history in its literature. Evelyn Lau's poetry explores the experience of a female sex worker with sometimes an ironic reflection.

The body of Chinese Canadian poetry demonstrates once again the discursive practice of employing a mainstream literary genre to reinterpret minority experiences. Since most of the Chinese Canadian poets use the poetic form to describe experiences, or to define and redefine concepts, such as origin and genealogy, Chinese Canadian poetry demonstrates narrative strategies of reflection and conceptualization. These strategies explain why many of the poets chose the more innovative and flexible form of prose poetry rather than verse. By fusing the generic boundaries of prose and poetry, poets who choose prose poetry have access to both, and yet are not exactly bound by either. In addition, Chinese Canadian poetry also demonstrates the significant role of the speaking subjects, or the first-person poetic personas, who are contemporary Chinese Canadians. Similar to the first-person narrator in an autobiographical novel or a nonfiction work, the I-narrator/persona in many poems discussed here refers back and forth to the poets' identifiable personal data for recurrent topics. This poetic practice emphasizes the personal and autobiographical references as relevant historical components of poetry as they are of other literary genres.

WORKS CITED

Eagleton, Terry. 1983. *Literary Theory: An Introduction*. Oxford: Blackwell.

Easthope, Antony. 1983. *Poetry as Discourse*. London and New York: Methuen.

Harlow, Barbara. 1987. *Resistance Literature*. London and New York: Methuen.

Ismail, Jam. 1991. "From Sacred Texts." In *Many-Mouthed Birds*, eds. Lee and Wong-Chu, 124-135.

Laiwan. 1991. "The Imperialism of Syntax." In *Many-Mouthed Birds*, eds. Lee and Wong-Chu, 57-58.

Lau, Evelyn. 1990. *You Are Not Who You Are*. Victoria, BC: Porcepic.

———. 1992. *Oedipal Dreams*. Toronto: Coach House.

———. 1994. *In the House of Slaves*. Toronto: Coach House.

Lee, Bennett, and Jim Wong-Chu, eds. 1991. *Many-Mouthed Birds*. Vancouver: Douglas & McIntyre.

Ng, Lucy. 1991. "From 'The Sullen Shapes of Poems'." In *Many-Mouthed Birds*, eds. Lee and Wong-Chu, 160-168.

Wah, Fred. 1985. *Waiting for Saskatchewan*. Winnipeg: Turnstone.

———. 1994. "Season's Greetings from the Diamond Grill." *Canadian Literature* 140: 8-11.

Wong-Chu, Jim. 1986. *Chinatown Ghosts*. Vancouver: Arsenal Pulp.

Woodcock, George. 1976. In *Literary History of Canada: Canadian Literature in English*, ed. Carl F Klinck. 2nd ed. Toronto: University of Toronto Press.

A Passionate Dance: The Poetry of Rienzi Crusz

CHELVA KANAGANAYAKAM

One can hardly miss the ironies inherent in the title of Rienzi Crusz's most recent collection of poems, *Beatitudes of Ice* (1995), or for that matter in the poet's decision to conclude this book with a poem that pays homage to a long line of poets who have in various ways influenced his writing. While Crusz has, in occasional poems and more specifically in his rare critical essay "Talking for Myself" that appeared in *The Toronto South Asian Review*, drawn attention to his indebtedness to British, European and Latin American poets, it is in that concluding poem that he acknowledges most fully the multiple traditions from which he gained both insight and formal sophistication. In it there is little "anxiety of influence" (to use Harold Bloom's phrase), and no self-consciousness about the politics of colonialism and "mainstream literature"; there is simply a frank admission of what it means to become a poet writing in English. The "drumbeat of Avon," the "psalms of David," the "melody" of Dylan and the songs of "good Manley" are all part of the process of learning "how to dance in this rarefied air" (*Beatitudes* 67–68). The poem thus stresses that whatever turns and twists his poetic career took over three decades, whatever poetic and political stances he adopted as a result of private and public circumstances, he has felt the need to differentiate between poetics and ideology, even if it meant reconciling two agonistic worldviews in the interests of his vocation.

If, however, among these diverse influences, one were to single out a particularly significant tradition—one that exerted the greatest force on his sensibility—it would probably be the poetry of Romanticism, particularly in its emphasis on the primacy of the imagination, the celebration of emotion and passion, and in its attitude to the benevolence of nature. Echoes of Modernism do appear in his poetry, particularly in the poems that establish an ironic distance from his subject matter or those that work with metaphors to displace and objectify an emotionally charged experience; but the consistent attraction has been to the kind of lyric that gives expression to the power of emotion and sentiment, even when it borders on sentimentality or hyperbole. It is a quality that Irving Layton, among others, recognized early in his writing as an attribute that sets him apart from the majority of contemporary Canadian poets, and one which Reshard Gool, in his introduction to *A Time for Loving* (1986), stresses repeatedly as a distinctive trait. As Gool puts it, "the verse rehearses grand risks, invention, resource" (vii). The much-earlier *Flesh and Thorn* (1974)—which, appropriately, chooses for its epigraph Sappho's "Love with his gift of pain"—is almost exclusively concerned with the exploration of passion, often in its allusion to one

> who once set fire to wet grass
> with torches in your limbs,
> coaxed suns like butterflies
> on to your open palms,
> spoke words as passionate
> as elephant trumpeting the moon.

("Pardon My Muted Ways," *Flesh*, n.p.)

The preoccupation with love, in all its facets but particularly passion, beauty, betrayal and despair, and with nature that both reflects and transforms subjective states, is hardly surprising since so much of his early poetry is linked with the personal circumstances that compelled his emigration to Canada.

Crusz was born in Sri Lanka (then known as Ceylon) into a middle-class, conservative, Burgher family in 1925, and grew up in Colombo, where he had his education at St Peter's College and later at the University of Ceylon where he read history. Whatever training in and exposure to English literature he had was gained from his father's library and from his brother Hilary, who later became a well-known zoologist and scientist, rather than from any formal training. He speaks candidly about this period of his life in "Talking for Myself" and insists that he came to "English on his own terms," which explains the absence of any juvenilia in his work. When, after a period of postgraduate training in England in library science, he returned to Sri Lanka in 1953, radical changes were beginning to take place in the newly independent nation and what seemed like a long and prestigious career as a librarian at the Central Bank was cut short, partly due to the changes in the political climate of a country committed to active decolonization but more specifically due to the breakdown of his marriage and the "raging chaos of love" that accompanied the departure of his wife. Very much a result of this desertion, his early poetry became a recollection of how "she rose like a zombie/and walked into her beloved Night" (*Flesh*, "Little Brown Boy," n.p.). Following the collapse of his marriage, he too then left the country in 1965, with his three children, to begin a new life in Canada, a decision that becomes the subject of his unpublished children's story "Bumpis, the Magic Elephant." If the relative stability of life in Canada and the passage of time have both assuaged the pain of betrayal and deflected the focus of his poetry, he has nonetheless remained very much the poet of passion, creating poems that, as Uma Parameswaran claims, go "singing into Canadian literature to the sound of Kandyan drums" (153).

If the sheer momentum and energy of lines such as,

And when like a bird
stoned in magnificent flight
I hurtled down, down
among dogs and flowers and kings,
their karmic tongues did not speak,
the Buddha eyes did not weep. . .

("The Sun-Man Looks at Pain," *Flesh*, n.p.)

has now given way to a much mellower and controlled poetry that is more reflective and more subtle in its evocation of moods, the impulse to work with emotion is as strong as ever. In the love poems written to his (second) wife Anne, the poems that describe his children, and even those in which the sun-man encounters racism, the imaginative and the passionate are still constitutive aspects. In an unpublished poem entitled "Libra" he rehearses his own death, with a defiance that recalls Blake and intertextually connects with Dylan

Thomas:

> No. I will not "go gently into that dark night"
> you'll first hear
> the Kandyan drums make fire
> under the dancer's anklet bells,
> the raven caw the breaking news,
> the elephant's last clear trumpet . . .

But Crusz's reputation as a Sri Lankan or hyphenated Canadian poet has been a result not of his love poetry or his elegiac lyrics but of those that deal with migrancy, with his status in Canada as an immigrant poet. Crusz's second collection *Elephant and Ice* (1980) has probably been the most influential in foregrounding the immigrant theme, although the notion of exile has never been far from his consciousness. "Elephant" and "Ice" have served as tropes in positioning his "public" self in a literary climate where ethnicity is a source of endless debate. In addition to the duality of these two images, the persona of the "sun-man," "winter man" and "raven," all of which the poet assumes to explore different facets of the migrant experience, serve as markers for relating the experience of living on the cusp of alienation, racism, identity and nostalgia. Despite his reservations about the ethnic label that defines his poetry and his identity, Crusz himself has courted this image with a substantial body of poems that move from one end of the spectrum of migration to the other, celebrating, critiquing and ironizing these two worlds. In "Elegy for the Sun-Man's Children Going" he speaks of "This immigrant poet,/whose road was never his, but went" (*Elephant*, 28) and in "Dark with Excessive Bright" he admits: "Dark I am/and darkly do I sing" (*Elephant* 90), all of which point to his own insistent concern with being an outsider in Canada.

The binaries in themselves are significant, and they find expression in the sensuous imagery of flowers, fruits and the beauty of nature in Sri Lanka, as against the cold, the snow and the bleakness of Canada. On the one hand the sun-man remembers

> how he once lived;
> on a fistful of rice,
> shred of dried fish,
> mango and pineapple,

coconut milk dripping
from his mouth . . .   (*Elephant*, 20)

On the other, in an alien land, the sun-man crawls

into his sun-dial nerves
and sleeps
with myths and shibboleths
as central heating steals
under his dark eyelids   (*Elephant*, 35)

If an awareness of the disparity between these two worlds and the predicament of exile are essential to any reading of Crusz, the emphasis on duality to the exclusion of an indeterminate middle ground has been both productive and frustrating. If the critical material about his exilic sensibility has served the function of establishing Crusz as a major "multicultural" writer, it has also had the consequence of obscuring the complexities of experience and of formal invention that frame his writing. Migrancy has thus been a mixed blessing, one which has brought him recognition in certain quarters as a poet who gives expression to the immigrant consciousness, and alienation in others as one who locates himself outside mainstream concerns.

Arun Mukherjee, for instance, has in several articles consistently referred to Crusz's capacity to reveal "what it is to be an immigrant and a non-white in a society that is so dissimilar from that of one's origin" (21) and praises the manner in which he negotiates the politics of otherness. Mukherjee sees in Crusz's writing the opposite of the impulses that run through Michael Ondaatje's poetry, which lack commitment to the social and political realities of Sri Lanka and foreground the aesthetic at the expense of the referential. Mukherjee is emphatic about her own standards that require literature to "say something" and within that paradigm Crusz succeeds where Ondaatje doesn't. While such formulations tend to imply a wholly tendentious bent in one and a belletristic impulse in the other, Crusz himself makes a distinction between the two in a poem called "Going for Broke" where he affirms his penchant for "batik profusion."

In contrast to the views of Mukherjee, Craig Tapping in a review of *A Time for Loving* that appeared in *Canadian Literature* has been sceptical of the poet's handling of the dualities of home and exile and sees in Crusz a "colonial's dangerous nostalgia" (147). For Tapping, Crusz is very much the essentialist whose recreation of "home" is a form of appropriation. Along similar lines, but in greater detail, Suwanda Sugunasiri takes to task all Sri Lankan poets writing in Canada for their lack of commitment, their distance from the realities of the country they left behind. For Sugunasiri, the differences between Ondaatje and Crusz are less important than the fact they both "fled the revolution" of Sri Lanka and have thus become self-imposed outsiders. For him Crusz is "no closer to being Sinhalese or Sri Lankan than Ondaatje, in his sensibility or rootedness" (67).

In a literary climate that is increasingly sensitive to the nuances of otherness, it is hardly surprising that the positioning of Crusz has become a matter of concern. Notions of essentialism, authenticity, appropriation and nostalgia are often invoked to celebrate or discredit the author's stance. While individual poems can be cited to prove one point or another, what is often inadequately recognized is the manner in which the poems resonate against each other to produce intersections that resist any easy taxonomy.

Andrew Stubbs is right in his observation that "the range of contrasts" in Crusz's poetry "narrate the endlessly repeating history of his journey from Ceylon to Canada" (1)—a retelling of the process of displacement. But it is also a narration that is constantly in a state of flux as the poet moves from the referential to the reflective, from the lyrical to the narrative, from celebration to acceptance. The shifts in persona counterpoint the fixity suggested by the pronominal "I" to explore shades of meaning, the uncertainties of Keats's "negative capability." If "the white silence of civilization" is stifling in one poem, the beauty of the burning bush is enough "to bring another Moses to his knees" (*Beatitudes*, 12) in another. This "white marshmallow land" is both his and not his. If, as he desires in a recent poem called "Love Poem for Anne #4" to

> tell the raven and the elephant
> that I still sing their extravagant song,
> parade their metaphors
> without compromise

and demonstrate that his sense of loss is undiminished, he is also conscious of the violence in the country, and speaks

> about Colombo's walking dead

42

the suicide-bombers, the blood
that flows so freely in the dusty North

and about the changes that have transformed the nation. Canada is still not home, but it is an "igloo of heaven" where he is at home and, as he remarks in another poem, he is

[a] brown laughing face
in the snow,
not the white skull
for the flies
in Ceylon's deadly sun.   (*Elephant*, 95)

The ostensible binaries can be deceptive in Crusz's work and, as he points out in his wonderful poem "Roots," his own identity, marked by hybridity, defies the easy dichotomies of East and West. Of his Burgher (i.e. Eurasian) ancestry and his ambiguous status in Sri Lanka, he says:

A Portuguese captain holds
the soft brown hand of my Sinhala mother.
It's the year 1515 AD,
when two civilizations kissed and merged,
and I, Burgher of that hot embrace,
write a poem of history . . .   (*Singing*, 42)

The syncretism does not invalidate the fondness with which the poet recalls the Sri Lankan landscape or uses it to contrast the bleakness of Canada, but he is aware of the ambivalence of his own inheritance. The colonial legacy is a complex one, clearly oppressive and hegemonic, as the rulers exploited the land and its people. He recalls

[h]ow your freighters coughed black,
then guffawed and left heavy
with coconut and tea,
cardamom, cinnamon and ivory.   (*Rain*, 2)

And yet, having learnt the language, the poet is inevitably a part of that tradition. In a context where decolonization and "writing back" are axiomatic, Crusz has consistently expressed this sense of divided loyalty. Quite rightly, Michael Thorpe sees him in relation to an older generation of postcolonial writers who could "appropriate the colonial legacy of Shakespeare and English without anguished breast-beating. . ." (130).

The land he left behind is where his ancestral memory resides, and the allegiance is rendered complex by his own Burgher status. He is an immigrant poet, but one for whom the cusp between worlds is both loss and gain. The challenge for him has been to create a system of mythology that transcends the referential and brings together the primordial relation to the land he has left. If the image clusters that make up this elaborate system have been mistaken for gestures of essentialism, it is at least partly because the fictive has been confused with the referential. Images of the elephant and the raven are part of the natural world that the poet alludes to, and they are part of the landscape he remembers, but his use of them as markers for the subconscious and the mythical is what gives to his poems their particular texture. It is the interplay of the real and the fictive that leads for instance, to the claim:

When the raven talks
listen,
it is God
in ultimate disguise.   (*Rain*, 44)

Here the raven in its referential mode is the other, the voice of the margins that is the target of discrimination. But the raven is also part of a mystical world, the symbol of a religious consciousness and the voice of God. Crusz is always conscious that language creates its own reality and if what is offered as the real is no more than a fictive construct, it is because his poetry rejects the various closures that ideological commitment demands.

It is hardly an accident that Derek Walcott appears time and again as an intertextual reference in Crusz's poetry. At its most obvious both share an awareness of racial mixture that flaunts hybridity; more significantly, they reveal a scepticism about nationalist narratives that employ a unitary model to legitimize a particular ideology. In both one sees a denunciation of the hegemony of colonialism and a cele-bration of the language that the rulers left behind. The self-reflexivity that surfaces constantly in Crusz's poetry is a reminder that at some level his concern is with language, with the power of metaphor not merely to reflect but also to shape experience. The large number of poems that are explicitly self-referential is again an indication that for

Crusz the relation between the fictive and the referential is hardly ever simple or straightforward.

Singing Against the Wind (1985), Crusz's third volume of poetry, begins with a poem entitled "The Elephant Who Would Be a Poet," which serves as an apologia for his poetry and as an illustration of the various preoccupations that run through his work. It is an example of the short, carefully structured, tonally perfect, witty and meditative poem that he often writes and is comfortable with. While it makes perfect sense as a stand-alone poem with its internal coherence and its formal structure, it is also part of a larger system of images—a private mythology—that he creates to anchor his ideas and give them resonance. The elephant, apart from its referential function in relation to the event described in the poem, serves also as a symbol of the landscape that the poet has left behind and that has been a shaping influence in his poetic career.

"The Elephant Who Would Be a Poet" is a poem about the process of writing poetry, about the isolation of the poet and his alienation from those around him, told through the image of the elephant and the mahout. After a day of tiring and monotonous logging, the elephant decides to relax in a most unusual manner:

> Without command
> he eases his huge body to the ground,
> rolls over,
> makes new architecture
> from his thick legs,
> four columns vertical
> to the sun.

Predictably, the mahout is taken by surprise and is confused by the display of dissent:

> The confused mahout
> refuses the poem
> in this new equilibrium,
> this crazy theatre of the mind . . .   (*Singing*, 9)

This, then, is the role of the poet—the outsider, the person who sees things differently and acts unconventionally, much to the annoyance and incomprehension of the reader who would prefer to see the poet in a much more conventional role. In different ways, the need to

45

define his craft and his own concerns become, inevitably, a central concern in all his published volumes. Rather than lead to self-indulgence and posturing, this self-reflexivity enables the poet to look at himself with ironic detachment, as in another poem in which his son Michael wonders, "What's so hot about dad's poetry?" (*Singing*, 68) and the poet, with characteristic self-awareness, admits that there is nothing particularly new "about this immigrant theme," and wonders why he chooses to flaunt it like a side of beef. While the convention of poets reflecting on their poetry is hardly new, its urgency and relevance for Crusz, who is sharply conscious of his hyphenated status, can hardly be underestimated.

In another poem, a reader is enticed by the pervasive "elephant image" and decides to give a "tiny crystal elephant" as a Christmas gift to the poet, thereby transforming the metaphoric into the metonymic. Wanting to pursue the relation between symbol and substance, the poet probes further about the friend's response to his poetry and is told to look again at the crystal elephant. He does, and "a very lopsided beast/was staring back at him with curious eyes" (*Beatitudes*, 57). Removed from the larger system of which it is a part, the beast looks awkward and exoticized, the symbol at once inappropriate, comic and irrelevant. Time and again the poetry is an affirmation and subversion of various stances. If the poet is defiant and serious in one, he is dismissive and humorous in another as he goes through various stages of introspection. There is hardly any finality, any closure, only a constant quest for a mode that would be both a narrative of a complex journey and a stay against the vicissitudes occasioned by the journey. The natural process of growth and decay concerns him and becomes the subject of his poetry. But he is equally concerned with the aesthetic, the capacity to detach the experience from its subjectivity to explore in metaphor the artistic appeal of the moment. Hence, the description of the mango leaf:

Now, cleanly autumned, scarlet,
at the feet of its mother tree,
with the sun veiling its small architecture
like a tabernacle,
and the tree smiling at its roots
for a death
so exotically done.   (*Elephant*, 52)

The self-reflexivity and the introspection are at least in part a consequence of a genuine concern with his own predicament of living on the cusp, of negotiating two worlds, of being anxious about his own directions. They also draw attention to all the areas of experience—the cosmic scheme—that occupy him. Very little attention has been paid, for instance, to all the poems devoted to his family, to his parents and his brother and to "the umbrella of doting children." In the poems devoted to his parents one finds a quality of unreserved adulation. If these poems in their concern with the narrative element sometimes lack the sensuous metaphoric dimension of his other poems, they still do occupy a central place in his work. And they shed light on the peculiar paradox of how despite a country that spurned him and a wife who deserted him, he still retains a profound sense of attachment to the land.

Some of the earliest poems published by Crusz in *Grail* have been about religion, no doubt inspired by his own convictions and his strong Catholic background. As early as in *Elephant and Ice* (59,66) Christian mythology and imagery resonate in his poems, and that is consistent with his education at a Christian school and his own admiration for Milton and Hopkins. However, the didactic poems which parade a religious sentiment are sometimes the least effective. Thus the tendentious edge of "Sermon in the Forest" reinforces the conventionality of the poem. Where the religious impulses come into contact (and conflict) with a secular imagination, the poems take on a richly textured and multiplicitous quality. A case in point is the first stanza of "The Gardener," which reads:

Since Adam
had fouled things up
by trying to live under God
with a naked woman, a serpent,
and an apple tree,
this gardener's ambition
was to remake Eden
in only a garden of roses.   (*Flesh*, n.p.)

In poetry that is as reminiscent of John Donne and Herbert Vaughn as it is of Indian *bhakti* poetry, Crusz demonstrates a resistance to any easy taxonomy. Religion becomes the occasion for satire, for exuberant wit, for the exposure of deep-seated hypocrisy and racism and for philosophical speculation about theology. "The Accepted One" remains a particularly important poem, written on the occasion of his brother's decision to give up priesthood, and ending with the reassuring thought,

> Father Magee opened
> a small door
> into a cockeyed world,

> and God did not pitch the sun
> with dark thoughts.   (*Still*, 69)

The tradition of *bhakti* poetry becomes clearer in those poems that adopt a tone of irreverence, of playful banter, of infusing a childlike innocence into what is ostensibly a religious poem. If in "Yes, in Our Father's House There Are Many Rooms" the gesture of asking God for a room and then a bungalow for his family satirizes the materialism of institutionalized religion, it also reflects that liberty and that deep sense of conviction associated with the best of *bhakti* literature.

It is tempting and perhaps not altogether wrong to offer a teleological view of Crusz's evolution as a poet. The very first volume is, as Uma Parameswaran and several others have observed, deeply personal, concerned for the most part with private sorrows and the struggle of living in an alien land, and the second volume is concerned with the two worlds of Sri Lanka and Canada and the trials faced by the poet who attempts to make the transition. It is here that one becomes conscious of the various binaries that later came to be associated with his oeuvre. *Singing Against the Wind*, as the title suggests, is about forms of resistance, about the need to go against the grain. The subsequent volumes are at once an assertion that the poet is still close to that world, despite the changes wrought by time, and an admission of the complexity of identifying "home"—of being nourished and abandoned by the rain. In Beatitudes, there is a greater affinity with the new home, a greater willingness to accept both worlds as essential to the poet. As Shyam Selvadurai rightly points out in a recent review, "suddenly the notion of his foreignness, his yearning for Sri Lanka are undercut and one is aware of a life lived, a history made here; a sense of belonging in spite of oneself" (25).

Such an evolutionary scheme serves as a defence against the notion that the poet's career has hardly evolved in the last two decades. It reveals a certain change of thematic emphasis in his writing. The taxonomy is convenient but it suggests a trajectory of growth and evolution that is hardly accurate. In fact something of the raw power of his earlier poetry is hardly ever captured in the more mellow and meditative later work. And there is a cyclical pattern in his poetry, a tendency to go back to themes that need to be expressed again. If a linear pattern is a necessary route for the reader, so is a synchronic one that draws attention to repetitive structures that inform his work.

To pay attention to the linear narrative of home and exile is to chart the complex journey of a poet who has moved from the personal to the public and from despair and pessimism to reconciliation and acceptance. In fact, that would substantiate the emphasis of his poem "Homecomings," which speaks about

> the journey's throbbing walk
> to this igloo of heaven
> or that sun-faced island of the elephant
> where I'm always at home,
> if not home.

But Crusz's claim to serious recognition lies not simply in the various stances, not even in the range of subject matter, but in the manner in which the poems relate to each other and resonate to create meaning and draw attention to themselves. What the image of the elephant communicates in one poem is complemented, subverted, questioned and built on in another. If the poet's birth is associated with Libra in one poem, that itself becomes the subject of another work and the promise of one poem is fulfilled in another.

The centripetal focus established by the network of imagery strengthens the rhythmic dimension of his poetry. Hardly a formalist, Crusz has written few poems that recapitulate established metrical forms. But the sonnet, the heroic couplet, the ballad and a whole range of stanzaic patterns are constant echoes in his free verse forms where each line and each stanza reflects that consciousness of metrical patterns in a manner that is unusual in contemporary poetry. While the minimalist poem, that highly condensed expression of experience, is not altogether unusual in his corpus, his strength lies in the more expansive mode where the line lengths, the enjambment, the counterpointing of metrical patterns, and the unfailing attention to the oral quality of poetry make his poetry striking in their appeal.

Even when the subject matter is overtly tendentious as in "Faces of the Sun-Man" one is struck by the sure sense of rhythm and the symbiotic relation between metaphor and prosody.

When Michael Thorpe, in a review of Crusz's *The Rain Doesn't Know Me Any More,* makes the grand assertion that Crusz is "arguably the best living Sri Lankan poet in English" (130), the claim is neither perfunctory nor casual. The comparison that the comment implies is an important one which brings into focus a number of poets writing in Sri Lanka, Australia and North America. Thorpe's comment establishes Crusz's ongoing concern with the Sri Lankan scene. Equally true is the poet's dialogue with the Canadian scene, where he is both marginal and mainstream, at odds with the restrictive conventions that label him as the other, and perfectly at home in the tradition of the sensuous lyric.

WORKS CITED

Crusz, Rienzi. 1987. "Talking for Myself." *The Toronto South Asian Review* 6: 29-35.

Gool, Reshard. 1986. Introduction to *A Time for Loving* by Rienzi Crusz. Toronto: TSAR.

Mukherjee, Arun. 1986/87. "Songs of an Immigrant: The Poetry of Rienzi Crusz." *Currents* 4: 19-21.

Parameswaran, Uma. 1992. "The Singing Metaphor: Poetry of Rienzi Crusz." *Canadian Literature* 132 : 146-54.

Selvadurai, Shyam. 1996. Review of *Beatitudes of Ice,* by Rienzi Crusz. *Books in Canada* 25: 25.

Stubbs, Andrew. n.d. "Keeping Iago: Rituals of Innocence In Rienzi Crusz's Recent Poetry." Unpublished.

Sugunasiri, Suwanda H J. 1992. "'Sri Lankan' Canadian Poets: The Bourgeoisie that Fled the Revolution." *Canadian Literature,* 132 : 60-79.

Tapping, Craig. 1988. "Front Lines." Review of *A Time for Loving* by Rienzi Crusz. *Canadian Literature* 117: 145-47.

Thorpe, Michael. 1994. Review of *The Rain Doesn't Know Me Any More* by Rienzi Crusz. *World Literature Today* 68.: 130.

The Singing Never Stops:
Languages of Italian Canadian Writers

JOSEPH PIVATO

J'ai changé, tout est neuf. I have changed, everything is new
FULVIO CACCIA

Canadian writers of Italian background have benefitted from the
cultural diversity of Canada by producing a body of literature that
exists in several languages: English, Italian, French, and Italian dialects. There are about 120 active Italian-Canadian writers, and while
most of them use only one language, all have a knowledge of one or
two of the other languages. And there is a small groups of writers
who work in two languages and the rare person who has published
in three. The result of this literary activity is that we have an unusual
situation in which not only is there a trilingual body of literature but
also are there writers who move freely among these languages and
translate between one and another for those who cannot reach beyond the language barriers.

The existence of this trilingual body of literature has some unusual
effects on the activities of the authors: on the nature of their writing,
their translations and their relations with other writers. This literature
makes demands on readers, who are expected to share in the knowledge of another language when they are reading English or French or
Italian. In fact it is necessary to read works in all three languages in
order to understand fully individual works and the body of literature
as a whole. This phenomenon is unusual for writing in North America, a continent apparently dominated by English language and culture.

As a direct response to this apparently predominant monoculture,

Montreal writer Fulvio Caccia and a number of friends founded *Vice Versa*, a trilingual literary magazine which promoted the idea of transculture, the production of books, plays and films, that transcend a single culture and demonstrate links with many different cultures, very much like music. A very successful example of such a body of work is Fulvio Caccia's own writing in Italian and in French. His book of French poems, *Aknos*, won the Governor General's Award for poetry in Canada in 1994. Another example is the Quebec film *La Sarrasine* by Paul Tana, which uses not only French, but also Italian, Sicilian and English.

Different Languages

An early Italian example of linguistic diversity in Canada is provided by Mario Duliani, who published *La ville sans femmes* in French in 1945 and one year later brought out his own Italian version, *Citta senza donne*. The Italian is not just a translation of the French but a different version for a different audience. These are two versions of the narrative of Duliani's experience as a prisoner in an internment camp during the Second World War. The Italian experience and perspective of these events are obviously different from those of a French Canadian, and this is reflected in the two versions. Duliani was a journalist for the Montreal paper *La Presse* and understood his audiences. This controversial book was translated into English only in 1994 as *The City Without Women*, by the Italian Canadian poet Antonino Mazza.

Currently we have a whole generation of writers who work and publish in more than one language. In Montreal Filippo Salvatore has published in Italian, in English and in French. His first collection of poems, *Tufo e gramigna* (1977) in Italian, was later produced in English as *Suns of Darkness* (1980). Salvatore has also produced a French play, *La Fresque de Mussolini* (1985), that implicitly compares the more extreme forms of Quebec nationalism to the fascist regime in Italy. By playing with the languages, rhetorics and perspectives of the two groups he is able to comment on both societies. Salvatore's primary languages have become French and Italian as he continues to add to the linguistic diversity of Quebec.

Another polyglot writer is Antonio D'Alfonso, who reflects the linguistic diversity of his upbringing and education in Montreal. In his book of French prose poems *L'autre rivage* (1987), he writes, "Meme l'italien est une langue appris."

In the English version of his book, *The Other Shore* (1986), this is expressed more fully, reading:

> Even Italian is a learned language for me. Language of the North, it is not the language my thoughts were formed in, nor the music I hear in my head at night when I cannot get to sleep. Already a transformation occurs: from Guglionesano, I must translate into Italian. When I write I translate. Sometimes no translation occurs. The words or phrases come directly into English or French. A linkage of differences. (109)

The linguistic strata in Antonio D'Alfonso's writing exemplify very well the four types of language identified by linguist Henri Gobard in his book *L'Alienation linguistique*. The first is the vernacular language, that of maternal origins, which in this case is the Italian dialect of Guglionesi. The second language is vehicular, the urban language of the state and commerce, which for D'Alfonso is English, the language of power. The third is the referential language, that of culture, which here is French. And the fourth is the mythic language of religion and beyond, which here is standard Italian. The cultural environment of a language has its effect on the writing itself. D'Alfonso openly acknowledges the roles of his languages in the following macaronic verse, a poem called "Babel":

> Nativo di Montreal
> eleve comme Quebecois
> forced to learn the language of power
> vivi en Mexico como alternativa
> figlio del sole e della campagna
> par les franc-parleurs aime
> finding thousands like me suffering
> me case y divorcie en tierra fria
> nipote di Guglionesi
> parlant politique malgre moi
> *steeled in the school of Old Aquinas*

queriendo luchar con mis amigos latinos
Dio where shall I be demain
(trop vif) que puedo saber yo
spero che la terra be mine   (57)

As a group these writers share their preoccupation with language, a kind of oversensitivity to the meaning and weight of words, English, French, Italian and dialects. They read each other's work, and they invite their Canadian readers to become aware of this diversity and the growing multidimensional aspect of Canadian literature. In their poetry and in interviews both Pier Giorgio Di Cicco and Pasquale Verdicchio epitomize this concern with the influence of Italian on their English writing.

Linguistic diversity has also emerged in the writing of other ethnic minority authors in Canada. West Indian writers like Austin Clarke are very effective in using West Indian dialects in their English narratives. The many languages of India are sometimes evident in the work of Rohinton Mistry and M G Vassanji. And in Calgary, Hiromi Goto is not afraid to use Japanese in her English novel *Chorus of Mushrooms* (1994).

Language Interference

When one language affects the use of another language we have language interference. This is a common phenomenon in the writing of ethnic minority authors. The first thing I should make clear is that despite, or maybe because of, all these language problems, Italian Canadian writers do not produce much experimental writing. Instead they tend to write very much in the realist tradition. The interference between languages in a work is not simply a clever literary device for them but a daily reality which they try to represent truthfully with all its ramifications.

D'Alfonso's "Babel," to me, is not a postmodern poem that deconstructs language but a slice of life: the language confusion which D'Alfonso and other ethnic students grow up with in Montreal.

In his French play, *Addolorata*, Marco Micone has the main character, Addolorata, explain her linguistic situation in Montreal with these words,

I can also speak English with my friends, French with the neighbours, Italian with the machos, and Spanish with certain customers. With my four languages, I never get bored. With my four languages, I can watch soaps in English, read the French TV Guide, the Italian fotoromanzi, and sing "Guantanamera" ... At the Bay, when I have Spanish customers, I introduce myself as Lolita Gomez. It's so much nicer than Addolorata Zanni. Addolorata is so ugly, that most of my cousins changed their name. The one living in Toronto calls herself Laurie. She is the cousin I like least. She is so weird—she studies things that are for men. She wants to be a "lawyer." She only speaks English. She says she also speaks Italian, but when she tries, she speaks have Italian, half English. I don't know where she is going to go with a language and a half. I have another cousin in Argentina. Her name is Dolores. (137-8)

For Addolorata there is not a confusion between one language and another, there is rather a confusion over her own identity. She has apparently compartmentalized herself into four linguistic identities for which she even has names. Is this a negative or positive situation for her, or is it rather simply a reality, a condition commonly found among ethnic minority characters ?

In the short stories of Dino Minni this shifting identity is often treated as a positive change, an opportunity for the character to make a new beginning, to take control of his or her own destiny. In his short story, "Details from the Canadian Mosaic," the little Italian boy, Mario, changes his name so that he has two identities to match his two languages:

He did not know at what point he had become Mike. One day looking for a suitable translation for his name and finding none, he decided that Mike was closest. By the end of the summer, he was Mario at home and Mike in the streets. (56)

Dino Minni is not writing from Quebec but from British Columbia where there seems to be great flexibility with different languages and cultures.

Entire works can demonstrate the effects of language interference in the widest sense. Caterina Edwards produced an English play which she originally called *Terra Straniera* ("strange land") but later changed to *Homeground*, with the opposite meaning. The difference is partially due to position and point of view. For an Italian immigrant Canada is a strange land. But for an *English-* speaking resident it can be home. The different languages then represent different perspectives. The play itself tries to communicate the Italian perspective and an Italian immigrant notion of *nostalgia*. This is not simply English nostalgia, but Italian *nostalgia*, a whole complex of ideas, relationships, obligations, regional ties, history, etc, which cannot be translated into English. *Nostalgia* is another one of those emotionally charged words. It takes the whole play to try to communicate some of this idea. The whole movement of the play is backward-looking, as the Italian immigrants will in the end leave Canada and return to Italy. The play is full of Italian terms, points of reference, rituals, folklore and cultural assumptions that can never be fully rendered into English.

In the play, the wife and mother Maria tries to recall the words of old Italian folksongs and at one point attempts to recall the recipe for an old ritual. She finds that she has forgotten it:

There is safety in the old ways, safety. The old rites. Oil and salt, flame and water. If I could remember the words. I only heard them a few times as a child, mumbled over my head or over that of my brothers and sisters. I left the valley before I had the age or the wisdom to learn from the older women. Each word must be exact. Oil and salt, flame and water—that I remember. The words, the words. (78)

To Maria the exact words are important; they cannot be changed or translated. A different language is a different frame of reference.

Homeground is constructed around this problem of different languages and cultures. The characters are recent Italian immigrants who, in the real world, would be speaking Italian to each other. In this Canadian play they speak standard English, but the dialogue is peppered with Italian expressions, "Senza pane tutti diventano orfani." There are also several verses of Italian folksongs, songs of nostalgia such as "Terra Straniera." Even the cold of the Alberta winter cannot make the singing stop.

In the context of the play the Italian words take on new meanings which emerge from the experience of these people in Canada. And the English words of these Italian characters change as well. Words like husband, son, job, house and bread take on meanings they do not normally have in an English Canadian context.

Even a word like "bread" does not mean the same thing in every language. It was not until I was twenty years old that my parents bought Canadian bread in plastic bags. Up to that point bread in plastic bags was foreign, something we did not even consider to be bread. To us, to me to this day, bread must have a crust, a texture and smell. How do you translate that lifetime experience of "bread" using merely words?

English is the main language of the play, but when used by these strange new people it is a language that is deterritorialized, subjected to a series of displacements that make it change pace, slow down, so that we have to reexamine the meanings of words. One character explains, " 'Pretty' from our mouths is not the same as 'pretty' from the mouth of Mr Edmonton." (62)

This language interference extends to the other languages used by Italian Canadian writers. Canadian writers who work in Italian use the language in a different way from writers in Italy. They may have to use an English Canadian expression because there is no equivalent word in Italian. But some Italian words take on new meanings when used this side of the Atlantic. The idea of migrant in English has two words: emigrant, the person who leaves, and immigrant, the new arrival who comes into the host country. In Italian there is only one word, *emigrante*, the person who leaves, since Italy was never a host country to new arrivals until the last ten years. In the Italian word *emigrante*, the person who has left has both positive and negative connotations. In Maria Ardizzi's Italian novel *Made in Italy*, the narrator is fascinated with the idea of *emigrante* because it seems to contain for her the idea of travel to exotic places and freedom. When she becomes an immigrant trapped in a ghetto in North America, the word has a different connotation. The perspective is no longer from one who is leaving but from one who has arrived and must make adjustments.

It should be noted that there are over one hundred books by Italian Canadians in standard Italian or in one of the dialects.

A Fourth Sound

Italian Canadian writers have produced a body of literature in three standard languages: English, Italian and French. But there is often a fourth language which may vary from writer to writer. For Antonio D'Alfonso, Filippo Salvatore, and Mary di Michele it is the Italian dialect Molise. For Dore Michelut, Marisa De Franceschi and Bianca Zagolin it is Friulan, the distinct language of the Friuli region of North Eastern Italy. For Pasquale Verdicchio and Corrado Mastropasqua it is the dialect and music of Naples.

For many Italian Canadians the other language is Italiese, that mixture of Italian and English which has developed as a dialect in Canada. Of the 120 active Italian Canadian writers *not one* writes in Italiese, not even for humour or dialogue. This is the everyday language for many Italian Canadians. It is the language many of us constantly hear, but it is not the language which we use in our writing. Rather it is the language we write against. It is the language against which we make our characters so articulate in one of the standard languages that they are sometimes hard to believe as realistic Italian immigrants. Hard to believe but not hard to understand. And this is the most important objective: to be understood clearly.

In a poem to his dead father, Pier Giorgio Di Cicco writes, "The roses dream with him / of being understood in clear english . . . " (31) Italiese is the language we reject as we reject the stereotypes of the "dumb wop" and the mafioso. In addition to clarity of communication, the languages we use also have the task of fighting that very heavy burden of the negative stereotype. For eighty years   North American film has depicted the Italian as either stupid or evil. But in the work of Italian Canadian writers one does not find figures from organized crime—even though Mario Puzzo made it fashionable and profitable in the United States to exploit the image of the Italian Mafia.

For Marco Micone the fourth language is that of silence. In his French plays Micone writes against the condition of being inarticulate. Micone's theatre begins with silence, the silence which he attributes to Italian immigrants in Quebec. In his first play, *Gens du silence* (1980), the Italians are not only voiceless but also invisible and powerless. The political conflicts in Canada between the English and the French have resulted in their marginalization, as indeed of other immigrant groups. In this first play, the immigrant daughter expresses the rootless condition in these words:

> I teach teenagers who all have Italian names and who have one culture, that of silence. Silence about the peasant origin of their parents. Silence about the reasons for emigration. Silence about the manipulation they're victims of. Silence about the country they live in. Silence about the reasons for their silence. (71)

Given their voiceless status, how does Micone make these immigrants express themselves? How does he break this silence with words comprehensible to both the Italo-quebecois and the Quebecois? Micone gives them a French voice with Italian and English accents. Nancy tells us,

> You must write in French so that everyone can understand you. Young people must find themselves in texts written by someone who lived like them, who understands and wants to help them. Their being different has to become a reason for them to struggle, and not a cause for complexes and passivity. (95)

Why do Italian Canadian writers use so many languages? The direct answer to this question is that they live in a Canada of different languages and reflect this in their writing. Italian immigrants come from an Italy of diversity, in which people normally use more than one language. They often speak the regional dialect at home and standard Italian in school and in communications with government officials and other authorities. It is natural for these people to deal with the ambiguities and translation processes of the different languages of Canada. They have produced a literature in three or four languages because they could not write it any other way.

As much as multiculturalism is attacked by neoconservatives, it is a reality in Canada. The work of Italian Canadian writers and other ethnic minority authors demonstrates that "there is settling into shape a nation" of great diversity.

WORKS CITED

Ardizzi, Maria. 1982. *Made in Italy*. Toronto: Toma Publishing.

Caccia, Fulvio. 1994. *Aknos*. Montreal: Guernica.

Buonomo, Leonardo. 1996. "Defining the Self through Memory: The Poetry of George Amabile and Pasquale Verdicchio." In *Memoria e Sogno: Quale Canada Domani*, edS Giulio Marra, A De Vaucher and A Gebbia. Venezia: Spernova.

D'Alfonso, Antonio. 1986. *The Other Shore*. Montreal: Guernica Editions.

———. 1987. *L'Autre rivage*. Montreal: VLB.

DiCicco, Pier Giorgio. 1990. *The Tough Romance*. Montreal: Guernica, 1990. First edition, Toronto: McClelland & Stewart, 1979.

Di Michele, Mary. 1980. *Bread and Chocolate*. Ottawa: Oberon Press.

Duliani, Mario. 1945. *La Ville sans femmes*. Montreal: Societe des editions Pascal.

Duliani, Mario. 1994. *City Without Women*. Translated by Antonino Maza. Oakville: Mosaic Press.

Edwards, Caterina. 1990. *Homeground*. Montreal: Guernica.

Gobard, Henri. 1976. *L'Alienation linguistique: analyse tetraglossique*. Paris: Flammirion.

Loriggio, Francesco, ed. 1996. *Social Pluralism and Literary History*. Toronto: Guernica, Editions.

Michelut, Dorina. 1986. *Loyalty to the Hunt*. Montreal: Guernica Editions.

Minni, C D. 1985. *Other Selves*. Montreal: Guernica Editions.

Micone, Marco. 1982. *Gens du silence*. Montreal: Quebec/Amerique.

———. 1984. *Addolorata*. Montreal: Guernica Editions.

Salvatore, Filippo. 1980. *Suns of Darkness*. Montreal: Guernica Editions.

_____. 1985. *La Fresque de Mussolini*. Montreal: Guernica Editions.

Padolsky, Enoch. 1996. "Ethnicity and Race: Canadian Minority Writing at a Crossroads." *Journal of Canadian Studies* 31: 129-147

Pivato, Joseph. 1994. *Echo: Essays on Other Literatures*. Toronto: Guernica.

Verdicchio, Pasquale. 1985. *Moving Landscape*. Montreal: Guernica.

_____. *Nomadic Trajectory*.1990. Montreal: Guernica.

Wallace, B. 1980. *Marrying into the Family*. Ottawa: Oberon Press.

Zagolin, Bianca. 1988. *Une femme a la fenetre*. Paris: Robert Laffont.

The Desire To Belong: The Politics of Texts and Their Politics of Nation

RINALDO WALCOTT

The Emergence of the Counter-Novel and the Requirement of a Deciphering Practice

The moment of what Sylvia Wynter calls the counter-novel has arrived for Black literature in Canada. Novels by Dionne Brand, Cecil Foster, Lawrence Hill, Austin Clarke, M Nourbese Philip, Suzette Mayr, André Alexis and a host of others have began to rework the novel's form and its conceptual premises, as it pertains to Black Canadians and their history, and to Black people more generally. These counter-novels are reshaping and refashioning both the literary landscape of Canada and rewriting Canadian historiography.

Wynter argues that the counter-novel must do more than what the traditional definition of the novel suggests is possible. In a discussion of what might be at stake in "Minority Discourse," Wynter argues that the counter-novel and Minority Discourse "is imperatively necessary, because [it is] linked to the motives of general human self-interest, rather than to the particular interests of specific groups" (Wynter 459). Thus, Wynter disputes the notion that Minority Discourse is too particularistic to speak to an assumed wider public. She further suggests that the counter-novel produces a " 'counter-exertion', one that will entail the transformation of both literary scholarship and our present organisation of knowledge" (459). She is intent on arguing that Minority Discourse, despite the misnomer, given the numeric evidence that those called minority are actually the majority, offers us the possibility of thinking differently about what might be at stake in refashioning what it means to be Human. Or, producing what she has termed in various essays, following the philosophers of science and culture, "new forms of human life."

Furthermore, in relation to the humanities as a site of knowledge production, Minority Discourse allows for "the liberation of the literary humanities themselves from the secondary role to which they have been logically relegated in our present episteme" (463). Wynter's insights are important to Black literature of the North because much of this literature creates universality from the gaze and words of those made subaltern. This is a universality that can be liberating. But it is sometimes a universality that can, in the case of some authors, partake of and reproduce dominant authoritative discourses situated within the differential power arrangements that make a numeric minority into a majority. The power of words are at stake in how we think about various positions on the questions of universality, minority and majority discourses, and their various contestations.

In this essay, I read and decipher the impact of three counter-novels that take Canada as a place and space of desire. I am particularly interested in the ways in which desire structures belonging. I suggest that different forms and expressions of desire are central to the notion of the counter-novel and its ability to effect and evoke new possibilities. This is an essay about the power of words to evoke and effect the desire for national belonging or something else. Lawrence Hill's *Any Known Blood*, Cecil Foster's *Slammin' Tar* and André Alexis's *Childhood* are all border-crossing texts set in Canada. Yet each of these texts depends upon a different kind of Black diaspora sensibility, one that is larger than national boundaries can contain. This border-crossing sensibility is useful for the narrative power of the text. Yet, despite the common ground of border-crossing in these texts, each displays a different set of political questions, concerns and implications for the nation. What this means is that border-crossings in these texts signify differently with different political and ethical concerns. Therefore the authors must be positioned differently in terms of the politics of their texts or what the texts are *intended to do*.

Politically, one might argue that these authors share little in common beyond being Black, but it is crucial to consider the kinds of repressions each of these works take up and why. Furthermore, what does the uncovering of repression in these works allow readers to see differently? And how does desire as a condition of belonging work in these novels? These questions impact on the different ways in which nation is understood and questioned or not questioned in these texts. The desire to concede to particular narratives of the nation is held up to scrutiny by each of these texts in very different ways. Or, put differently, critics might read different implications for the nation in each of these texts. These implications come with different political utterances and stances.

Sylvia Wynter suggests that "[u]nlike a critical practice which must seek for the 'meanings' of the text in the text alone . . . a deciphering practice will seek to function correlatively at four levels" (267). These four levels, complex and interrelated are: A) the signifying practices of the text itself; B) the specific social environment or cultural dimension of the text as its performative complex of meanings produce a "'symbol-matter information system' that is structured by the behaviour-regulating code that brings it into being as such an environment/dimension" (267); C) the third level brings the results of A and B together. This is important because this level requires us to consider what the performative and representational signifying practices of the text or its meanings are *"intended to do*—that is, *what* collective behaviours they are intended to induce and how precisely their practices of signification" (267) provide ways to shift, alter and/or retain the status quo of our habits; and D) the last level, then, is the place from which we might constitute the beginning of a critique of present conceptions of the Human and move towards a rethinking of what it means to be Human or to constitute "new forms of human life." What Wynter offers in her complex argument for a deciphering practice is a challenge to think beyond current conceptions of the Human and its order/containment/regulating "metaphysico-epistemological" premises. It is in this regard that I read each text for what it might occasion us to do with knowledge, nation, citizenship and the potential for being Human.

Childhood *and the Myth of Belonging*

André Alexis's *Childhood* has been one of the most celebrated Black texts in recent Canadian literary history. In 1999 Alexis won the Chapters/Books in Canada First Novel Award and shared the prestigious Ontario Trillium Award with Alice Munroe. The novel has been nominated for numerous other literary awards. Its publication and promotion has been heralded in very interested ways and its Canadian publishers McClelland and Stewart (M&S) secured international publishing rights for it even before the book was published. Recently, on the televisual "magazine" show *Hot Type*, Alexis was the only Black Canadian writer mentioned as one to look out for in terms of future promise. Interestingly, another Black Canadian writer, Dionne Brand has been named by the *New York Times* as the Canadian writer to look out for and most recently the New York *Village Voice Literary Supplement* featured her among eight other writers on the "verge."

Childhood has been interestedly promoted with little reference to Alexis as a black man. The promotion of the book on those terms has prompted the critic Peter Hudson to write in a review that Alexis "came across as an Artiste: as a cool, erudite Negro whose commitment to pure aesthetic form transcends the vagaries of race" (35). Hudson's insight speaks back to a racist discourse that often reads the concerns of "Black art" as political rather than artistic, therefore helping to shape conversations concerning what art must do. The promotion of the text as one being in excess of "Black art" seems to carry the implication that a link to blackness in the text would in some way damage its craft. But it is precisely the repression of the text's blackness and Alexis's blackness and the Caribbean genealogy of that blackness that I want to address in my response to the narrative and artistry of Alexis's text.

There is no doubt that Alexis is a fine and talented writer. His craft is tight and he can turn words and keep one's attention to the most banal of details in a way few writers can. This is important to point out because *Childhood* is a text almost about nothing. But the politics of his writing and his art can and might be questioned. Border-crossing pervades Alexis's text both in terms of its artistry and in terms of its narrative. Yet the reception of his book has ignored the border-crossing sensibility of the text. Reviews have focused on the language and style of the book but have failed to address what these are attempting to keep under wraps. I want to focus my comments on the narrative. However, I feel it necessary to say that the border-crossing of the art is a certain kind of forced postmodern aesthetic and practice which often does not work, even though it interestingly disrupts reading practices. I think the earnest postmodern quality of the text speaks to the repression of other border-crossing moments in the narrative.

Childhood is the story of a thirty-something-year-old man who looks back on his life. The question of memory and its reliability is at stake in Thomas MacMillan's look back. By looking back, MacMillan crosses a number of interesting borders. The narrative is an account that plays with the magic of memory as an attempt to convey the ordinary things about life that makes it livable. In the process of this "trip" down memory lane the narrative reveals a number of interesting thematic issues. In particular, one of the issues which the narrative reveals is the question of just what is "a Canadian experience"—or should we say "condition"? By this I mean that the characters in *Childhood* could well all be Trinidadian—and in fact a number of them are. Yet, this major detail has not been addressed in the reception of the text. As well, this major detail has been missing in M&S's promotion of the text. A certain kind of repression is being enacted in the cultural milieu surrounding the book. To understand this milieu effectively requires that we decipher the text and its related meanings.

The themes and langauge of *Childhood* must be deciphered to uncover what is buried behind the surface of *Childhood's* thin membrane of remembering and memory. According to Wynter, to decipher a text is to "identify not what texts and their signifying practices can be interpreted to mean but what they can be deciphered to do, and it also seeks to evaluate the 'illocutionary force' and procedures with which they do what they do" (266-67). This injunction of Wynter demands that we move beyond an analytic model which attempts to read the surface of texts for potential meanings. Instead, she requires and challenges us to decipher what the texts allow us to do within the contexts of larger questions of cultural and political mobilization.

In many ways Cecil Foster's and Lawrence Hill's counter-novels take us much further along the road to putting into use the analytic possibilities of a deciphering practice. I shall explicate this assertion a bit more clearly below. But I return to *Childhood* to further attempt what Michel Foucault calls an "interpretive decipherment" (11) and a "decipherable memory" (64). *Childhood* is a text in which the aesthetic qualities of the language masks some other things going on that might have much to say about what it is possible to do with the text in its political and socio-cultural environment.

In recounting his childhood, Thomas MacMillan reveals to us that he lived with his grandmother until the age of ten, when she died. Shortly after her death his mother (Katarina) appears with a man, her boyfriend (Mr Mataf) to take him to Montreal. Along the way mother, son, and boyfriend engage in petty shoplifting of food and sleep in their car or in a tent. Katarina's relationship falls apart on the trip and Mr Mataf leaves mother and child stranded on the road. Thomas and his mother make their way to Ottawa, where his mother pays a visit to a Mr Henry Wing and the remainder of the adult Thomas's remembering unfolds at the house he inherits on Cooper Street after Wing's death.

Travelling from Petrola to Ottawa, a number of borders are crossed. Alexis invokes the tropes of Canadian landscape and geography to demonstrate effectively his qualifications for belonging. A certain kind of anxiety to belong is displayed in some of his representations. The most symbolic border-crossing in the text is through language. Thomas, Mr Mataf and his mother intermittently speak French. It becomes less used when they live in Ottawa. The text performs a central dynamic of the myth and assumption of belonging to Canada. This is a white Canada, not a "settler-invader" Canada. Therefore it is not difficult to take the other step and argue that the bilingualism of Alexis's text works to preempt discussions of his blackness and to secure his affiliation with this normative Canada.

I am not suggesting that other Black writers in Canada do not use French or write in French. The use of bilingualism is strategic and important but it also leaves us with the question, What is it intended to do? Therefore, what I am asserting is that Alexis's use of bilingualism is a strategic border-crossing deployed to make his place in the nation appear secure and correlatively less "Black." What can we read off the surface and below the surface of his text? It is this question that I hope to address by discussing the representation of the domestic (Mrs Williams) in Henry Wing's house in Ottawa.

Also of symbolic importance is the text's border discourse—the ways in which some pages are divided with footnotes and other devices like lists and figures or diagrams. In fact Thomas MacMillan's way of bringing order to the everyday details of his life and his memory is a compulsion to make lists. These border-crossing postmodern practices are crucial I believe to Alexis's display of an assumption to belong to a particular construction of the (post)modern nation-state of Canada. As I already asserted Alexis's postmodern textual performance is somewhat forced and this at times undermines his otherwise smart and witty observations. However, the question of how a certain kind of postmodern aesthetic, (mind you, one that I am in no way hostile to) plays itself out textually and extratextually in Alexis's work is crucial to my argument. Following Hal Foster, we might say that Alexis represents a conservative postmodernism.

In both *Childhood* and Alexis's interestingly conceived collection of stories *Despair* he walks a margin of Caribbean exoticism which he uses to spice up his mainly contemporary French literary (post)modernist-influenced aesthetic imitations, translations and revisions. However, I want to and intend to read Alexis's border-crossing as otherwise. The otherwise that I am reading for is the repression of the Caribbean "spice" in Alexis's work and what that symbolic repression might mean within the contexts of desiring to belong to the nation (in *Childhood* one of the first encounters of tension between the domestic Mrs Williams and Kata concerns itself with a scotch bonnet pepper used to bring some heat/spice to Caribbean cooking).

I caution that I am fully aware of reducing imaginative works to sociology and I resist the impulse to do so. However, what is at stake here is what literature is intended to do. The Canadian postcolonial critic Diana Brydon reminds us that when we consider contemporary literatures we should also recognize that "social policy and political implications as well as specifically disciplinary repercussions within the university" (12) accrue from how we read and interpret the words we engage. I therefore read *Childhood* as an earnest assumption and assertion of belonging. The border notes and the bilingualism of the text are deeply implicated in a kind of repression. To address this repression I want to spend some time discussing the representation of the domestic in the text. Almost immediately after Thomas and Katarina arrive in Ottawa a certain kind of tension appears between his mother and Mrs Williams, the domestic. This tension plays itself out in small ways: like Katarina's insistence that peppers not be used in the cooking. Henry Wing's love for Kata, as he calls her, overrules Mrs Williams's desire to use peppers, making it clear exactly who the "lady" of the house is. The tension comes to a head when Mrs Williams is accused of stealing by Katarina and eventually fired by Henry Wing. The accusation is untrue, but it is supported by Thomas, who is asked to do so in advance by his mother.

Mrs William's representation in the text and her eventual dismissal speaks to a larger history of domestic labour in Canada and the gross exploitation of domestics. In Alexis's text there is no hint of irony, nor critical questioning surrounding the portrait of Mrs Williams. She wears a yellow head rag and is quite reminiscent of the stereotype of the historic Aunt Jermima. In fact, Alexis pulls out all the old and tired tropes of the mammy stereotype: the kid who becomes deeply attached to the domestic help, the domestic helper who comes to see the child as almost her own, the eventual betrayal, and the domestic as a wonderful storyteller. Thomas is torn between his love for Mrs Williams and carrying out his mother's request to lie to Henry Wing about her having stolen his mother's shoes.

What is at stake in Alexis's representation of the domestic? That representation and memory appears twice in the text. I find this doubling interesting and important. I think that at stake is a particular kind of positioning, an attempt to put distance between those who belong and those who might not. The Caribbean domestic is deeply embedded in contemporary Canadian history. Alexis's assumption of belonging to the nation on terms which do not articulate any critical response to this representation reads like a desire to place distance between domestics and the "real" citizens of Canada. In fact, like the farm workers whom Foster's text pays homage to, the domestic is "not-quite a citizen." However, the "symbol-matter" of Alexis's story is so dependent on the stories that his immigrant parents and others they exposed to him must have told, that in this particular textual repression those narratives refuse to disappear.

Instead, these repressed tales recur in the repeated preoccupations with food—Caribbean food, which the narrator has not had for a long time. In fact, since Mrs Williams "left"—as Thomas remembers her departure—he has had no Caribbean food, because he cannot prepare it himself. As we all know, food is one of the central markers of outsider multicultural status in Canada. It is difficult not to recognize in the representation of Mrs Williams a certain kind of "Canadian" disdain for those whose labour is needed but whose citizenship, whose belonging, is not wanted. Alexis's craft, his language, his word/image representation falls apart for me here because it does not and in fact refuses to engage the historicity of the representations of Black women, who historically were forced to labour in the privacy of other peoples homes. These representations are markedly different from those of the domestics we might meet in Austin Clarke's Toronto Trilogy. But more to the point these representations seem to eschew over twenty-five years of solid critique and public debate concerning domestic workers in Canada. Alexis's representation is definitely different from those women we meet in the nonfiction, oral narrative of Makeda Silvera's now classic *Silence*.

The crossing of the border from Trinidad to Canada is repressed in the novel and even more so in the publicity surrounding the novel. While much of M&S's publicity states that Alexis was born in Trinidad, that is as much as we get about what Trinidad might mean in terms of his writing. I am not one to argue for some kind of valorization of the place in which we were born—as though birthplace is inherently meaningful—but in Alexis's case the relation to birthplace is meaningful in that Trinidad plays a crucially important shadowy force in his themes. While symbolically and otherwise his work is forcefully Canadian, Trinidad keeps echoing in his texts.

Yet, it seems that Alexis assumes belonging to the nation also means that Trinidad must be repressed. It is only through a reading practice of interpretive deciphering that Trinidad can be surfaced and placed within the discussion of Alexis's work. But I might add that for this to happen it requires that critics not position themselves as capable only of speaking for specific nations as though those nations were discrete, stable entities. *Childhood* is a text which might teach us how the requirements of becoming a full citizen in a nation like Canada is one of forgetting. The forgetting required is one that supports the notion and idea that to linger on the past is to refuse national belonging. This assumption is conservative in its manifestations, because it suggest a very narrow definition of the nation and what it might be capable of including.

Floating the Borders

Slammin' Tar *and the Desire to Belong*

The problem of the nation as discrete entity is immediately evident in Cecil Foster's text. In *Slammin' Tar*, Foster's third counter-novel, the question of border-crossing is approached from another political position, one which has different implications for the nation. Foster's text is about the desire to belong. A desire which always seems to come up short for those with the desire to belong. Foster's text has been roundly critiqued for its lack of proper editing, and so, in the process the story that he attempts to tell has almost gone unnoticed. However, recently the local CBC News at Six did an in-depth story on the farm workers program in Canada, and in Ontario more specifically. The story was followed by an interview with Foster concerning *Slammin' Tar*. The convergence of the "human interest" story and the Foster interview pose a number of questions and concerns which are the premise and foundation of the notion of the counter-novel. Despite the editorial problems of Foster's text, it has partially provoked a conversation concerning questions of the Human. In this case it has provoked a conversation concerning the ways in which those who play a major role in getting food to Ontario's tables are never really given the opportunity to become full citizens.

Slammin' Tar is the Barbadian demotic for walking really fast or running. But in Foster's use of the term, I can't help but also read it as a critique of the Canadian governmental policy towards farm workers. A policy which basically says to farm workers to "keep on movin' " because achieving citizen status here is unattainable. In Alexis's *Childhood* Mrs Williams has the patriarchal signifier "Mrs" to mark her marital status. But no husband is evident. This is one of the fallouts of domestic labour programs. Domestics could not migrate with their families. Foster's text is an interesting contrast with Alexis's, because the latter gives us the other side of the story of migratory work relations. Foster's text is very much within the tradition of social realism, a tradition which has been important to Black diaspora writing, some might say from its inception. In his representation of the male farm workers, men who have also been forced to leave their families behind and are strictly monitored in a controlled chain of capitalist exploitation, questions of nation, patriarchy, sexuality and citizenship are central to understanding the dilemma of belonging.

Slammin' Tar recounts the story of migrant farm workers from Barbados who have been travelling to Edgecliff, a farm outside of Toronto, for many years. The text centres on what might be the final trip—due to the farmer's growing debt, the aging and death of some of the workers, and other capitalist factors. Foster attempts to look at one slice of current capitalist relations and by so doing to grapple with the multiple contradictions of contemporary global capitalism. His novel describes the difficulty of farming as an industry, the relationships between the men, who live most of their lives in Canada and are unable to easily move out of the program and become full-fledged immigrants and citizens, and the deaths of at least two workers (one in Barbados just before the trip out, and the other, a suicide on the farm) both men apparently afflicted with a disease which Foster the author and Brer Anancy the narrator refuse to name.

The inability to name what appears to be HIV/AIDS is an interesting and useful silence. The spectre of death haunts *Slammin' Tar*. Therefore, more than the farm workers program is at stake in the text. The question of race, sex and illness as these become implicated in national and governmental policies like retirement plans, health benefits, and so on are also at stake. At the heart of Foster's text, thus, is the question of community. Concerning questions of community and AIDS, I turn to the philosopher of historiography William Haver, who writes that "[an] absolute exigency, [which] is given to us to think when it is AIDS we are attempting to think, concerns the question of community" (23). Haver's thinking concerning representations of AIDS is useful when reading Foster. Haver is clear that:

In representation, an object—AIDS, for instance—can be both the trace of a Real that resists comprehensibility absolutely *and* the occlusion of that radical incomprehensibility in its status as an Imaginary object (the object, that is to say, with which one identifies, or—in disgust, fascination, and disavowal—refuses to identify, thus identifying with and as that refusal) (22).

The unspeakability of the word HIV/AIDS in Foster's text speaks to the ways in which desires to belong might limit what we think it is possible to say. But if HIV/AIDS is the unspeakable in Foster's text it works similarly to the repression of Trinidad in Alexis's text. That is, both repressions continue to return and along with these returns are much more virulent questions concerning the desire to belong and the assumption of belonging. What therefore becomes ultimately at stake is the question of what must be contained and what contaminants must be thrown out to suture the myths of the nation.

Slammin' Tar is narrated to us by Brer Anancy and another, younger female storyteller, who bring us the stories of Johnny and Winston, the younger and most recent entry into the program. Winston represents either the last possible person to have such an opportunity or the next generation of workers. To say that Foster's text is patriarchal is too easy. Foster's narrator is consumed with tradition and he unabashedly relishes in it. Therefore, he is conservative and conservationist on many fronts. This is partly why the naming of HIV/AIDS is almost an impossible utterance. So while the silence or inability to name HIV/AIDS might be the condition of its utterance, what is even more apparent is the un-nameabilty of homosexuality. If you will, the spectre of homosexuality which HIV/AIDS continues to signal in contemporary culture haunts *Slammin' Tar*. But there is a long tradition of naming homosexuality without naming it—the thing that dare not speak its name. These men then are consumed with questions concerning sexuality—whether it is discussions concerning prostitutes or condoms or health—a sexual anxiety pervades the text and articulates its conservative stance.

Foster's is a text where the question of deciphering is urgently necessary. On the one hand the politics of the text seems apparent. That it is a story concerning the injustices farm workers face is very clear. However, Foster's choice to have Brer Anancy appear as an unambiguous male figure, the role of illness and death, the representation of women, cross-racial desire and a host of issues require that we decipher what his text intends to do. One thing is evident, the text speaks clearly, if not always coherently, to a desire to belong. It attempts to articulate the desires of those whom Wynter terms "subject[s] of the jobless archipelagoes" ("Rethinking . . . " 272). Therefore, while this is a work of fiction, it attempts to articulate an intended project that might be read as one concerned with social and economic justice. *Slammin' Tar* is thus a text which ushers in at least one aspect of the counter-novel. It utters a different and contested history of

Canadian labour relations and it speaks back to (and this I think is important for Foster) Black men's contributions to Canada.

Any Known Blood *Or, Just Who Belongs and Where?*

The centrality of Black men to a rewriting of Canadian history might be most evident in Lawrence Hill's text. Hill's *Any Known Blood* has been described as the story of five generations of Langston Cane men (yes they all share the same name). These Langston Canes take their name from two African Americans associated with the Harlem Renaissance—the first name from poet and playwright Langston Hughes and their surname from the title of Jean Toomer's 1923 polyvocal novel *Cane*. This intertextual dialogue between Black Canadian contemporary literature and history and African American history and literature is crucial to Black literatures of the North. Immediately a cross-border identification is made in a lovingly (un)antagonistic fashion. Naming in the text is one of the most obvious instances of Hill's border-crossing sensibilities. Writing against a nationalist grain that would guarantee a reading of Canada as distinct from the United States, Hill's text seems to suggest that it is impossible to make sense of some aspects of Black Canadian history without a serious and sustained consideration of the place of the US in that history. This counter-novel makes the method of a deciphering practice urgent in Black Canadian literature.

Langston Cane V takes us on a border-crossing investigative "tour" to the United States, which eventually stops in Baltimore. The "tour" reveals as much about Canada, more specifically Oakville, Ontario, as staying at "home" would have allowed. Before we consider the cross-nation movements of Hill's text, it might be useful to consider the ways in which his entire project is intended to question discretw and separate boundaries. The text opens with Langston Cane the fifth telling readers "I have the rare distinction . . . of not appearing to belong to any particular race, but of seeming like a contender for many" (1). After providing some instances of how his racial identity is misread and how he takes advantage of various racial misreadings, it becomes clear that Hill is concerned to unsettle the ground of any too-easy claims concerning nation, race, ethnicity and belonging. *Any Known Blood* is a text intended to rupture and breach assumptions concerning race, community, nation. But *Any Known Blood* is also a text concerned with memory and remembering, and the political implications thereof.

Cane's return to Baltimore and his "recovery" of a family history informs the ways in which we might make sense of Black people's historical relations to both nations as fraught with border-crossings of various sorts. In fact, from the very beginning of the family genealogy we are forced to contend with the ways in which the Cane family occupies the site or place of North American border-crossing in terms of its inter-raciality. This practice by Hill forces the reader to attend intricately to the ways in which the metaphors of race and nation work and are unmade in the text. Hill's text is different from both Foster's and Alexis's because it refuse the idea of a stable nation that one might join.

Any Known Blood is the cannibalized story of Hill's actual family but it is based on other historical details as well. But it would be misguided to read the text as "real," for Hill recreates with such irreverence that it might almost be necessary to disregard the ways in which he works with "factual" evidence. In fact Hill's text is good evidence of how we might both read into fiction as social realism and simultaneously resist reducing literature to only its social manifestations. Instead, Hill clearly challenges the writing and the genres of literature, autobiography, and history as a discourse and form that we can be certain about. *Any Known Blood* rewrites Canada's history, opening up the possibility of claims of belonging that are different from both Alexis's and Foster's claims. In this regard Hill's work sits in relation to the work of many Black diaspora counter-novelists—Caryl Phillips, Toni Morrison, Sherley Anne Williams, Erna Brodber, Ishmael Reed and Paule Marshall to name a few. The works fill in what Toni Morrison calls "the blank spaces" of historical writing, making their texts "critical fictions" and counter-novels.

Any Known Blood is a serious recounting of Black Canadian history which allows for a telling to occur that has been largely absent from imaginative writing and critical fictions by Black Canadians. It is a text of many twists and turns and it is witty and hilarious in many places. It cross-references Hill's earlier novel *Some Great Thing* and it sheds much needed light on the ways in which reading histories as discrete and singular might be one of the great fallacies of contemporary thinking. *Any Known Blood* uncovers the lies of the Canadian nation as a white-only space and ask its readers to move beyond such a conception of the nation. *Any Known Blood* contentiously speaks to *Childhood's* conception of nation, and one can venture to say the latter charts a too narrow notion of national desire.

The counter-novel must and does more than provide what appears to be a seamless narrative. Instead it engages in not only refashioning the novel as a form, which historically speaking was said to be beyond the capacities of Black people, but also engaging any number of issues that might not find space in other forms of writing or expression. *Childhood* makes tangential and exotic any trace which might reconstitute the myth of Canada. In *Childhood* there exists an interesting dilemma. It is a dilemma which presumes that to belong entails forgetting or repression of elsewhere. The idea of forgetting is held up to scrutiny in *Any Known Blood*. Remembering as posed by Hill is the active resistance offered to and for rethinking the nation.

Despite the promotion of *Any Known Blood* as a story of five generations of Cane men, I want to insist that such a reading does not do adequate justice to it. In fact, I want to suggest that the text might be interestingly read as Milicent Cane's story. Milicent is central to the unfolding of the narrative, because it is through her that Cane V is able to complete his investigation. Milicent is the sister of Cane V's father. She is involved in a long-term dispute with her brother, who married a white woman (Cane V's mother) and Milicent cannot tolerate the relationship. Therefore, she refuses to engage her brother in a familial friendship. But Milicent's rejection of her brother's choices concerning his spouse is not a knee-jerk Black nationalist position but firmly grounded in her experience and interpretations of history. In particular, Milicent cannot put behind her the experience of Aberdeen, who was threatened and attacked by the Klu Klux Klan in Oakville when his intention to marry a white woman was made known. Thus Milicent's response to her brother's marriage is founded in a traumatic experience which she must and will eventually work through and recover from. It is also partly because of this experience that Milicent has lived most of her life in "exile" in the United States. A rather interesting response to Canada as different from the United States on matters of racial terror.

In many ways "Aunt Mill" is the holder of the family's story despite Cane V's assertions about his father's ability to tell a good tale. The text actually rests on the tension between orality and the scribal tradition. The text does not performatively display an anxiety concerning this tension but merely incorporates it as something assumed. The relation between Mill's remembering and archival research is crucial to Hill's critique of official forms of history writing. His father is however never prepared to risk the details of the family history. But when Milicent decides it is time to cross borders she does so with full gusto. Not only does she share her personal records with Cane V, but also she dedicates her time, energy and money to aid the recovery of the family's story and by extension the story of the back-and-forth crossings of Blacks across the Canada-US borders. In fact, by the end of the text Milicent returns to Oakville to make reparations with her brother and his wife and to spend her last days with her childhood protector Aberdeen.

Milicent's return is interesting for many reasons. As she crosses the border, she takes charge of what it means to be a citizen in a way that provides for the easy passage of Yoyo (an African journalist and satirist) who is entering Canada somewhat like a fugitive slave of the postmodern moment. She does so by asserting family status—in this instance her unquestioned belonging to the nation as well as her relation to the two men in the car. She is also able to pull this off because of her age. Here Alexis's Mrs Williams and Foster's farm workers are present too, because Hill is mapping the contours of Black movement as those movements reshape history, nation and citizenship. Hill's concern with border-crossing begins with the arrival of the first generation of the Canes. The first Cane is a fugitive slave. The Canes and their story move back and forth across the border. Various Cane men try to secure a decent living for their families wherever possible—in Canada or the United States. Cane V's father came to Canada as an ex-GI shortly after World War II, escaping to Canada not unlike a fugitive slave. These escapes link the histories of Black Canadians. But importantly, the practices and experiences of five generations of Cane men also link the histories of Black people in North America to the whites. Hill demonstrates that this linking is not always easy, but the denial of it might be much more dangerous for our future. Thus his insistence on unsettling the racial categories and the assumptions of community that the discourses of racial sameness suggest is crucial to the politics of his text.

Just What Might Be Intended: Genealogies of Place, Space and Desire

These three texts take up space in a Canadian literary landscape with different implications. What is lovely about the space and place these texts occupy is the plurality of the conversation concerning Blackness. The silence on Blackness in *Childhood* is its very utterance and in that utterance is an unintended expansion of the nation. Hill and Foster appear to intend works that are much more far reaching in terms of fundamental rethinkings of the nation. The genealogies present in each text bears a trace to something beyond the nation, disturbing its boundaries and requiring of us that when we think with and about these texts we also think beyond the notion of singularity. If community is at stake in these texts, it is a community that requires the active working out of the category. Notions of the national community are breached by these texts and readers are required to think within and beyond the desire for community to confront the difficulties of the ethical.

What I have been arguing about these three texts is that the politics of each has very different implications for how we might understand Blackness in the nation. I am also suggesting that we must do more than interpret them: we must decipher their politics. Aware of reducing literature to acts of sociology, I am strongly suggesting that literature nonetheless has much to offer conversations concerning how one's citizenship might be imagined. And this is in part the power of words, to ascribe way beyond our imagined selves moments of immense meaningfulness. If such a project does not fit with some conceptions of art, then we must rethink what art can, must, and does do. Hill's project does not assume belonging; it instead calls into question the very terms of belonging. But even more radically, it articulates an ambiguous and ambivalent relation to nation. Yoyo, the African immigrant who must be smuggled into Canada from across the border is very much Hill's comment on at least four hundred years of Blacks in Canada. Yoyo comes full circle from Mattieu de Costa, the alleged first Black person to appear on what is now Canadian soil. Foster's project articulates the desire to belong that is merely one episode in the larger history that Hill reconstructs.

Yet the importance of this episode should not go unnoticed, because of the serious editorial problems with Foster's text. While Alexis assumes what is required to belong and then merely performs the myth of belonging, it is still possible to do a subversive deciphering of his text. Such a reading would decipher what other cultural elements makes his art possible, returning the repressed elements and querying them. As Alexis reproduces "the economy of stereotype" he leaves behind the traces of a past which can never be completely put behind or repressed. While Hill and Foster might be read as troubling stable notions of what the nation means, it is only through the generosity of an interpretative decipherment that one might read Alexis alongside them. If we insist that art speaks for some kind of politics, then we are confronted with the question of what kinds of politics as pedagogues we engage in when we choose what we will introduce our students to in certain works of art. All three of the texts considered here will find their way into university classrooms (they will be in my classes. How will we approach what these texts tell us about the conditions of citizenship for Black people in Canada? How will we decipher the different politics of these texts and the impact of those politics in the actual world? And, finally, how will we read these texts without reducing them to only one tiny place of resistance or subversion of either the nation or Blackness, without understanding what kinds of desires motivated the creative process? I conclude with these questions because such questions should animate the power of words in the university in the struggle for a genuine multicultural citizenry in Canada.

WORKS CITED

Agamben, G. 1993. *The Coming Community*. Translated by M Hardt. Minneapolis: University of Minnesota Press.

Alexis, André. 1998. *Childhood*. Toronto: McClelland & Stewart.

Brand, Dionne. 1991. *No Burden To Carry: Narratives of Black Working Women in Ontario 1920s to 1950s*. Toronto: Women's Press.

Brand, Dionne. 1996. "All Our Possibilities: A Foreword." *The Austin Clarke Reader*. B Callaghan, ed. Toronto: Exile Editions.

Brydon, Diana. 1995. "Introduction: Reading Post-coloniality, Reading Canada". *Essays in Canadian Writing*, 56: 1-19.

Foster, Cecil. 1998. *Slammin' Tar*. Toronto: Random House of Canada.

Foster, H. 1985. *Recordings: Art, Spectacle, Cultural Politics*. Seattle: Bay Press.

Foucault, Michel. 1989. *The Archaeology of Knowledge*. London: Routledge.

Haver, W. 1996. *The Body of This Death: Historicity and Sociality in the Time of AIDS*. California: Stanford University Press.

Hill, Lawrence. 1997. *Any Known Blood*. Toronoto: HaperCollins.

Hudson, P. 1998. "Alexis' Uninvolving Therapeutic Fiction". *Word*, 35.

Morrison, Toni. 1990. "The Site of Memory." In *Out There: Marginalization and Contemporary Cultures*. R Ferguson, M Gever, T T Minh-ha and C West, eds. New York: The New Museum of Contemporary Art and The MIT Press.

———. 1992. *Playing in the Dark: Whiteness and the Literary Imagination*. Cambridge: Harvard University Press.

Nancy, J. 1991. *The Inoperative Community*. Translated by P Connor, L Garbus, M Holland and S Sawhney. Minneapolis: University of Minnesota Press.

Rukszto, K. 1997. "National Encounters: Narrating Canada and the Plurality of Difference." *International Journal of Canadian Studies* 16:. 49-162.

Walcott, Rinaldo. 1997. *Black Like Who? Writing Black Canada*. Toronto: Insomniac Press.

Wynter, Sylvia. 1990. "On Disenchanting Discourse: 'Minority' Literary Criticism and Beyond." In *The Nature and Contexts of Minority Discourse*. A R JanMohamed and D Lloyd, eds. New York: Oxford University Press.

———. 1992. "Rethinking 'Aesthetics': Notes Towards a Deciphering Practice." In *Ex-Iles: Essays on Caribbean Cinema*. M Cham, ed. Trenton, New Jersey: African World Press.

In Pursuit of Eden: The Displacement and Relocation of Vision in Josef Skvorecky's Fiction

BRUCE MEYER

The perspective on the past that Josef Skvorecky has presented in *The Cowards* (1958) and later in *The Engineer of Human Souls* (1977) is a subtly conservative, nostalgic one where the author attempts to freeze time by looking back on the fabric of his own experience and the history that surrounds it. The question is "Why would he want to do this?" After all, twentieth-century literature is full of nostalgics. D H Lawrence in *The Rainbow* and its sequel *Women in Love* laments the passing of a pastoral and somewhat innocent England. D M Thomas's fascination with Freud is in many ways the ultimate nostalgia where his protagonist longs to return to the protection of her mother's womb. Perhaps, as Thomas Wolfe pointed out, we may try to go home but there are always those impediments—change, entropy, and growth—that prevent the return. What so many writers carry with them is not the loss of Happy Valley but the memory of a Rasselasian escape from it and the memories of a former place from a former time that are constantly measured against the inadequacies of the present. Like Voltaire's *Candide*, it is of little matter as to what the world offers in the here and now: what is remembered is that some place, long ago, was the best of all possible worlds. For Josef Skvorecky, that best of all possible worlds is hard to measure because, to so many of his readers, it seems the worst of all possible times and places; yet the experiences of occupied World War Two Czechoslovakia that he relates so lovingly and so faithfully through the youth and adulthood of his recurring protagonist, Danny Smiricky, remain a constant source of wonder, the standard against which everything else in the protagonist's life is measured. For Smiricky, the wonder and confusion of youth, even in a time and a place that is harsh and brutal, is a period that contains all the lessons and challenges that the character faces throughout the rest of his life. To have lost that time and that place, to have fled from its cradle into the perplexing circumstances and inadequacies of a new world, is the problem that Skvorecky addresses again and again in his fiction. What the reader is presented with is not a portrait of a paradise lost or paradise regained but of a crucible of the self that a personality refuses to relinquish.

Youth, for both Skvorecky and Smiricky, represents a kind of Eden, a state of heightened awareness where the mind is vigilant to understand what is happening, a place that was innocent in the manner that Lear's simple yet knowing Fool is innocent. It is a period in time that is lost even as it happens, a fleeting "now" that his protagonist hopes will be long enough to comprehend fully but passes away in the blink of an eye. Skvorecky's attempts to capture this in *The Cowards* explains, in part, the sense of stream-of-consciousness that invades the author's prose during Danny's meditations and observations. It hallmarks Skvorecky's style in such a manner that the reader is caught up in the breathlessness of the anticipated moment that cannot, in prose, contain all the wonder of its experience. *The Cowards* contains numerous moments in which the character makes an important discovery about the nature of life only to see those epiphanies vanquished by the ebb and flow of the history in which he is caught up. All the time, the lessons of youth, taught against the backdrop of the writer's homeland, are set against the desire to find the outlets for inalienably free expression, the chance to voice the pains, the sufferings, the joys and the desires of an individual growing into himself. For Skvorecky, those moments of free expression are embodied in two timeless and ahistorical conduits that throughout the Danny Smiricky novels and stories (in particular *The Cowards, The Engineer of Human Souls, The Swell Season* [1975] and *The Bass Saxophone* [1977]) connect the character's personal past to his personal present: jazz and literature.

Jazz and literature, as Skvorecky perceives it, are the two arts that articulate the kind of Eden that he hopes exists in the world. They are the means by which individuals find and express the essential truths that cannot be troubled or disrupted by ideology. As one of the publishers of a samizdat house, 68 Publishing, Skvorecky pitted literature against ideology in an effort to maintain a semblance of imaginative freedom·in Czechoslovakia in the years following the Russian invasion of 1968. The jazz band in which Danny Smiricky plays the bass saxophone in *The Cowards*, *The Swell Season* and *The Bass Saxophone* is a visible symbol of defiance against the Nazis who outlawed jazz as a decadent and culturally destructive music. Both literature and jazz, as both Skvorecky and Smiricky see them, are the ways in which human beings find their personal Edens while kicking against the social and political systems that would crush the pursuit of happiness. Literature and jazz offer hope, yet they are not the solutions to the problem.

Skvorecky uses both literature and jazz as framing devices for his narrative in *The Engineer of Human Souls*. The chapters in *The Engineer of Human Souls* (with the exceptions of "Conrad" and "Lovecraft") are named for various American authors—Poe, Hawthorne, Twain, Crane and Fitzgerald—not only because they represent benchmarks in the year's worth of English curriculum that Smiricky is teaching but because they signal the tone, the cadence and the theme of *Engineer*'s chapters. What the reader is meant to see is the necessity of having meaning in literature, didactic as it may seem, and the need for readers, either Eastern bloc or Western alliance, to see that culture is something that must constantly inform, educate and warn the individual into an astute awareness of the world's inherent dangers. Skvorecky's structure takes up where Alexis de Tocqueville's admonitions against the "mediocratization of democratic life" leaves off: he perceives that Eden, politically, can never be totally safe in the hands of the intellectually complacent. For Smiricky, American culture and all the great aspirations that it represents—aspirations that became the dream of a young bass saxophone player in Occupied Czechoslovakia—is a demi-Eden, a Land of Cockaigne, where the freedom and plenty that has been enjoyed by Smiricky's students has translated into a laggard state that is stupid and beneath innocence. What Smiricky longs for is a kind paradise where the citizens are armed with ideas and intellect—a notion similar to one expressed by fellow Czech writer Milan Kundera in *The Unbearable Lightness of*

Being. Smiricky's Eden is an Arcadia of artists and philosophers (not unlike that little ante-room at the entrance of Dante's *Inferno* where the great minds of the classical world dream and wait) because that is the only way that the values of any social, public, and political Eden can be maintained.

Writing in his essay "Red Music" in *The Bass Saxophone*, Skvorecky explained his personal sense of dislocation, of being in a place that is not necessarily his place:

> To me literature is forever blowing a horn, singing about youth when youth is irretrievably gone, singing about your homeland when in the schizophrenia of the times you find yourself in a land that lies over the ocean, a land—no matter how hospitable or friendly—where your heart is not, because you landed on these shores too late. (29)

This is a similar sentiment to one echoed by V S Naipaul in *A Bend in the River* (1979) when the protagonist, Nazruddin, visits his friend Indar in London only to find that the former energetic businessman is despairing at the fact that he, too, had arrived too late and that the entire city was "one big cleaning establishment." What both Naipaul and Skvorecky are grappling with is not just the shock of being transplanted to a new place: what they must come to terms with is the dilemma of entering a world that is composed of an entirely different perception. In Naipaul's case, there is no cure for the shock of displacement and he hypothesizes in *A Bend in the River* that all of history is a constant series of displacements and dislocations. Skvorecky, on the other hand, takes a slightly different approach. For him there are some consistencies between places that one can hold on to. In the case of Danny Smiricky, those consistencies are the great expressions of cultural freedom, literature and jazz. Both literature and jazz are the benchmarks and signposts of Smiricky's youth; and they are the seeds he carries with him to the new world, the blueprints for a new Eden to replace the lost paradise (if there ever was one) of Smiricky's youth. Skvorecky's thesis, in a rather roundabout way, is that paradise is not a place but a perception. Happiness is something that is possible under even the worst conditions. What is lost, in the end, is not a time or even a place, but the ability to locate oneself in those imaginative values where the voice of the inner artist, the voice that emerges in both jazz and literature, is allowed to speak freely.

In a strange, almost paradoxical way, paradise for Smiricky is a state of longing. At the conclusion of *The Cowards*, as the war and all the experiences of his youth are coming to an abrupt and confusing conclusion, the young Smiricky laments to himself:

> Everything I had lived through before had been lovely. But what I was feeling now—all this nostalgia and regret and despair— was silly and dumb. Still, let the mood pass and things would look up again. That's the way it always went. I knew that. I knew damn well that nobody's ever really happy, or happy on time, since happiness belongs to the past. (348)

The realization that there can be no "Edenic" now is all the more overwhelming for the young character in that his youth, the flower of his life, has been spent making aircraft parts for the Nazis in a forced-labour factory under the constantly oppressive watch of the Gestapo. What becomes a key element in Smiricky's personality is cynicism, an essential distrust of the possibility of happiness even when that happiness looks him straight in the eye. For Smiricky, Eden, or at least the psychological manifestation of inner peace and certainty, is something that cannot be trusted. His paradise is a fallen world. It is no wonder, therefore, that when the possibility of an Eden, a kind of "hedgerow" type of learning environment presents itself, it is a bleak place of unrealized possibilities, frustrations and indifference for the mature Professor Smiricky. Skvorecky's protagonist is more of an emigre than an immigrant. He arrives in Canada after the Russian invasion of Czechoslovakia in 1968, a dissident and exile who must grapple not only with a new round of oppression courtesy of the Soviets, but with the inane and stupefyingly complacent mentality of Canadian students. The setting for this paradox, this no-man's land between two absurdities, is a figurative paradise lost, Edenvale College.

Edenvale is a thinly disguised representation of the University of Toronto's Erindale College in Mississauga. In the summer Erindale is a pleasant campus consisting of two main buildings, the Science building near the parking lot and the Arts or "South" Building which is situated at the end of an idyllic forest path known as "The Five Minute Walk," a route that winds through clumps of wild lilies and patches of shady pines. Skvorecky's Erindale, however, as presented in the opening pages of *The Engineer of Human Souls*, is a cold, bleak wasteland of snow and desolation, an Eden removed to the top of Mount Purgatory:

> Edenvale College stands in a wilderness. In a few years the nearby town of Mississauga is expected to swell and envelop the campus with more variety and colour, but for the time being the college stands in a wilderness, two and a half miles from the nearest housing development. The houses are no longer all alike: people have learned something since George F. Babbitt's time. Perhaps it was literature that taught them. (3)

The final comment, "Perhaps it was literature that taught them," subtly reiterates one of Skvorecky's key themes in *The Engineer of Human Souls*, that the only hope for either the individual or humanity to escape the nightmare of history is to refine and develop the articulate imagination. In what amounts to a challenge to his complacent and bovine-minded students in a literary seminar, Smiricky asks "'those who can do, those who cannot and suffer enough because they can't, write about it.' Does anyone know what that quotation comes from?" The answer, of course, is Faulkner, and it is a quote that Skvorecky returns to quite often—he cited it in a 1978 interview with the student magazine *University of Toronto Review*—as the way in which literature can reverse the tide of suffering that history and political thought have wreaked upon the twentieth century. What Smiricky is confounded by is the "innocence" in the eyes of his students. What Skovrecky is communicating, however, is the warning that freedom does not give one a licence to commit intellectual laziness.

Freedom, Skvorecky constantly asserts, is a valuable condition where, in a very Miltonic sense, free will is the power to choose between right and wrong. The educated mind, the mind that can either maintain Eden or restore it, is the mind that is constantly challenged and sharpened by the imaginative possibilities inherent in the world around oneself. To this end, the greatest good one can do for one's society is to become an artist. The artist is the individual who sees through the charades of society, the voice that not only mocks false truths but articulates the alternatives. What frustrates Smiricky is the failure of North Americans both to defend their own freedom by defending their imaginative intellects and their inability to realize just what a paradise they have. Like Johnson's Prince Rasselas in *Happy Valley*, the realization of paradise is only possible once one has lived in the fallen world of almost Blakean experience and suspicion. Skvorecky seems to be grasping at this concept in his work—that the exile is one who lives in a perpetually "fallen" world. He cites Evelyn Waugh's lines as an epigraph to *The Swell Season*, his collection of short stories that pre-quels the events in *The Cowards*: "To have been born into a world of beauty, to die amid ugliness, is the common fate of all us exiles."

One must question what the idea of "homeland" means to Skvorecky. On the surface that concept means Danny's home town of Kostelec or "Czechoslovakia," the place of the protagonist's personal past. During Smiricky's exile years, however, that concept becomes considerably readjusted. *The Engineer of Human Souls* contains numerous nostalgic letters that are shared not only by those who have been separated from their homeland, the Czech dissidents in Canada, but also by those who have become separated through time from their youth. As digressional instruments in the narrative they serve to background and complement Smiricky's contemporary experiences and bring the reader up to date on events that were detailed in earlier excursions into the Smiricky chronology in *The Cowards, The Swell Season* and *The Bass Saxophone*. The intriguing yet challenging aspect of the Danny Smiricky saga is that the reader should read all of the works of the on-going Danny story in order to comprehend the subtleties of *The Engineer of Human Souls*. Set against the full scope of the Smiricky saga, *The Engineer of Human Souls* becomes an even more poignant essay on the meaning of freedom and the power of the individual voice to articulate its own statement even when facing the odds stacked against it by oppressive political regimes. In this light, the art of jazz becomes not only a nostalgic sidebar to an earlier period in the protagonist's life, but also a metaphor for what freedom really is: the chance to say exactly what one needs to say. It is this honesty that lies at the heart of Skvorecky's on-going pursuit of Eden.

For Skvorecky, there is an undeniable link between his fascination with jazz—the music of the individual asserting himself against imposed structures—and the fact that his characters, like Skvorecky himself, have constantly been faced with the need to improvise, often solo, in a strange new setting. Not only does his recurring protagonist, Danny Smiricky, fight the pressures and challenges of dislocation, he also must struggle with the impact that twentieth-century history has had on the individual. The result is the story of a character who is constantly in pursuit of a moment when he, at least, was innocent in a world that denied innocence. What Skvorecky pursues is a vision of an Eden, part art, part reality, but entirely sincere, that offers more than just solace from a world gone mad, promising a unique vision of redemption.

What should be remembered in any discussion of freedom in relation to Skvorecky is the message of Milton's *Paradise Lost*: paradise, in whatever form it takes, is not a question of prolonged or fleeting happiness or even political doctrine but of the ability to choose one's own course of action through informed decisions. When free will is stymied, either by Nazis or Communists, the result is not Utopia or even a mediocre Land of Cockaigne, but a dangerous and nightmarish dystopia where only the inner voice of the individual, unarticulated, survives. Literature and jazz, as private possessions of the mind, offer Smiricky the respite from the outer world. As Danny sits on the bar stool of Toronto's Colonial Tavern, a favourite haunt of jazz greats such as Errol Garner, he is connected to an understanding of himself and of the world that is beyond the reach of ideologues and secret policemen who turn Smiricky's external world into a suspicious and recurring nightmare. In this context, perhaps part of the De Tocquevillian prophecy is true: that the same democracy that is capable of creating mass mediocratization is also a free space where the individual can pursue his or her own desires.

In one of the most poignant statements from the conclusion of *The Cowards*, Smiricky fixes the position of jazz in his life:

I didn't have anything against anything, just as long as I could play jazz on my saxophone, because that was something I loved to do and I could be for anything that was against that. And as long as I could watch the girls, because that meant being alive. For me, then, two things meant life. (392)

In the final analysis, Skvorecky's Eden, that place that Danny Smiricky longs for in his heart, is the inner happiness of being able to lose oneself in something that is beyond the control of the conscious world. That Eden is the happiness of both art and literature; it is not a place but a state of mind. It is a mentality that is aware of what it must do to survive and what it must say to protect itself and the circumstances that would foster and promote such happiness. As the Second World War ends and an era in Smiricky's life passes before him, the protagonist of *The Cowards* laments the state of happiness as he perceives it:

But what I was feeling now—all this nostalgia and regret and despair—was silly and dumb. Still, let the mood pass and things would look up again. That's the way it always went. I knew that. I knew damn well that nobody's ever really happy, or happy on time, since happiness belongs to the past. (348)

The sad, strange aspect to Smiricky's happiness is that the past is constantly reinvented. Like a myth of paradise that one carries deep inside as one passes from an old world to a new world, the past is something that is continually reinvented, retold, a story that is reshaped in the image and according to the demands of a present that can never be totally appreciated. For Skvorecky, the new world is always that longed for release from the here and the now.

WORKS CITED

Skvorecky, Joseph. 1970. *The Cowards*. London: Penguin Books.

———. 1975. *The Swell Season*. Toronto: Harper Perennial.

———. 1977. *The Bass Saxophone*. Toronto: Hugh Anson Cartwright.

———. 1984. *The Engineer of Human Souls*. Toronto: Harper Collins.

Locating M G Vassanji's 'The Book of Secrets': Postmodern, Postcolonial, or Other-wise?

JOHN CLEMENT BALL

When M G Vassanji's first novel, *The Gunny Sack*, came out in 1989, its publisher gave it a high pedigree. "Africa's answer to 'Midnight's Children'" gushed an unattributed blurb on the front cover. It would be easy to dismiss this as pure hype, wishful thinking by the Heinemann marketing department — as the pre-emptive and presumptuous hoisting of a new work by a then-unknown writer into the upper echelons of literary influence. It would be easy, that is, if the remark weren't so provocative. Does "Africa" really *need* its own *Midnight's Children*? Should we assume that Africa too is "a continent finding its voice," as the cover blurb on Salman Rushdie's novel once so New York-centrically proclaimed? If so, is Vassanji, a Canadian East African of Indian ancestry, the writer to articulate that newly-found voice?

Midnight's Children and *The Gunny Sack* do have some striking similarities: both contain isolated, self-conscious narrators named Saleem (or Salim); each writes an ancestral family history covering several generations through a loosely linear procession of characters, stories, and intrigues. Both novels use a fragmented form and dense, high-velocity prose suggestive of orality and cultural richness—a proliferation of stories eager to be told and virtually bursting the seams of narrative. To this admittedly rather reductive set of similarities one would want, in a full-fledged comparison, to note the many differences between the two books. But what interests me most about this positioning of Vassanji in Rushdie's company is a theoretical question: how is Vassanji's work served by the two categorizing labels under which Western critics most often discuss *Midnight's Children*: postmodernism and postcolonialism?

Helen Tiffin cites Rushdie's novels as "classic examples of works which have been . . . appropriated" under both "isms" (vii), and he is certainly the most prominent author to be so doubly located, or doubly claimed. In the comparatively small amount of criticism on his work published so far, Vassanji has not been formally ushered into either the postmodern or the postcolonial embrace. His 1994 novel *The Book of Secrets*, however, affiliates itself even more strongly than *The Gunny Sack* does with various formal conventions, themes, and political positions associated with postmodernism and postcolonialism. The theoretical question prompted by the earlier novel and its audacious blurb can, I believe, be most productively investigated in connection with the more recent novel. This case study of *The Book of Secrets* aims to illuminate some uses and limitations of the postmodern and postcolonial rubrics and to consider what is at stake when we read Vassanji's novel through the lenses of theories with such influence and explanatory power. By negotiating Vassanji's theoretical location, we can also begin to address the question of how he and his work are linked to "Africa"—its histories, its nations, and its literatures.

The Book of Secrets exhibits many of the attributes claimed for postmodern fiction by such prominent theorists as Linda Hutcheon and Brian McHale. From the Western point of view that postmodernism presumes, it can be seen to contest master narratives of history and progress, to set models of difference, marginality and "ex-centricity" over against the "center" (Hutcheon, *Poetics* 57-73), and to refuse closure by hoarding some of its secrets and declining to resolve contradictions. Like other postmodern fictions, it problematizes knowledge, history, borders, subjectivity, and conventions of realist representation. The novel's narrative mode makes it a natural fit with Hutcheon's privileged subspecies of the postmodern, the "historiographic metafiction" (*Poetics* 105-77). The reader watches as the narrator, Pius Fernandes, fabricates from fragmentary texts and oral witnesses a historical narrative covering 75 years. Pius explicitly comments on the status of his serendipitous narrative as constructed

(8), calling it an "incomplete . . . book of half lives, partial truths, conjecture, interpretation, and perhaps even some mistakes" (331-32). The 1913 colonial administrator's diary that prompts Pius's project is described by him as brittle, torn, stained, full of silverfish and cockroach eggs, and "often unreadable" (6). In paradoxical postmodern fashion, history as textual object—the diary—is both devalued by nature and fetishized by humans. It can be many contradictory things at once: a commodity whose ownership and monetary value can be discussed; a source of spiritual comfort and superstitious worship; and a transcendent symbol of and point of access to personal, familial, racial, communal, and national histories. Like one of Canada's earliest "postmodern" novels, Robert Kroetsch's *The Studhorse Man*, Vassanji's book has a marginal narrator who begins as a would-be "objective" biographer of others, but ends up writing autobiography; he moves into the narrative centre and increasingly asserts his subjectivity. The process of writing is foregrounded, and both novels can be seen in Hutcheon's terms to use and abuse, install and subvert various textual conventions of representation (*Poetics* 3).

But what is notably different between Vassanji's Pius and Kroetsch's Demeter is part of what makes *The Book of Secrets* less postmodern than other novels to which it bears affinities. Postmodern narrators and protagonists commonly reflect their "ex-centricity" psychologically and behaviourally—as the kind of obsessive lunacy and totalizing, self-assertive megalomania exhibited by Kroetsch's Demeter and Madham, Rushdie's Saleem and Gibreel, or J M Coetzee's Foe. As self-deconstructing power mongers, such figures embody the postmodern paradox of simultaneous exemplification and critique. Vassanji's Pius, however, does not fit this model. He remains rational, modest, and apparently reliable to the end; any doubts the reader may have about the "truth" of his narrative are disarmed by his own candid, self-reflexive musings. His takeover of narrative focus—the move from biography to autobiography—appears not, as in many postmodern novels, as dangerous will to power and centrality, but rather as a reluctant acknowledgement of necessity: tracing the diary's history as an artifact through the lives it has touched makes the telling of Pius's own story inevitable, especially once Rita makes her claim. Pius's marginality is a function of his ethnicity (Goan Indian), his occupation (schoolmaster), and his economic status in both pre- and post-independence Tanzania; it is not metaphorically represented as abnormal consciousness or pure textual play, but is carefully grounded in the material world. Pius possesses a degree of historical specificity and referential agency that Kroetsch's characters never achieve nor want to achieve. Even Rushdie's Saleem disqualifies himself from a referential identity or a stable marginality when he insists on expanding his subjectivity allegorically to encompass all of India.

Vassanji's metafiction is ultimately less playful, less deliberately deceptive and disruptive of realist conventions and ontologies than most exemplars of postmodern fiction; it lacks their "in your face" quality. Its use of the supernatural (Pipa's conversations with Mariamu's ghost) can be explained psychologically. When he places a historical figure like Winston Churchill in his narrative, Vassanji does not flout the historical record. The novel *can* be read as what Brian McHale calls "apocryphal history"—a supplement to the official record that claims to restore what has been lost or suppressed. But it does not, despite its title, participate in what McHale calls "secret history"—a more transgressive subcategory of apocryphal history that purports to displace the official record by telling (as fiction) what *really* happened and why (90-91). (*Midnight's Children* is a prime example of postmodern secret history.) Neither Vassanji nor his narrator wants to violate or invalidate the historical record; this novel, like *The Gunny Sack*, does want to supplement and pluralize that record by inscribing the communal and racial memory of Indians in East Africa. After all, as he has said in an interview, the communal histories he narrates include "subjects that had never been dealt with before" his first novel (Ball 3). In an early essay, Vassanji constructs postcolonial writers as preservers of collective traditions; they give themselves a history, he says, by recreating the past from memory otherwise obliterated by the rapid transformation of the world. This act of reclamation is often "the first serious act of writing," so important that "A future historian of that culture will have no recourse but to walk those imaginative landscapes" ("Postcolonial" 63). The emphasis here is on construction rather than deconstruction, on retrieving and legitimizing elusive narratives that are crucial to self-knowledge and group identity, rather than on debunking and delegitimizing oppressive structures of knowledge, master-narratives, and humanist concepts of identity.

The contrast I am drawing out here is one commonly made in critiques of postmodernism by leading postcolonial critics. As Helen Tiffin writes, "While the disappearance of 'grand narratives' and the 'crisis of representation' characterise the Euro-American post-modernist mood, such expressions of 'breakdown' and 'crisis' instead signal promise and decolonisation potential within post-colonial discourse" (x). Bruce King summarizes this critical preference as a rejection of "post-modern eclecticism, with its European notions of exhaustion and the end of history" by those favouring "the vitality and challenges of the post-colonial" (8-9). Does Vassanji's apparent compatibility with postmodernism suggest a misleading interpretive emphasis? Would his novel be better positioned within postcolonial paradigms?

Sylvia Söderlind begins *Margin/Alias*, a study of Canadian and Québécois fiction that uses postcolonial, postmodern and post-structuralist theories, by proposing that novels can be both postcolonial and postmodern, and that despite the differences between the two discourses, there need not be any contradiction in using both terms (5). The postcolonial's more secure referential grounding, she argues, gives it a more material antagonist—imperialism in its traditional and "neo" forms—than postmodernism, which typically opposes abstractions like realist representation and totalizing power. As a result the postcolonial is less inclined to "metaphorize" or "aestheticize" its arguments, and to have greater political force because it stays rooted in real political issues and agencies (229-34). Postmodernism, according to those postcolonial critics who most strongly resist its use on literatures from former colonies, overvalues the antireferential and the deconstructive at the expense of the referential assertion and vocalization that marginalized groups are compelled to perform. For Rajeswari Mohan, postmodern readings involve a "decontextualization . . . whereby politically charged and historically urgent discursive and textual elements are reduced to purely formal and aesthetic properties of the text" (37). According to Simon During, the postmodern is "deterritorialized" (368). Like Tiffin, he argues that it threatens to neutralize and absorb postcolonial *opportunity* for self-representation by reading texts in light of a European *crisis* of representation and authority. Postmodernism, according to some critics, is so enamoured of its contradictory impulses of complicity and critique that it promotes only stasis, sterility and the status quo. As Diana Brydon succinctly puts it, "The name 'post-modernism' suggests an aestheticising of the political while the name 'post-colonialism' foregrounds the political as inevitably contaminating the aesthetic, but remaining distinguishable from it" (192).

The point behind such critiques is that postmodernism is not simply a set of formal and thematic traits and conventions that can be read into or out of various contemporary works of art. As a "cultural dominant," it originates in the West—specifically a late-capitalist, commodity-culture West, as Fredric Jameson has influentially argued (55). That cultural grounding may not do justice to places that have different histories and economies, and that have experienced specific power differentials with Western nations. Using postmodernism as a critical rubric becomes a loaded act; it can determine certain kinds of readings and preclude others. Moreover, if we interpret Vassanji's metafictional moments as lessons in the textuality and plurality of history, the contingency of truth, and the problematics of discursive authority *in general*, are we not having him show us what dozens of other "postmodern" fictions have already demonstrated (to say nothing of the exhaustive theorizing and cataloguing projects of Hutcheon and others)? Are these ideas the most valuable, interesting, or original rewards Vassanji's text can offer us?

I believe not. Vassanji, I would argue, uses certain conventions associated with postmodernism almost casually. David Adams Richards does something similar in his novel *For Those Who Hunt the Wounded Down* (1993), which also uses multiple points of view, a fragmented narrative, and unresolved contradictions to show the impossibility of true, unitary knowledge of a turbulent episode in a community's recent past. As I read them, however, what the Richards and Vassanji novels share is an emphasis on what *can* be known and represented, however incomplete. The acknowledgement of what *cannot* be known—and thus what cannot be transparently represented through an authoritative narrative — may be necessary, but it is not the main point or achievement of either novel. It is not a cause for anxiety or despair. That an acknowledgement of partial, incomplete knowledge *is* built into these texts may be because so-called "postmodern" strategies are almost *de rigeur* in contemporary fiction;

as Hutcheon says, "novels today often seem to find it hard not to display their suspicion of certain literary conventions that they were once able to take for granted" (*Canadian* 15). But that acknowledgement, that "suspicion," is also for Vassanji an unavoidable aspect of his raw material: the stories of a specific community, whether from the long-ago or recent past, must by definition be fragmentary, plural, and subjective. And the step from giving voice to those histories to foregrounding the imperfect processes by which they circulate in and influence the present seems a logical one for authors such as Vassanji and Richards who, when they aren't resembling postmodernists, look a lot like realists. That which looks most postmodern in their books is, in fact, a function of their referential contents and contexts.

These theoretical distinctions may be illustrated by an episode from *The Book of Secrets*. During the Great War, the British officer Maynard recruits several Africans from both sides of the border with German East Africa into a spy ring. They become information gatherers, assisting British intelligence. Scraps of paper, photographs, sketches, maps—"all crumpled, stained, smelly"—become grist to the mill, the fragmentary raw materials by which Maynard as "indiscriminate scavenger . . . would piece together a truth, a story, the secrets of the enemy" (154). The parallels between this activity and Pius's narrative activity are obvious. Yet neither act is what Söderlind would call a politically disempowering "metaphorization" or "aestheticization" of the other. Maynard's research is materially rooted and has life-and-death consequences—both for the German soldiers who may get bombed as a result of his knowledge (however inchoate that knowledge may be), and for the spies from the German side, who will die if caught participating in his project. The project's potential power is far more important than its epistemological limitations. Something of this power reflects by association on Pius's scavenging act, but his narrative also possesses power in its own right. It obviously does not have (or desire) the power to kill, but it does have the power to sustain, to give voice, to retrieve knowledge and memories from the past that can benefit characters inside the novel as well as the East African Indian diaspora outside its covers.

That constructive power is one way in which *The Book of Secrets* makes its postcoloniality apparent, but a number of other features of the novel fit with theories of postcolonial literature. Its language displaces "standard English" with a local variant that uses Swahili and Indian vocabularies; as Bill Ashcroft would say, Vassanji makes "language variance . . . *metonymic* . . . of cultural difference" ("Constitutive" 71). The novel provides numerous models of cultural syncretism, hybridity, and what Kwame Anthony Appiah calls the "contaminated" identities of postcoloniality (354). Moreover, the broad historical sweep of its recuperative, referential project can be seen as paradigmatically postcolonial. The narrative begins in colonial times, embarking from a presumption of white British textual and political authority symbolized by Alfred Corbin's diary. The diary, in however piecemeal a fashion, narrativizes power. It does this through its content—reflections on the administering of justice—and by its subordinating inscription of African Indian characters and stories as elements of Corbin's personal adventure. Much as Chinua Achebe does in *Arrow of God*, set during the same era in Nigerian history, Vassanji shows us the blinkered colonialist and racist discourses of Africa and its people that were disseminated by British agents. Corbin uses familiar imperial-masculinist metaphors of penetration and compliance when he talks of "entering" a "dark continent . . . now opening up to European civilization" (23). Maynard's favourite saying is the Conradian observation that "This is a savage country, it makes a savage out of you" (21). As in *Arrow of God*, such remarks are self-satirizing in the context of a narrative that elaborates alternative versions of African reality, and that enables the detailed articulation of specific African subjectivities. The novel takes local possession of Corbin's appropriating narrative and appropriates it back — reworking it and pressing it into the service of local needs and knowledges. The diary was first stolen in 1914 by Mariamu, who may have feared it contained her secrets or stole her soul; in 1988 Pius takes this colonial remnant and paradoxically places it at the centre of, but subordinate to, a communal narrative of Indians in East Africa. The novel thus exhibits the two forms of resistance that Slemon wants to read into postcolonial texts. He calls for a criticism that "would draw on post-structuralism's suspension of the referent in order to read the social 'text' of colonialist power and at the same time would reinstall the referent in the service of colonized and postcolonial societies" (5). By incorporating into his narrative both colonial and postcolonial social spaces and texts, Vassanji encourages the reader do two things: first, to suspend the referents proposed by the diary's more ideologically and epistemologically limited colonialist perspectives, and second, to respect the postcolonial referential assertions of a specific community newly inaugurated into fiction—a community whose possession and use of that diary is now of greater significance than any British claims in it or to it.

It is these competing textualities that make *The Book of Secrets* seem paradigmatic: as Leela Gandhi has recently written, texts as sites of power and struggle are the dominant focus of postcolonial literary theory (141). But its 75-year historical span makes the novel appear to be comprehensively postcolonial in two further and related ways. First, it moves from an examination of colonial engagements and subjectivities to a consideration of the post-independence aftermath as experienced by a diasporic migrant questioning his national affiliations and sense of home. As the largely local story of Corbin, Maynard, Mariamu, and Pipa gives way to a more international focus on Pius, Gregory, Ali, and Rita, we encounter between the covers of one novel the major elements of what many critics see as the overall development of postcolonial literature and theory in the latter half of the twentieth century. For Gandhi, this is a shift from novels concerned with a "textual mapping of the colonial encounter" to "the new 'migrant' novel" (152-53) and, as a function of this, from texts concerned to interrogate the hierarchical binaries of colonialist discourses to those informed by concepts of hybridity, diaspora, and migrant 'homelessness': from Achebe's *Things Fall Apart*, for instance, to Rushdie's *The Satanic Verses*, and from the oppositional critical models of Frantz Fanon to the fluid cosmopolitan rootlessness of Homi Bhabha. Though admittedly reductive, this schematic view of the postcolonial project's shifting emphases can be connected to a second movement: from the "nationalistic" to the "transnational" postcolonial "moments," as Christian Moraru names them (174). Revathi Krishnaswamy, following Appiah, similarly diagnoses a shift from "first generation" to "second generation" postcolonial novels in terms of a move from nationalist politics and realist writing to anti-nationalist politics and the repudiation of realism (125-26). As Gandhi describes this same process (which she and Moraru both connect to a shift from Marxist to post-structuralist and postmodernist influences on postcolonial thinking), the dominant postcolonial texts and theories have increasingly steered away from an anticolonial nationalism grounded in a dualistic struggle over colonial (or ex-colonial) territory to a more detached "postnationalism" that eschews binaries and distrusts the inclusive and exclusive claims of nationalist discourses (Gandhi 102-66).

These are powerful models that astutely summarize some general shifts in postcolonial theory and fiction, especially in Africa and South Asia. But we will misrepresent Vassanji's novel if we thus try to read it as a nationalist critique of colonial power (in Part One) that adopts a postnationalist (or transnationalist) thematics (late in Part Two and in the framing sections). Its firm grounding in a minority subcommunity of the colony/nation gives *The Book of Secrets* a uniquely ambivalent relationship to both empire and to the postindependence nation, and puts it at odds with many novels by black Africans, despite the structural and thematic resistances to imperial power mentioned above. The history of the Ismaili Muslims (Vassanji's fictional "Shamsis"), like that of other Asian communities in East Africa, is largely ignored in histories and literary histories of the region. Yet as economic and social historians like Robert Gregory (43-87) have shown, Indian entrepreneurs—shopkeepers and traders—played a crucial role in what are sometimes called the "opening up" and "development" of East African colonies. Beginning in the 1890s, Indian entrepreneurs followed the new railway lines that Indian indentured labourers were helping to build, and by setting up shop they introduced Africans to such aspects of modernity as a money economy and consumer goods. Yet whether colonial East African society is constructed as a three-tiered hierarchy of aristocratic European settlers, Indian businessmen, and African labourers, or alternatively as a two-tiered structure of bourgeoisie and proletariat, Indians get caught in the middle. Their social exclusivity and successful dominance of certain sectors of the economy inspired envy, resentment, and racist treatment from both white and black populations in the colonial era. As Gregory shows, beginning in the 1930s the climate of pioneering free enterprise in which Indians thrived was increasingly curtailed. More and more restrictive policies and regulations governed their activities, and an awkward mix of *laissez-faire* policies and more socialistic government management of the economy was introduced by paternalistic colonial rulers wishing to assist the rise of Africans (Gregory 78). In the postindependence years of the 1960s and 1970s, things got much worse for Asian East Africans. They were expelled from Idi Amin's Uganda, and in Tanzania, where Vassanji's novel is largely set, a policy of nationalizing private enterprise impoverished entire Indian families in a stroke.

This history of a specific racial and socioeconomic group finds expression in the novel—most obviously in the story of Pipa the shopkeeper. His progression from the meagre proceeds of a rural shop to the wealth produced by a large urban one, only to suffer the obliterating effect of nationalization, can be seen to stand for a whole class's historical experience. But as an in-between, comprador group often regarded by whites as dishonest and exploitative (Gregory 76) and by blacks as "colonizers by proxy" (Meister 266), Asians benefitted from many aspects of colonial power structures, and often occupied mediating roles between Europeans and black Africans. In *The Book of Secrets*, therefore, Pius talks of how "Our world was diminishing with the Empire" (274), and of the Indian shopkeepers' animosity to the Mau Mau rebellion and incomprehension as to how "the mighty British [could] give way to the African, the servant" (264). The politics embodied by the novel's main characters can be seen as conservative, even reactionary. Nostalgic for Empire, socially isolationist, at odds with black nationalism and postindependence policies, Indian communities cannot be easily linked to the anticolonial nationalist politics of various black African novels. Even though Vassanji's negative portrayal of postindependence regimes has some affinity with critiques of neocolonialism by black African authors such as Achebe, Ngugi, Ayi Kwei Armah, and Wole Soyinka, neocolonial oppression in this novel is only seen affecting Indians. Here, as in Vassanji's other African fiction, the black majority is virtually invisible (although probably no more so than Indians are in Ngugi's books).

If we read the history of East African Indians as that of a middle class squeezed off its secure and promising socioeconomic perch by pressures from both Europeans and Africans—"above" and "below"—Vassanji's sympathetic engagement with that history is at odds with dominant models of African resistance. The ethnic novelty of this "Tanzan/Asian" African novel (see Nazareth) forces us to

reconsider the Manichean binary of black-white opposition that Abdul JanMohamed, following Fanon, proposes as the cornerstone of an
African aesthetics. Indeed, while resistance and critique are part of
the novel's texture, they do not seem to be its main purpose. It
contains very little anger or accusation. A sense of gentleness and
balance pervades the novel's ironies, a sense of acceptance its rises
and falls. A black character like Khanoum, unjustly abandoned by her
adopted Indian community when her husband dies, is handled at
least as sympathetically and movingly as the Indians disenfranchised
by socialist black nationalism. The diary of Alfred Corbin, the novel's
central symbol of colonial authority, may represent on one hand what
Chris Tiffin and Alan Lawson identify as the containment and control
of imperial textuality (6): it contains secrets and even the soul of
Mariamu, and it affects and inhibits Pipa for most of his life. But on
the other hand the diary functions as an enabling device once it is
appropriated by Pius in the service of the very communal subjectivity
that it originally knew only as the object of its gaze. As Shane Rhodes
astutely points out, this dual association of Corbin's diary with both
"colonial rule" and "neocolonial recuperation and critique" is mir-
rored in the African crowd's awe-struck fingering of the novel's other
important diary, that of Livingstone (Rhodes 185). While JanMohamed may emphasize the corrective and antagonistic stance of the
native towards colonialist literature, then, Vassanji's non-native narrator Pius is more interested in appropriating than opposing, more
inclined to use and supplement than correct. Like Ngugi, writing in
his prison diary, Vassanji begins from a premise that "diaries and
memoirs of the leading intellectual lights of the old colonial system
contain full literary celebration of this settler culture" (Ngugi 34);
unlike Ngugi, he wants to discover the knowledges these documents
can offer, not just their ethnocentrisms and blinkered imperialist
ideologies.

In the novel's nuanced positions on colony and nation we can find
the key to its special blend of postcolonial and postmodern affiliations. Rosemary Marangoly George, in a fine reading of *The Gunny
Sack*, writes that for "marginal" Indians in Tanzania, the event of
independence was like "a wedding where the best seats are taken for
family members": concepts such as "nation" and "national subject"
proved simply not "large enough" to contain them (195). *The Book of*

Secrets envisions the nation and its people from a similar basis. Carefully negotiating commitments and detachments derived from a specific community's experience, the novel allies itself neither with the dualistic critiques of anticolonial nationalism nor with a free-floating cosmopolitanism, though it flirts with both. It belongs neither with the first-generation realist African novels that legitimated the nation, nor with the antirealist second-generation novels through which disillusionment with nationalism's failures was expressed. Those novels properly belong to writers of the black majority, whose anticolonial agitations prompted decolonization and the emergence of new African nations under black governance. Although wary of structures (such as colony and nation) that claim to define and contain a place and its people, *The Book of Secrets* still remains firmly committed to the grass-roots experiences of particular people (Indians and others) inhabiting a specific place (the East African lands now called Tanzania and Kenya); when the narrative ventures abroad it, like its narrator, does so only fleetingly, always returning to the home base that it, like Pius, "will never shed" (316). Despite the migrant status of its narrator and its author (who now lives in Toronto), the novel does not celebrate postnationalist diasporic migrancy in the manner of Rushdie, Bharati Mukherjee, or Amitav Ghosh, nor does Vassanji really, despite the "postmodern" aspects of his frame, abandon the realist novel's legitimating project for the delegitimating play of antirealism—whether postmodern or otherwise. Indeed, without legitimating the nation per se, he does want to legitimate and realistically represent the experiences of the "Tanzan/Asian" community within it, a group that he has been largely responsible for ushering into the realm of historical fiction.

While offering itself in many ways as a typically postmodern and exemplary—even comprehensively—postcolonial novel, Vassanji's book resists easy assimilation into either of these categories. This is appropriate; as Arun Mukherjee, Anne McClintock, and many other critics have warned, such enticing terms can dangerously homogenize and distort the diversity and particularity of the texts they presume to describe. While I don't agree with these critics that we should thus reject them altogether, I believe that they should be negotiated rather than applied, and the subsumptive explanatory power they often claim should be treated with suspicion. It is both the value and the drawback of the influential comparativist theory texts like *The Empire Writes Back* and the Hutcheon postmodernism books that they seem to offer instant access to the agendas of a broad variety of works. They may tempt us to use categorical or generic labels as the endpoint of discussion rather than the beginning. As with generic terms such as "satire" or "epic," these labels come equipped with so many models and assumptions regarding what they designate that they can become shortcuts to interpretation. However relevant the discourses of postmodernism and postcolonialism may be, for this text or any other, they must be tested, qualified, and supplemented. Every novel has something uniquely its own that no paradigm can reveal. The best literary criticism tempers the allure of mastery with a respect for the book's special mystery.

As its title suggests, Vassanji's book is full of mysteries and secrets. Some are explained or revealed; many are not. In *A Theory of Literary Production*, Pierre Macherey examines secrets as a function of narrative, and he discusses how mystery and detective novels simultaneously create and suppress a secret in order to propel the story. Narrative exists only as long as the secret is withheld, its revelation postponed; once the secret is out, narrative is abolished as a now redundant means to truth and meaning. At least, so it may seem. In fact, Macherey argues, meaning and enjoyment reside in the narrative journey, not in the final truth revealed. "The depths" of truth or revelation, he says, are ultimately "less fascinating than this frail and deceptive surface" of narrative (29). The narrative seems to be an interlude, after which normality returns, but, he says, "this interlude is actually interminable. There is no end to the birth and death of secrets" (34). Macherey relates the idea of "secret" to the idea of "other" in various complex ways; in one typically oblique passage he writes, "The discovery of the secret motives of the other is not the least of the mysteries in the house of illusions" (33). At one point near the end of *The Book of Secrets*, Pius the narrator-detective is urged by Rita, his interlocutor and oral history source, to bury the past, bury the narrative he is constructing. "[W]hat arrogance," Rita says, "to presume to peep into other lives—to lay them out bare and join them like so many dots to form a picture. There are questions that have no answer; we can never know the innermost secrets of any heart. Each dot is infinity, Pius, your history is surface" (297). Surface is what

Macherey values, however, and Pius's history does come to light as published narrative, even though it does not presume to join all its dots or reveal all its secrets. As for the critic, perhaps, after suggesting some interpretations, a time will come when it makes sense to take a cue from Macherey, Rita and Vassanji: to acknowledge that the revelation of a narrative's secrets is not always possible or desirable, and that the critic—even one armed with every label on the shelf—will never be as "other-wise" as the novel itself.

NOTE

Earlier versions of this paper were presented at the Universities of Guelph, British Columbia and New Brunswick in 1994 and 1995. I am grateful to the audiences at all three institutions for their questions and responses, and also to the honours and graduate students at the University of New Brunswick who have subsequently studied the novel with me, and from whom I have learned much— particularly Shane Rhodes, whose now published essay on the novel I am pleased to cite in this revised version of my own.

WORKS CITED

Adam, Ian and Helen Tiffin, eds. 1990. *Past the Last Post: Theorizing Post-Colonialism and Post-Modernism.* Calgary, University of Calgary Press.

Achebe, Chinua. 1964. *Arrow of God.* rev. 1974. London: Heinemann.

Appiah, Kwame Anthony. 1991. "Is the Post- in Postmodernism the Post- in Postcolonial?" *Critical Inquiry* 17: 336-57.

Ashcroft, W D. 1989. "Constitutive Graphonomy: A Post-Colonial Theory of Literary Writing." *Kunapipi* 11, 1: 58-73.

Ashcroft, W D, Gareth Griffith, and Helen Tiffin. 1989. *The Empire Writes Back: Theory and Practice in Post-Colonial Literatures.* London & New York: Routledge.

Ball, John Clement. "Interview with M.G. Vassanji." *Paragraph* 14,3-4: 3-8. Rpt. as "Taboos: M.G. Vassanji" in *The Power to Bend Spoons: Interview with Canadian Novelists,* ed. Beverley Daurio, 200-09. Toronto: Mercury.

Brydon, Diana. "The White Inuit Speaks: Contamination as Literary Strategy." In Adam and Tiffin, 191-203.

During, Simon. 1985. "Postmodernism or Postcolonialism?" *Landfall* 155 (Sept. 1985): 366-80.

Gandhi, Leela. 1998. *Postcolonial Theory: A Critical Introduction.* New York: Columbia UP.

George, Rosemary Marangoly. 1996. *The Politics of Home: Postcolonial Relocations and Twentieth-Century Fiction.* Cambridge: Cambridge University Press.

Gregory, Robert G. 1993. *South Asians in East Africa: An Economic and Social History, 1890-1980*. Boulder: Westview.

Hutcheon, Linda. 1988. *The Canadian Postmodern: A Study of Contemporary English-Canadian Fiction*. Toronto: Oxford University Press.

————. 1988. *A Poetics of Postmodernism: History, Theory, Fiction*. New York and London: Routledge.

Jameson, Frederic. 1984. "Postmodernism, or The Cultural Logic of Late Capitalism." *New Left Review* 146 : 53-92.

JanMohamed, Abdul. 1983. *Manichean Aesthetics: The Politics of Literature in Colonial Africa*. Amherst: University of Massachusetts Press.

King, Bruce. 1996. "New Centres of Consciousness: New, Post-colonial, and International English Literature." In *New National and Post-Colonial Literatures: An Introduction*, ed. Bruce King, 3-26. Oxford: Clarendon.

Krishnaswamy, Revathi. 1995. "Mythologies of Migrancy: Postcolonialism, Postmodernism and the Politics of (Dis)location." *ARIEL* 26, 1: 125-46.

Kroetsch, Robert. 1970. Reprinted 1988. *The Studhorse Man*. Toronto: Random House.

Macherey, Pierre. 1978. *A Theory of Literary Production*. Translated by Geoffrey Wall. London: Routledge & Kegan Paul.

McClintock, Anne. 1992. "The Angel of Progress: Pitfalls of the Term 'Post-Colonialism.' " *Social Text* 10,2-3: 84-98.

McHale, Brian. 1987. *Postmodernist Fiction*. New York and London: Methuen.

Meister, Albert. 1966. *East Africa: The Past in Chains, the Future in Pawn*. Translated by Phyllis Nauts Ott. New York: Walker & Company.

Mohan, Rajeswari. 1992-3. "Dodging the Crossfire: Questions for Postcolonial Pedagogy." *College English* 16, 3-17, 1: 28-44.

Moraru, Christian. 1997. "Refiguring the Postcolonial: The Transnational Challenges." *ARIEL* 28, 4: 171-85.

Mukherjee, Arun. 1991. "The Exclusions of Postcolonial Theory and Mulk Raj Anand's 'Untouchable': A Case Study." *ARIEL* 22, 3: 27-48.

————. "Whose Post-Colonialism and Whose Postmodernism?" *World Literature Written in English* 30, 2 : 1-9.

Nazareth, Peter. 1990. "The First Tanzan/Asian Novel." *Research in African Literatures* 21, 4: 129-33.

Ngugi wa Thiong'o. 1981. *Detained: A Writer's Prison Diary*. London: Heinemann.

Rhodes, Shane. 1998. "Frontier Fiction: Reading Books in M G Vassanji's 'The Book of Secrets.' " *ARIEL* 29,1: 179-93.

Richards, David Adams. 1993. *For Those Who Hunt the Wounded Down*. Toronto: McClelland & Stewart.

Rushdie, Salman. 1982. *Midnight's Children*. London: Pan. Original edition, 1981.

Slemon, Stephen. 1990. "Modernism's Last Post." In Adam and Tiffin, 1-11.

Söderlind, Sylvia. 1991. *Margin/Alias: Language and Colonization in Canadian and Québécois Fiction*. Toronto: University of Toronto Press.

Tiffin, Chris, and Alan Lawson. 1994. "Introduction: The Textuality of Empire." In *De-Scribing Empire: Post-Colonialism and Textuality*, ed Chris Tiffin and Alan Lawson, 1-11. London: Routledge.

Tiffin, Helen. "Introduction." *Past the Last Post: Theorizing Post-Colonialism and Post-Modernism*. In Adam and Tiffin, vii-xvi.

Vassanji, M G. 1994. *The Book of Secrets*. Toronto: McClelland & Stewart.

———. 1989. *The Gunny Sack*. Oxford: Heinemann.

———. 1985. "The Postcolonial Writer: Myth Maker and Folk Historian." In *A Meeting of Streams: South Asian Canadian Literature*, ed. M G Vassanji, 63-68.. Toronto: TSAR.

Anti/Modern Spaces: African Canadians in Nova Scotia

LESLIE SANDERS

Blacks first arrived in Nova Scotia in 1783; although some were slaves, most came from the new American state as Loyalists, in response to the Crown's promise that service in its name would result in freedom. Granted plots of barren land (if any at all), ill served by white neighbours and white governance at every turn, members of this first migration fared poorly indeed. In 1790, one of their number, Sergeant Thomas Peters, successfully appealed to the Crown for relief in the name of his people and was offered, as alternative, land grants and full political participation in Sierra Leone. In 1800, this first group was followed by almost all of the 550 Maroons who in 1796 had arrived in Nova Scotia, part of a ceasefire agreement in their native Jamaica. The next major migration of Blacks to Nova Scotia, 1200 refugees, arrived during the War of 1812, again because the British had promised freedom to those who sided with them. These settlers stayed and, along with those first remaining Loyalists, formed the ancestral core of the Blacks of Nova Scotia.

Subsequent history, as yet largely unwritten, bespeaks a desperately poor community struggling for survival in wretched circumstances. Scattered throughout the province, itself since the late nineteenth century one of the poorest in Canada, Black Nova Scotians sought a living in subsistence farming, in menial labour, in the mines of Sidney and Sandhill, and on the sea. Although usually included in regional industry, blacks served largely as a residual labour force in all forms of employment, rarely succeeding in establishing themselves in other than work defined as "black specialties, such as,

106

cooperage, porterage and domestic work" (Clairmont and Wien, 158).

For purposes of synopsis in *Banked Fire: The Ethnics of Nova Scotia*, Donald Clairmont and Fred Wien divide Nova Scotian Black history into three phases, their caption for each in itself resonant. From earliest settlement (both slave and free) to the founding of the African Baptist Association in 1854 they call "Establishing the Patterns"; the second phase, ending with the establishment of the NSAACP in 1945, they call "Hanging In There." Finally, they term subsequent history "Making Changes." Notable in all three periods is migration, subsequent to 1800 not of large groups or to Africa, but of individuals seeking a better life elsewhere in Canada and the United States. Their flight was a response to white Nova Scotia's obdurate racism, enshrined in segregation by custom and by law, for example of schools, and blatant neglect. This constant erosion, particularly of its elites, accounts for many of the small (approximately three percent of the population) and somewhat scattered Black community's difficulties.

Between 1964 and 1967 occurred an event that crystallized for Nova Scotia Blacks their position and condition. In the name of urban reform and social improvement, and also because it wanted the land, the city of Halifax relocated the residents of Africville, a poor black community within its limits, and razed the dwellings they left behind. The wrench was profound and heartbreaking. Although only four hundred people, about eighty families, were affected, Blacks all over the Halifax area and elsewhere in Nova Scotia felt the callousness and disrespect that marked the negotiation leading to the removal, and its execution. Now a memorial park, the site has become, for the community, a monument of their near erasure.

The historical erasure of Africville, in fact, and, for purposes of this discussion, as represented in *The Spirit of Africville*, a collection published by the Africville Genealogical Society(1992), map the problematic I wish to address in this paper. In an emotional speech concerning the destruction of Africville, a long-time Halifax resident and immigrant from Jamaica punctuates his remarks with the refrain, "I did not see any flowers." He, like the proponents of urban renewal with whom he worked at the time, saw only a slum, while the residents insisted that the dirt road, virtually unserviced, and the utterly impoverished enclave on the edge of downtown Halifax, was a tightly knit and vital community with over a century of history, and a testament to the African presence in Nova Scotia.

"Kind of reminds you of the country, even though we're still in Halifax" (18), George R Saunders depicts a resident saying, in his 1959 fictional piece, "A Visit to Africville," contained in the collection. Written as a walking tour in which the community emerges through the voices of the residents, this work maps Africville not only by descriptions of the space it occupied, but also by the genealogy of the residents of each house and a gossipy recounting of familial and communal relation. Saunders's piece is, discursively, in marked contrast to the other works in the collection: a history of Africville, an account of the removal, and a transcription of the film that is primarily a record of a 1989 conference, which gathered participants ranging from former residents and their descendents to the former mayor of Halifax and external experts consulted at the time, to discuss Africville and its meaning. The historical pieces rely on a dispassionate and balanced accounting of events, separating out "facts" from their various interpretations. Not all the residents, for example, were against the appropriation of their property and removal. The city had long sought the Africville location for industrial purposes, and the community there was marginal, underserviced, and cut off from the structures and activities of urban Halifax—it was "pre-modern" and its presence was an affront to the modern city that Halifax was becoming. As the film *Africville Remembers* and its text carefully record, the debate about Africville twenty-five years later had lost none of its urgency. Several players in the decision to demolish, including the former mayor and the man who saw no flowers, confessed that they now would have acted to preserve the community.

The meaning of Africville, whether as historical fact, or as expression of the community that has come to identify with it, is by no means resolved in this collection. It is no accident, however, that coming to grips with the destruction of Africville has produced a profusion of artistic work. Maureen Moynagh suggests that the debate over Africville's meaning must be understood within the context of a general Maritime antimodern sensibility, and even more specifically "the hegemonic discursive paradigm conditioning cultural production in the province . . . of Nova Scotia as a community of traditional, rural folk," which, Moynagh adds, according to Ian

McKay in *The Quest of the Folk* became the way Nova Scotia developed its image for tourism. "One of the most pervasive articulations of anti-modernism privileged rural life as place of moral, psychic, and social regeneration, a refuge from all the ills of urban industrialism and modernization," she writes. Moynagh cites McKay as arguing that this commerical antimodernism allowed Nova Scotia to present its economic and political decline as the choice of a simpler, more traditional way of life. According to McKay, blacks and natives were specifically excluded from this folk world (Moynagh, 16-17).

The rhetoric of the antimodern and the project of inscribing blackness upon Maritime antimodernity provide one context for the analysis that follows. Colina Philips and George Elliot Clarke, the artists under consideration in this paper, strategize this project in different ways, each illuminating the possibilities and pitfalls of such representation. Each fashions a way of rendering the tensions of "the country" as "anti-modern." However, constructing a useable history—and present—without inscribing what seems only prior, backward, nostalgic, is particularly a problem for artists for whose subjects are both not-modern and "other" in societies where modernity overwhelmingly determines majority sensibilities and where the attribution of "backwardness" infuses an already racist discourse.

In "History: Geography: Modernity," the geographer Edward Soja argues, that "[a]n essentially historical epistemology continues to pervade the critical consciousness of modern social theory. It still comprehends the world primarily through the dynamics arising from the emplacement of social being and becoming in the interpretive contexts of time: in what Kant called *nacheinander* and Marx defined so transfiguratively as the contingently constrained 'making of history.' This enduring epistemological presence has preserved a privileged place for the 'historical imagination' in defining the very nature of critical insight and interpretation" (136). Virtually absent—"occluded" is Soja's term—has been consideration of how "the lifeworld" constructs itself in space, in geographical as well as historical landscapes. He calls for "a transformative theorization of the relations between history, geography and modernity."

Soja locates Foucault as the one modern historian who gestures towards a history of spaces and occasionally acknowledges its importance. A central text for his discussion is "Of Other spaces," in which

Foucault defines a taxonomy of space in terms of heterotopias, specific spaces defined by their use and place in the rituals and desires of human existence. A characteristic of heterotopias, for Foucault, is their typical link to "slices in time," for which he coins the word "heterochroncis." "The heterotopia begins to function at full capacity," he writes, "when men arrive at a sort of absolute break with their traditional time." His example is the cemetery. But, he continues, heterotopias always "presuppose a system of opening and closing that both isolates them and makes them penetrable," and they function "in relation to all the space that remains." Concerning this last characteristic, he writes:

> Either their role is to create a space of illusion that exposes every real space, all the sites inside of which human life is partitioned, as still more illusory . . . Or else, on the contrary, their role is to create a space that is other, another real space, as perfect, as meticulous, as well arranged as ours is messy, ill constructed and jumbled . . . the heterotopia, not of illusion, but of compensation, and I wonder if certain colonies have not functioned somewhat in this manner (27).

Using Marshall Berman's *All that's Solid Melts in Air: The Experience of Modernity*, Sojo defines modernity as engaged in a continually changing "culture of time and space"and an interplay between modernization and modernism.

Where in all this is the meaning of Africville? In the African American classic *Invisible Man*, Ralph Ellison's unnamed protagonist rejects the historicism that situates African American migrants to Harlem as "the old ones . . . the agrarian types . . . Thrown on the dump heaps and cast aside . . . they don't count . . . History has passed them by" (290-1). Moreover, he later comes to see the zoot-suited Harlem youth on the subway, as "outside of historical time" (440). The story of a man who has taken up residence underground, Ellison's narrative gestures instead towards a history of African American spaces, an alternative to, and in terms of this text, a necessary retreat from the utterly deceptive historical account that promises the move from south to north as one from bondage to freedom.

Historical discourse allows few options for delineating the lives of those who do not engage with modernity, or even modernization. Premodern implies the inevitability of progress. Constituting antihistorical discourse, the pastoral and the romance, essentially heterotopic, transfigure these lives into a rejection of the "real";they express the artist's memory and desire, while their own desires remain tacit. The modern artist who wishes to fashion a mode of representation that insists upon the simultaneity and contemporaneity of these lives is hard put to escape labels and discourses. In Foucault's words, the artist needs to construct a space "that is other, another real space," while refusing the perspective that completes Foucault's sentence: "as perfect, as meticulous, as well arranged as ours is messy, ill constructed and jumbled." For that space, too, is messy, ill-constructed and jumbled; it acts, as Paul Gilroy suggests about the African diaspora, in *The Black Atlantic, Modernity and Double Consciousness*, not only as a counter-discourse of modernity but, indeed, a counterculture.

Colina Phillips's eighteen- minute film *Making Change* meditates upon the life of her father, a coal miner in Donkin, Nova Scotia, who was also a gifted musician, and who desperately longed to pursue his art . Shot primarily in black-and-white, but framed in colour, the film is silent, except for a brilliant jazz score, a musical work created, she relates, a year before the film was composed. Thus the primary narrative is musical: beginning lyrically, but with an undertone of dread, moving to a harsh and discordant reflection of her father's conflict, and ending in haunting melody. His instruments, and those of the score, are the piano on which he composes and the clarinet which is his love. Set in the 1930s in rural Nova Scotia, the film opens, in colour, with a backshot of the filmmaker—all that is evident are her dreads—typing its title and the details of its setting into a laptop computer. She faces a window from which one glimpses an urban landscape, remote from the setting of the narrative itself. In the opening shot of the body of the film, a figure approaches the viewer; he is striding through a field overlooking the sea. The camera greets and then follows him; it cuts to a dirt road bordered by tall bushes and trees. Again he approaches, snatches some flowers from the side of the road, turns into the vegetation through which we glimpse a house. We are in the house: the film is now black-and-white, and remains so until the final few minutes.

It is a simple house, the living room dominated by an upright piano, a table. His wife and young daughter greet him, delighted at his return from work. Shot: the flowers in a vase on the table; shot: wife and daughter glimpsed pumping water in the kitchen. His wife brings him tea, spilling it on the musical score over which he is bent. His daughter plays haphazardly on the piano. Later in the evening his wife casts finger rabbit-shadows on his score, lovingly wraps her apron around him and lures him to bed. Afterwards she sleeps, holding onto him; he lies awake. The next morning, he runs out of the house still dressing.

Miners approach the camera, dimly visible by the light of the lamps on their hardhats. In this first mine scene, the father applies his pickaxe carefully. Two more scenes in the mine are interspersed with scenes outside and in the house. In an early scene, he and his daughter fly a kite and become enmeshed in its string. They roll on the ground laughing. But later, the jaunty confidence of his initial stride, during his journeys to and from work, diminishes; depression slows his gait. On the road, he is handed a flyer advertising a band scheduled to play the following weekend. He fantacizes: dressed in a slick white suit with the band behind him, he plays his clarinet for an admiring audience. In the mine, he slumps in despair. In the house, his daughter interrupts his musical labours, scribbling on his score, knocking down his music stand. His wife, now with infant, hushes her. Late one night, as he struggles with his music, a pickaxe falls on to the table: in anger he sweeps off the table and the piano, smashes the light. His wife comes, tries to soothe him, sees the flyer and enters her own fantasy: hair done up, fashionable dress, she sings before a microphone. That night he sleeps with his head on the table, she on the couch still clutching his thermos. The next day, instead of his lunch box he brings his clarinet to work. Deep in the mine, he plays a jaunty melody and another miner dances in delight.

In the final shots, he leaves the house dressed for the road. He turns, not down the path but toward the camera, and enters a colour frame: on the edge of the cliff, overlooking the sea, he dances, holding up his clarinet, playing a joyful melody. Before the credits, the camera lingers over family photographs, ending with a musical score that bears his name.

In terms of the problem I am examining in this paper, *Making*

Change may be seen as providing a discourse, not of utopic spaces, but of those that are messy, ill constructed and jumbled. Within the narrative there are three: house, mine, and outside. The father's conflict between his family and his art are played out in both house and mine, the latter virtually a narrow space between "a rock and a hard place." Family not only chains him to the mine, but also within the home continually interrupts his artistic labour. These interruptions are expressions of familial love, but his daughter's playfulness, his wife's affection are a source of torment because his musical desires cannot accommodate them. The camera angles mirror his emotions: sometimes long shots create a sense that the space is ample; at others, sections of the room are shot from a variety of angles producing the sense that each element of the domestic space produces its own oppression. The house is also clearly presented as the scene of women's labour; for example, one striking shot looks down at a sewing machine, material still attached. In another, wife and child work in the kitchen, while the father gazes at them from the next room. The camera always returns to him, his face, even in repose, weighted down with care or anguish.

In the second scene in the mine, just before his night-time outburst, he is almost in tears, and the shot that follows him across the field duplicates the opening shot in which he strode so confidently towards the camera. Now his gait is heavy, but the setting remains the same. The outside space is country: country is not nature—as opposed to the binaries modernity associates with it, culture and urbanity—but rather simply the environment in which this family enacts its life. The family and its life is located through the ways in which the film recounts cinematic history, its initial contemporary frame, its colour in the opening and closing scenes, its black-and-white core, and, of course, its being a silent film accompanied by music. The only sound that seems to emanate from the action on the screen is that of the kitchen water pump from which mother and daughter draw water. When the father plays his clarinet, it is especially clear that the film is silent, for the father merely mouths the instrument, while the score provides the music being played. Imagistically, the film moves back into time as well. The image of the opening frames, the laptop computer, the urban view out the window, and even the presentation of the filmmaker herself—her dreads in contrast to her mother's straight(ened?) hair tied back, or processed, in her fantasy—all are in marked contrast to the setting of the narrative.

Yet other details mark the story as contemporary: miners labour now as they did sixty years ago; the landscape is as yet unchanged. Moreover, the principal conflict, that of the artist enmeshed in domesticity, is remarkably contemporary: this film is the first representation of which I am aware where the male conflict is portrayed as one enacted within domesticity itself.

The film's power is that it does not function as memory, although it is a loving representation of the filmmaker's father. The closing credits offer the film as tribute to miners everywhere, again insisting on its contemporaneous frame. Mining continues to fuel modernization; the film's historical details, the old car that drives by, the details of daily dress and fantasy fashion, perhaps the kitchen pump—though in rural Nova Scotia still not everyone has running water—mark and signal the past, but it denies the difference between "then" and "now." Moreover, its silence is not simply filmic retrospective because its score is absolutely contemporary, a musical narrative itself rather than a reproduction of an era. In fact, set as it is in the country, its visuals seem to demand blues rather than the modern jazz score which forms the film's predominant narrative. And jazz is the African North American musical idiom in which modernity found its rhythm. *Making Change* refuses either to romanticize or to historicize its subject; rather, it posits it squarely within the modern sensibility.

George Elliott Clarke's *Whylah Falls* meditates on the reality of what seems past to modern eyes in a quite different fashion. Important to his project in this text is the term he prefers to use when speaking of black Nova Scotians: "Afracadian," a term welding African ancestry to Acadian space. The relation of Acadia to imaginary pastoral world (Arcadia) is, reputedly, a deliberate reference, contained in the original naming, a tribute to the land's beauty ("Genealogy"). The idyllic, then, is imbedded in Clarke's conception of Nova Scotian African Canadians, and this imbrication of an ideal or romanticized imaginary will have implications for the complex task he set himself in his most extended representation of his fictional Black folk community. A narrative consisting of a collection of poems, *Whylah Falls* is the story of the poet X, who has been away from home, and his courtship of Shelley, whose family is the centre of the story. The impetus for the story comes, in part, from historical incident, the 1985 acquittal in Weymouth Falls, Nova Scotia, of a white man by a racist judge on the grounds that his victim "Graham Cromwell, a country and western tenor, father, woodsman, and *bon vivant*, had been 'a mean drunk.' " Clarke was much involved in the resulting protest; his poetic response, "Weymouth Falls Suite," marked the beginning of this volume of poetry, set in the 1930s, in which Weymouth becomes a mythical town of Whylah, the Sissiboo river, the Sixhiboux, Digby County, Jarvis.

The collection is utterly hybrid in poetic form. For example, its seven sections are each prefaced with an *Argument* reminiscent of Milton's *Paradise Lost*; within each section, it moves easily between prose, blues, *vers libre*, and even haiku. Essentially a pastoral, in the course of its narrative, however, *Whylah Falls* alludes to virtually the entire canon of British literature from Chaucer to Pound and Eliot, adapting and adopting form and image to its portrait of the Clemence family and the lives of those among whom they live. Clarke's appropriation and re/visioning of British and American poetic traditions has an effect somewhat like that of a cubist painting: familiar planes and surfaces rendered new by rearrangement and juxtaposition on a flat surface. It is almost a maxim that hybridity marks the postcolonial style; however, it is as well a mark of the modern, where it comprises a re-reading that investigates the meanings of the past within the context of the rupture that modernity seems to be.

Names also signal Clarke's re-reading: for example, the brother Othello, who is cruelly murdered, is killed by a man who believes he has slept with his wife. Jack Thompson, the Iago figure, is in fact the culprit, although he does not pull the trigger; his malicious act is revenge for Othello's protection of his sister Amarantha, after whom Thompson lusts. Fuelling these details is the racial context: Thompson and Seville, the murderer, are the story's only white characters. This reclamation of *Othello*, the play, through Othello the character, provides a "community" perspective on Shakespeare's Moor. Throughout this work, Clarke seeks to situate the British literary canon in the meadows, vales, gardens and homes of the people of Whylah Falls. In a prose piece peppered with blues lyrics called "Bringing It All Back Home," X says: "After Howlin' Will Shakespeare, Blind Jack Milton, and Missouri Tom Eliot, I'm just one more dreamer to hoist a guitar and strum Sixhiboux Delta Blues. Oh yes." In "Each Moment Is Magnificent," the phrase "Sweet Sixhiboux, run softly till I end my song" evokes Eliot's "Sweet Thames, run softly till I end my song" in *The Wasteland*, a line Eliot borrows from V Spencer's *Prothalamion*. Clarke's piece, too, depicts how lovers engage a river, linking his mythical Sixhiboux to London's Thames, and so three worlds: Renaissance and Modern London, rural, contemporary Nova Scotia, Afracadia.

Clarke concludes one of the prose/blues pieces that portray the riotous goings on as lovers and musicians pile in and out of Cora's house: "And this song is Canadian literature." Towards the book's end, having gained more insight, in another passage that mixes prose with poetry, X concludes—immediately following a quote from Chaucer: "Literature be the tongue you do your lovin' in." This juxtaposition of Chaucerian and colloquial black English also insists on the poet's right—and that of his community—to a range of traditions. In interviews, Clarke has repeatedly insisted on a Maritime fondness for blank verse, and for "disciplined verse" (Compton, 147-8); in *Whylah Falls*, he displays his loyalty to that tradition. But within the text, an array of language is summoned to the task of recording the community. Like X, the other characters speak variously. For example, in an extravagant display of the demotic, in the poem called "The Symposium," Cora gives her stepdaughter the advice she herself should have followed ("I'm gonna learn you 'bout the mens so you can 'scape the bitter foolishness I've suffered. A little thoughtful can save you trouble"). Blues lyrics abound.

Music is, in *Whylah Falls*, almost continually present. It links the community to a quite different tradition, that of the "black Atlantic," especially the United States, but also the Caribbean and Mediterranean. Amarantha Clemence's black lover is the flamenco guitar playing Pablo, a troubadour who has drifted from Cuba to Canada, longing for a "gentler imperialism." His melodies are "Moorish," and they mingle with the playing of other characters. In the piece entitled "Four Guitars," for example, the Clemence brothers Othello and Pushkin play "Baptist hymns . . . infernal hollers . . . ," nursery rhymes and blues in varying styles, while Pablo "nudge[s] O" into a Latinate version of "I be's troubled" and adds his "Moorish sense to that spiritual salvaged from two centuries of bad luck." Finally the Clemences' stepsister Missy contributes "a dark mandolin . . . adopts Poor Girl tuning, mumbles her debt to Bessie Smith and Amy 'Big Mama' Lowell, [and] booms, 'I've got Ford engine movements in my hips' " and finally a balladlike lyric:

Come and love me, darling one,
In sweetest April rain.
Kiss me until life is done:
Youth will not come again. (92-94)

When the characters are not playing music, they are listening to the radio: Duke Ellington, Billie Halliday, jazz and blues, and also the news. The radio, like the train that brings X to Whylah Falls, or takes Shelley to Yarmouth for her summer job on a ferry, links the community to the modern world from which they remain isolated. Allusion, then, is one strategy through which Clarke situates his characters in worlds beyond the literal and imagined rural context in which they are figured, and in which they live. And music is so present that it comprises virtually a continual mode of commentary and interaction, situating them also in a world beyond their own..

The dominant mode of *Whylah Falls,* however, is pastoral. Most of its poems concern themselves with pastoral themes: principally, the lush beauty of nature and the adventures of lovers within its protected space. The cycle of the seasons ensures that death is followed by resurrection. Two bitter stories disrupt the too-ing and fro-ing of the lovers. Othello's murder fills one complete section of the work, his death played and replayed, mourned by his community, unimportant to the world outside it. The murderer, we are told in the section's argument, will be acquitted. The state has no interest in the crime, and no thought of pursuing justice for this community. The other tale of horror is the story of Saul Clemence and his wife Cora. Fifty years a miner, "Who dast blame this man if he makes his stepdaughter his lover and his wife his foe? Yes, jury of readers, there is no defense for these social crimes . . . " we are told in the argument. The poems in this section are few and most are grim, depicting in his voice and in Cora's, the actions that lead inevitably to Saul's violence towards Cora, her suffering, his suicide when Missy abandons his bed. Yet the structure of *Whylah Falls* is cyclical, beginning and ending with "The Adoration of Shelley," each of the the two chapters taking their epigram from the *Song of Solomon*. The Argument reads: "Ten months have passed. All things must pass . . . *There is a time to mourn and a time to cease form mourning* . . . "

The poem "Quilt," which occurs towards the end of the section on Pablo and Amarantha's courtship, and just before the murder of Othello, suggests how these elements of the modern and the space that this community inhabits might be arranged:

Sunflowers are sprouting in the tropical livingroom.
Pablo, I am falling away from words.

The newspaper scares me with its gossip of Mussolini and the dead

of Ethiopia.
The radio mutters of Spain and bullets.
Only the Devil ain't tired of history.

Yesterday, I saw—puzzled beside the railroad tracks—a horse's
bleached bones.
Roses garlanded the ribs and a garter snake rippled greenly
through
the skull.

The white moon ripples in the darkness of fallen rain.
The sunflowers continue in the living room.
The latest reports from Germany are all bad.

I quilt, planting sunflower patches in a pleasance of thick cotton.
We need a blanket against this world's cold cruelty.

Quilts are an artform of spaces: each square, regardless of pattern or image, bonded to the patches that border onto it. There is no bleeding in a quilt; in the viewer's eye, however, the patches assemble and reassemble in a variety of patterns, and from a variety of persepctives. In *Slave Culture*, Sterling Stuckey suggests that certain slave quilts, fashioned from scraps of fabric, and used to wrap the

newly baptised, "bore a remarkable resemblance to Dahomean appli-
que cloth," and that their patterns derived from African religious
iconography (91). During slavery, more overtly referential story quilts
hung by the roadway mapped the path for escaping slaves. Quilting,
then, is wonderfully suggestive symbol of the space occupied by
black Nova Scotians in the modern world.

In a different vein, in her epilogue to *Picasso*, Gertrude Stein comments:

> When I was in America I for the first time travelled pretty much
> all the time in an airplane and when I looked at the earth I saw
> all the lines of cubism made at a time when not any painter had
> ever gone up in an airplane. I saw there on the earth the min-
> gling lines of Picasso coming and going, developing and de-
> stroying themselves, I saw the simple solutions of Braque, I saw
> the wandering lines of Masson . . . (50)

Stein, the quintessential modernist, too saw the twentieth century in
terms of spaces; cubist painting configures the world in a manner not
unlike that older women's art form of the quilt.

In some ways, Clarke's representation of the community in *Whylah
Falls* also functions in the way that Foucault suggests heterotopias do.
Underpinning his narrative is a mythic space, seasonal, pastoral,
healing. He alludes to several possible frames for his tale of love and
death: the cyclical movement from summer to spring is one. Another
is biblical and religious, for the "Song of Solomon" provides the
epitaphs of the opening and closing sections, both called "The Adoration of Shelley." Other sections are titled: "The Witness of Saul";
"The Witness of Selah"; "The Passion of Pablo and Amarantha"; "The
Martyrdom of Othello Clemence": and "The Gospel of Reverend F R
Langford." In each section, in the tradition of Black music, where
gospel and blues partake of the same musical tradition, the titles are,
in some sense also profoundly secular. The passion is sexual: Selah's
witness is to the carnality of the many men she beds, including the
poet X; Saul Clemence beats his wife Cora and beds his stepdaughter
Missy. Reverend Langford's sermon is countered by various members of his congregation, and at one point he too lies drunk on the
Clemence kitchen floor.

It must be noted that the romantic narrative thread in *Whylah Falls*, and the positioning of the community's chronicler, the poet X, as lover, threaten to undermine the ways in which the work does succeed in being topical rather than heterotopical. The latter is defined by need and desire—or as Foucault would have it, serves the purpose of "illusion" or "compensation." The heteroptic text, the space, cannot, rid itself of the desire that motivates its creation. Yet the world depicted in *Whylah Falls* understands contradiction profoundly, and itself continues to create a discourse that stands as a challenge to modernity's belief in rationality and progress.

In "Africville, An Imagined Community," Maureen Moynagh argues that Africville has come to serve, for African Nova Scotians, the kind of imaginary that disrupts the hegemonic imaginary of province and nation. Her analysis of recent representations of Africville's history and destruction concludes, in the words of a poem by Fred Ward, "we are Africville." But this identification resolves none of the tensions of the antimodern or, in her terms, the nonindustrial life. Despite Nova Scotia's official policy regarding "the folk," modernity leaves us few options for their representation without romanticism, condescension, yearning and retreat. This may be why, for me, Colina Philips's film succeeds in its representation while Clarke's volume of poetry is not entirely successful. *Making Change*, through its construction of human desire and aspiration, bursts its frame(s). That other place is not delineated, but it is articulated both visually and muscially, and it is not heterotopic. *Whylah Falls*, enclosed in the romance form, the cyclical, the pastoral, suggests a kind of stasis, and the impossibility of change. Saul will forever beat his wife and bed his stepdaughter; Othello will be murdered over and over, with the killer always exonerated. Pastoral is not a resolution. Yet the deeply felt debate about the meaning of Africville is nothing less than a desire to turn the quilt, so rich and ambiguous in New World African history, into a liberatory politics, and the works of these and other artists serve to clarify and illuminate how that might come to be.

WORKS CITED

Africville Genealogical Society. 1992. *The Spirit of Africville*. Halifax: Formac Publishing Company.

Clarke, George Elliott. 1990. *Whylah Falls*. Winlaw BC: Polestar.

———. 1989. "George Elliott Clarke's Weymouth Falls Suite." *New Maritimes* (January/February).

Clairmont, Donald and Fred Wien. 1978. "Blacks and Whites: The Nova Scotia Race Relations Experience." In *Banked Fires: The Ethnics of Nova Scotia*, Douglas F Campbell, ed. Port Credit ON: Scribblers' Press.

Compton, Anne. "Standing Your Ground: George Elliot Clarke in Conversation." *Studies in Canadian Literature*, 23.2.

Ellison, Ralph. 1989. *Invisible Man*. NY: Vintage.

Foucault, Michel. 1986. "Of other spaces." *Diacritcs* 16: 22-7.

Gilroy, Paul. 1993. *The Black Atlantic: Modernity and Double Consciousness*. Cambridge MA: Harvard UP.

Moynagh, Maureen. 1998. "Africville, an Imagined Community." *Canadian Literature* 157: 14-34.

———. 1996. "Mapping Africadia's Imaginary Geography: An Interview with George Elliott Clarke." *Ariel* 27, 4: 71-94.

Pachai, Bridglal. 1987. *Beneath the Clouds . . . of the Promised Land: The Survival of Nova Scotia's Blacks: 1600-1800*, Volume One. Halifax: Black Educators Association.

Phillips, Colina. 1995. *Making Change*. Film.

Sojo, Edward. 1993. "History: Geography: Modernity." In *The Cultural Studies Reader*, ed Simon Durang. NY: Routledge.

Stuckey, Sterling. 1987. *Slave Culture: Nationalist Theory & the Foundations of Black America*..

Stein, Gertrude. 1959. *Picasso*. Boston: Beacon.

Walker, James W St G. 1985. *The Black Identity in Nova Scotia: Community and Institutions in Historical Perspective*.. Halifax: Black Cultural Centre.

———. 1997. "Allegories and Orientations in African-Canadian Historiography: The Spirit of Africville." *Dalhousie Review* 77,1: 155-178.

Winks, Robin. 1971. *The Blacks in Canada*. New Haven: Yale UP.

The Shahrazadic Tradition: Rohinton Mistry's 'Such a Long Journey' and the Art of Storytelling

AMIN MALAK

While in Mistry's first book, the collection of short stories entitled *Tales from Firozsha Baag* (1987), the three finest and most exciting pieces switch between Bombay and Toronto, the narrative in his second book, the novel *Such a Long Journey* (1991), is set entirely in India.[1] Lengthier, more assuredly detailed and variant, *Such a Long Journey* nevertheless shares numerous features with its predecessor, the most obvious being the imaginative depiction of residential complexes (Firozsha Baag and Khodadad Building respectively), inhabited mostly by middle-class Parsis. The Parsis are a tiny but vibrant Bombay community whose religious and ethnic roots go back to the Iranian prophet Zoroaster (c 1400 BC). The choice of such a setting reveals the author's penchant for groups of characters that exhibit diverse temperaments and rich potential for drama. One is almost tempted to say that Mistry's strategy aims at producing characters *en masse*, yet the tone and texture of the narrative suggest a design that situates the individual within a context, be it family, ethnic community, or nation, whereby the narrative becomes humanized and historicized. Subsequently, the discourse can evolve effortlessly and interchangeably, moving from private to public, from ethnic to national, from local to universal. Significantly, the vehicle that readily serves to express such a vision is storytelling, an art whose influence, according to Walter Benjamin (83-109), has diminished in the technologized cultures of the West, yet still flourishes as a popular narrative form in the oral tradition of numerous other civilizations.

Such a Long Journey tells the story of a sympathetic bank clerk, Gustad Noble, whose devotion to his family, loyalty to his friends, and love for his Parsi community are continually tested through a series of mimetically rendered events and situations. Loyalty and journeying constitute two major contrasting patterns in his life: the first entails constancy and commitment; the second mutation and metamorphosis. Gustad Noble is well delineated and centrally positioned amongst a host of other characters; as his name suggests, his touching, tolerant self appeals to our best instincts, at times even movingly evoking pathos. Mistry illustrates that a decent, ordinary person can be unassumingly heroic. Unlike the larger-than-life gods of myths and legends, the characters of oral stories and folk tales are creatures of average, often mundane, qualities: they experience failures and frustrations but also entertain hope, express joy and reap rewards. Mistry's modest Noble, because of his closeness to our humanity, recurrently excites then fulfils our anticipation of his reactions to situations that are, at times, beyond his control or comprehension. Through well-timed flashbacks, we become aware of how this middle-class clerk is still haunted by his father's degrading bankruptcy years ago, an event that disrupted and dashed his hopes for an advanced education. We can thus appreciate his current troubles with a son, Sohrab, who prefers arts to studying at the prestigious Institute of Technology, thereby denying the father the vicarious pleasure of achieving what cruel destiny had denied him. And this is not the only preoccupation that disturbs Noble's relative tranquillity: his close but mysterious friend, Major Bilimoria, asks a favour that requires risky, if seemingly legal, financial transactions, connected, as is revealed later, with Indira Gandhi's secret scheme for funding guerrillas in Bangladesh while deceptively embezzling the money for her family's use. This high, breathtaking drama, at times stretching the limits of credibility is handled competently through the use of prolepsis and analepsis. (Genette 40)

But the novel, as I suggested earlier, is more than the tale of the one individual's life, touching and riveting as this aspect is; it is a microcosm of a community, an image of a "tribe" invented through the imagination of its storyteller. We are presented with a gallery of characters of diverse types and temperaments, such as dabblers in magic, an ageless aphrodisiac vendor, a barefoot pavement painter of ecumenical saints and gods, a malcontent who hurls defiances at God, the disabled Tehmul (perhaps Mistry's finest creation) who exhibits "a child's mind and a man's [sexual] urges," (*Such a Long Journey*, 303) and a Dr Jekyll/Mr Hyde secret agent who seems to be everywhere and nowhere.[2] "It is a tidal wave of humanity," one reviewer comments (Ross). Another articulates quite colourfully the role of the minor characters:

> They come and go like ghosts, as they do in life, as anyone who has lived through an Indian afternoon will know . . . To walk down a crowded Colaba street on an afternoon is to come into contact with more people than one would in the course of a lifetime in Sweden. In the West, because of the climate, people get to know each other in rooms. Relationships form. So do characters. In India, the human face, being part of a river of faces, refuses to lend itself to characterization, disappears, like a hint, soon after appearing, remains ghostly, without inwardness. This sense of humanity as at once endlessly replenishable and dispersed, Mistry powerfully suggests through his minor characters. (Chaudhuri, "Parsi Magic")

Mistry's skillful blending of his characters' personal affairs with communal concerns situates them and lends them significance as social beings. This conception of characters and the engaging, simple, yet subtle, narrative are but two of several aspects of Mistry's strategy of harmonizing the secure style of storytelling—whose paradigms are refined in the Shahrazadic tradition—and the generic exigencies of the novel, an essentially European product. The challenge is to reconcile respectfully and synergetically the compatible features from both practices, without denigrating either, as E M Forster does when he calls storytelling "this low atavistic form" (41). Accordingly, it is appropriate to enumerate below the salient features of storytelling that have bearing on our reading of *Such a Long Journey*.

Sense of Audience

In any story told orally, the audience's comprehension, engagement, response, and sympathy are crucial. Its approval of, indeed participation in, the way the story is told means in essence that it partakes in shaping it. That is to say the audience's confidence in the integrity of the storyteller is as crucial as the story's merit and the excitement it generates. Here the audience has to trust *both* the tale and the teller. As Salman Rushdie affirms, "the first and only rule of the storyteller is to hold his audience: if you don't hold them, they will get up and walk away. So everything that the storyteller does is designed to keep the people listening most intensely" (1985, 1). In *Haroun and the Sea of Stories*, when Rashid Khalfa's storytelling talent is restored to him after the defeat of the evil Khattam Shud, Rushdie describes it thus: "And it was plain that he was okay again, the Gift of Gab had returned, and *he had the audience in the palm of his hand*" [emphasis added].(206)

Sense of Heritage and Values

That both the storyteller and the audience share common codes speaks volumes about the social function of the storyteller as a repository of the community ethos, recorder/reminder of shared perceptions, and spokesperson articulating feelings, attitudes and judgements. The storyteller, then, distils and defines individual experiences while registering and retaining community history; as Walter Benjamin puts it:

> Experience which is passed on from mouth to mouth is the source from which all storytellers have drawn . . . In [storytelling] the love of faraway places brought home by a much-travelled man is combined with the love of the past, as it best reveals itself to natives of a place. (85-85)

Interestingly, for a traditionalist like R K Narayan, whose fiction provides yet another illustration par excellence of the dominance of storytelling strategies in his narrative, stories can be unabashedly utilized to confirm common creed: "Since didacticism was never shunned, every story has implicit in it a moral value, likened to the fragrance of a well-shaped flower" (9). Significantly, Narayan underscores the difference between oriental and Greek visions of good and evil.

Reliable Reporting in Private and Collective Memory

If I may venture a tentative definition of storytelling, I would say it is a form of imaginative reporting about something that happened to someone elsewhere, earlier—witness the formula "Once upon a time . . ." Of course in order to accept and appreciate the report(ing), one needs a trustworthy reporter; one needs to establish *rapport* with the *rapporteur* (puns intended). A striking quality of *Such a Long Journey* is the large amount of reporting that occurs throughout: characters often tell each other what happened to themselves or to others elsewhere. Exceptionally, however, one report assumes pivotal significance: it involves the confessional claim Major Bilimoria makes about how corruption goes to the top of the Indian political establishment, implicating that "strange . . . very strong woman" (272) (i e Indira Gandhi), who double-crossed him with a large sum of embezzled state funds.[3] Given the delicacy of the contention, Mistry depicts Bilimoria making those allegations elliptically while in the grips of delirium and death, thus making the claim twice removed from the reader; this situation is not unlike what Rushdie's Gibreel Farishta undergoes as he "dreams" those risky, controversial reports in *The Satanic Verses*.

Reporting can also take other forms: self-reporting through memory, the most prominent being Gustad Noble's recurrent, private recollections of his father's shattering business failure. There is also collective memory symbolized by traditions (such as the dramatic details of Parsi burial rituals in the novel) and community codes, as well as the history of the nation, India, especially as it relates to the saga of wars with troubled/troubling neighbours: China, Pakistan, and Bangladesh.

Blending Modes and Moods

Storytelling as a craft involves at times blending different modes of expression to serve stylistic and thematic intentions. In Mistry's fascinating story "Squatter," which employs the form of a story-within-a-story, a bright, young listener, Jehangir, comments appreciatively on the technique used by Nariman, the storyteller who enchants the boys of Firozsha Baag:

> Nariman sometimes told a funny incident in a very serious way, or expressed a significant matter in a light and playful manner. And these were only two rough divisions, in between were lots of subtle gradations of tone and texture. Which, then, was the funny story and which the serious? [The boys'] opinions were divided but ultimately, said Jehangir, it was up to the listener to decide. (147-8)

Not only do storytellers blend modes but also genres. In *Such a Long Journey*, Peerbhoy, an aphrodisiac vendor with a multifaceted personality and a parody of sorts of Shakespeare's Polonius, turns to storytelling during the mobilization for the war in Bangladesh; his "tale" mocks General Yahya, the Pakistani potentate then, referred to as the Drunkard:

> In defence to the mood of the country and the threat from without, Peerbhoy Paanwalla had mobilized his talents for the common good, using his skills to weave a tale that defied genre or description. It was not tragedy, comedy or history; not pastoral, tragical-comical, historical-pastoral or tragical-historical. It was not a ballad or an ode, masque or anti-masque, fable or elegy, parody or threnody. Although a careful analysis may have revealed that it possessed a smattering of all these characteristics. But since things such as literary criticism mattered not one jot to the listeners, they were responding to Peerbhoy's narrative in the only way that made sense: with every fibre of their beings. They could see and smell and taste and feel the words that filled the dusk and conjured the tale; and it was no wonder they were oblivious to the gutter stink. (306)

While storytelling is not quite that amorphous a process, it does enjoy solid, resourceful possibilities that could befit variations in mood, situation, time, audience and comprehension level.

Digression

Given that *Such a Long Journey* characterizes not only Gustad Noble's private odyssey but also the lives of a community of other characters relating to him, befriending him or coming in contact with him, the narrative often shifts—quietly, imperceptibly, but intentionally—into the histories and preoccupations of these others. According to Tzvetan Todorov's analysis of the narrative technique of *Alf Laylah wa-Laylah: 1001 Nights*, the appearance of any new character necessitates inserting a new story within the preceding one—a process which he labels as *enchâssement* (embedding or encasement):

> L'apparition d'un nouveau personnage entraîne immanquablement l'interruption de l'histoire précédente, pour qu'une nouvelle histoire, celle qui explique le "je suit ici maintenant" du nouveau personnage, nous soit racontée. Une histoire seconde est englobée dans la première; ce procédé s'appelle *enchâssement*. (82)

As the most striking feature of storytelling, these digressions are meant to defy or de-emphasize linearity, rigid narrative cohesion, or self-indulgent insularity. Replying to a question on the role of digressions in *Midnight's Children*, Salman Rushdie affirms that "they are absolutely crucial":

> The digressions are almost the point of the book, in which the idea of multitude is a central notion. When I started writing, I just tried to explain one life, and it struck me more and more that, in order to explain this life, you had to explain a vast amount of material which surrounded it, both in space and time. In a country like India, you are basically never alone. The idea of solitude is a luxury which only the rich people enjoy. For most Indians, the idea of privacy is very remote. When people perform their natural functions in public, you don't have the same idea of privacy. (22-3)

On another occasion, Rushdie eloquently describes how storytelling aborts linearity:

An oral narrative does not go from the beginning to the middle to the end of the story. It goes in great swoops, it goes in spirals or in loops, it every so often reiterates something that happened to remind you, and then takes you off again, sometimes summarizes itself, it frequently digresses off into something that the storyteller appears just to have thought of, then comes back to the main thrust of the narrative. Sometimes it steps sideways and tells you about another, related story which is like the story that he's been telling you, and then it goes back to the main story. Sometimes there are Chinese boxes where there is a story inside a story inside a story inside a story, then they all come back . . . So it's a very bizarre and pyrotechnical shape. And it has the appearance of being random and chaotic, it has the appearance that what is happening is anything the storyteller happens to be thinking, he just proceeds in that contingent way. It seemed to me in fact that it was very far from being random or chaotic, and that the oral narrative had developed this shape over a very long period, not because storytellers were lacking in organization, but because this shape conformed very exactly to the shape in which *people like to listen* . . . [emphasis added] (1985, 7-8)

The vibrant character of Haroun in *Haroun and the Sea of Stories* deploys a juggling metaphor to describe the dynamics of storytelling: "I always thought storytelling was like juggling . . . You keep a lot of different tales in the air, and juggle them up and down, and if you're good you don't drop any. So maybe juggling is a kind of storytelling, too." (1990, 206)

Put briefly, then, one can assert digressions are not redundancies but variations that are integral parts of the narrative strategy, leading towards the *enchâssement* phenomenon, mentioned earlier in Todorov's observation and which he further underscores by calling it "the narrative of narrative": *le récit d'un récit.* (85)

Orality/Literacy

Storytelling is obviously a phenomenon of the oral tradition; the novel is a product of literacy. Each practice is defined by the artistic and social functions attributed to it by its relevant civilization. According to Walter Ong, for oral culture narrative functions crucially in two ways: "to store, organize, and communicate much of what they know" and "to bond a great deal of lore in relatively substantial, lengthy forms that are reasonably durable and repeatable" (140-1). Of course when narrative becomes choreographed and typographed, the needs for warehousing and durability are satisfied, but at a price. Features—such as open-endedness, spontaneity, intimacy, drama—and functions—such as audience participation, singing, dancing and playing music—have to be abandoned and/or curtailed substantially. In *Resisting Novels: Ideology and Fiction*, Leonard J Davis argues that "the shift from storyteller to novelist carries with it the move from craftsperson . . . to professional" (143) whose financial and cultural success changes narrative into professionalized novel form—breaking the story away in objectified form—as opposed to the lived and contextualized folk tale or storyteller's tale. In the newer form, character becomes established as the ideological representation of personality, plot plows the disorder of modern life into orderly lines, the natural flow of time is broken up into commodified units which appear serially in magazines or individual numbers to maximize sales. The novelist, as professional, gains with this the "universal" authority of a cultural, financial, and creative paragon. (Davis, 144)

Walter Benjamin astutely articulates a different perspective on this shift from storyteller to novelist:

> The storyteller takes what he tells from experience—his own or that reported by others. And he in turn makes it the experience of those who are listening to his tale. The novelist has isolate himself. The birthplace of the novel is the solitary individual, who is no longer able to express himself by giving examples of his most important concerns, is himself uncounseled, and cannot counsel others. To write a novel means to carry the incommensurable to extremes in the representation of human life. In the midst of life's fullness, and through the representation of this fullness, the novel gives evidence of the profound perplexity of the living. (87)

The epistemological and phenomenological differences separating storytelling from novel writing make the task of a postcolonial writer like Mistry who straddles the two traditions quite challenging. The task of the storyteller-cum-novelist is to accommodate, reconcile, and integrate the demands of both practices: *Such a Long Journey*, qua hybrid, contains calculated, negotiated features, reflecting different geneses. Accordingly, the attitude of the postcolonial novelist towards his profession becomes Manichean, quite similar to his attitude to the English language he uses; as the Indian novelist Raja Rao puts it succinctly, "One has to convey in a language [or a medium] that is not one's own the spirit that is one's own." From reading Mistry's two books, one senses the confidence and dexterity with which he handles his material. The subject-matter may, thus far, be limited in scope, namely Parsis living in residential complexes, but when it contains such variety of tones, textures, and temperaments, and when it is so consummately constructed and conveyed, our satisfaction with the final product is guaranteed. Mistry's secret success as a writer relates to the fact that he, the *bona fide* storyteller, is comfortably intimate with the situations and experiences that he deals with. "To write well," Mistry says, "I must write about what I know best. In that way, I automatically speak for my 'tribe' "(Hancock, 145).[4]

Significantly, for the title of his first book written about his "tribe," Mistry chooses the term "tales" over the obvious alternative "stories"; *Tales from Firozsha Baag*. Such a choice clearly evokes oral narrative. M H Abrams gives us a convenient, if fairly bland, distinction between the two: a tale focuses on the "course and outcome of events" while a story focuses "instead on the state of mind and motivation, or on the moral qualities, in the protagonist" (172). This distinction is not of much help here, for Mistry's tales are more than mere episodes. By opting for the less fashionable and ambitious of the two terms, Mistry, who modestly calls himself "a traditional writer" who is not trying to break new ground or pioneer new technique" (Hancock, 148), renounces claims to moral depth and stylistic sophistication that should legitimately be his. Indeed, his characters' motivations are clearly delineated and their action is convincing and consistent. (The only exception I would make here relates to a few unconvincing coincidences in *Such a Long Journey*.) Accordingly, the boundary between tale and story in Mistry's case is not only shifting and ambiguous but also false and irrelevant.

Let me conclude by venturing a proposition: the art of storytelling not only rewards us aesthetically, but also provides an infinite source of inspiration and hope. There is a common saying uttered by the wise men and women of Baghdad, the city of *Alf Laylah wa-Laylah: 1001 Nights,* when they or their friends face a crisis or a depressing situation: "It shall pass and become one more story to tell." The story thus becomes a register and repository of our experiences, signalling the distilled, civilizational wisdom derived from them. Moreover, it represents a sure worry-defeating, life-embracing vehicle that confirms confidence and instills hope by holding out not only on the possibility of survival but also of a quasi-creative reward of telling a wise, enduring story to oneself and to others. As Mistry says "there is a latent desire in all of us to be story-tellers. In the best of all possible worlds, all of us would be story-tellers and listeners" (Hancock, 150).

To tell a tale then means that someone has witnessed, experienced, and survived something; equally important, another person or other people are sharing it with her through listening, responding, and appreciating. I tell a story, therefore I am; you listen to it *ergo* you are.

NOTES

1. For an analysis of *Tales from Firozsha Baag,* see my "Insider/Outsider Views on Belonging: The Short Stories of Bharati Mukherjee and Rohinton Mistry."

2. From this impressive gallery of portraits, I find Tehmul and the nameless painter the two most potently suggestive, self-contained "minor" characters. While respectively manifesting reticence and a speech impediment, they nevertheless speak through their actions. Functioning jointly as the novel's conscience, they symbolize innocence and creativity and illustrate its plea for compassion and tolerance.

3. In an informative review of the novel, Arun Mukherjee states that Mistry is giving a narrativized rendition of a real incident popularly known in India as the Nagarwala case. To Mukherjee, Mistry "picks up [a] thread from the rich fabric of narrative—imaginary and real—woven around India's unofficial royal family and tells us his version of a story that has been told and retold in India millions of times."

One should point out, however, that Mistry does not represent the minority situation as entirely one of victimization, but sees it as a challenge one is *forced* to face. Consequently his narrative method frequently employs humour and irony.

4. Whether Parsis in India or South Asian immigrants in Canada, Mistry's "tribe" is permanently positioned as a minority and his discourse articulates it as such. In one effective instance, he voices Gustad Noble's acute pain with his son's disregard for his vulnerable status as a minority in an ethnically turbulent society:

> What kind of life was Sohrab going to look forward to? No future for minorities, with all these fascist Shiv Sena politics and Marathi language nonsense. It was going to be like the black people in America— twice as good as the white man to get half as much. How could he make Sohrab understand this? How to make him realize what he was doing to his father, who had made the success of his son's life the purpose of his own? Sohrab had snatched away that purpose, like a crutch from a cripple. (55)

WORKS CITED

Abrams, M H. 1988. *A Glossary of Literary Terms*. 5th ed. New York: Holt, Rinehart and Winston.

Benjamin, Walter. 1968. "The Storyteller: Reflections on the Works of Nikolai Leskov." Translated by Harry Zohn. In *Illuminations*, ed. Hannah Arendt. New York: Harcourt, Brace and World, 1968.

Chaudhuri, Amit. 1991. "Parsi Magic." *London Review of Books*, 4 April.

Davis, Leonard J. 1987. *Resisting Novels: Ideology and Fiction*. New York: Methuen.

Forster, E M. 1927. *Aspects of the Novel*. London: Edward Arnold.

Genette, Gérard. 1985. *Narrative Discourse: An Essay in Method*. Translated by Jane E Lewin. Ithaca: Cornell UP.

Hancock, Geoff. 1989. "An Interview with Rohinton Mistry." *Canadian Fiction Magazine*: 65.

Malak, Amin. 1989. "Insider/Outsider Views on Belonging: The Short Stories of Bharati Mukherjee and Rohinton Mistry." In *Short Fiction in the New Literatures in English*, ed. Jacqueline Bardolph. Nice: Université de Nice.

Mistry, Rohinton. 1987. *Tales from Firozsha Baag*, Toronto: Penguin.

___. 1991. *Such a Long Journey*. Toronto: McClelland and Stewart.

Mukherjee, Arun. 1992. "Narrating India." *The Toronto South Asian Review*. 10.

Narayan, R K. 1989. *A Story-Teller's World: Stories, Essays, Sketches*. New Delhi: Penguin.

Ong, Walter. 1986. *Orality and Literacy: The Technologizing of the Word*. New York: Methuen.

Rao, Raja. 1938. Foreword to *Kanthapura*. London: OUP.

Ross, Val. 1991. "Keeping the World at Bay." *The Globe and Mail*. 30 November.

Rushdie, Salman. 1982. Interview. *Kunapipi*, IV.

___.1985. "*Midnight's Children* and *Shame*." *Kunapipi*, VII.

___.1990. *Haroun and the Sea of Stories*. London: Granta.

Todorov, Tzvetan. 1971. *Poétique de la Prose*, Paris: Seuil.

New Voices in Indo-Caribbean Canadian Fiction

FRANK BIRBALSINGH

In October 1960 when *The Tamarack Review* took the bold step of devoting an entire issue to West Indian writers who were just emerging, mainly in England, the gesture was warmly received by the writers themselves and by their countrymen, who regarded it as a mark of international recognition for their small, poor and undeveloped region. To West Indians it confirmed an historic pattern of Canadian generosity to the English-speaking Caribbean, and to Canadians it was another example of their generosity to third world nations, and their role as peace maker and negotiator between the United States of America and the Union of Soviet Socialist Republics, both armed to the teeth and apparently ready to plunge the world into nuclear holocaust. But whether West Indians reacted with gratitude or Canadians with smugness, the *Tamarack* special issue on West Indian literature can now be seen as the herald of a literary partnership between Canada and the West Indies that has taken root and bloomed.

In 1960 there were few West Indian immigrants in Canada and fewer writers among them. Today that has changed completely: not only are there many more immigrants—there are estimates of over 400, 000 Caribbean Canadians, including the children of immigrants born here—but West Indians are probably as active in literature as almost any other immigrant group in Canada; and if prizes are any indication of quality, two Governor General literary awards have so far gone to Caribbean Canadian writers, both women—the 1994 award for biography to Rachel Manley, a Jamaican Canadian, and the

1998 award for poetry to Dionne Brand, a Trinidadian Canadian. So established has the tradition of Caribbean Canadian writing become that it is now possible to detect two fairly distinct generations of writers, one which became active in the 1960s and 70s, and another which first emerged during the 1980s and 90s. Austin Clarke is undoubtedly the most prominent representative of the earlier group, and probably the best known of all Caribbean Canadian writers, while the later group consists of names such as Dionne Brand, Neil Bissoondath, Cecil Foster, Makeda Silvera, Marlene Nourbese Philip and many others. While Clarke's first novel appeared in 1965, the writing of the later group first appeared in the 1980s.

In addition to this division by age, Caribbean Canadian writing may also be divided by ethnicity into Afro-Caribbean and Indo-Caribbean categories. By the time Sonny Ladoo (1945-73), the first Indo-Caribbean Canadian writer produced two novels—*No Pain Like this Body* (1972) and *Yesterdays* (1974)—Austin Clarke, of Afro-Barbadian origin, already had several novels and one collection of stories to his name. Clarke's work included a distinguished trilogy of novels—*The Meeting Point* (1967), *Storm of Fortune* (1973), and *The Bigger Light* (1975)—which provided the first detailed, fictional account of the day to day lives of Black, West Indian immigrants in Canada. Since Ladoo's career ended prematurely when he was killed during a visit to his native Trinidad, his claim to be the first Indo-Caribbean Canadian writer may be factually correct, but his work left no lasting influence, and his novels, both set in Trinidad, do not even consider the experience of West Indian immigrants in Canada. For these reasons the Guyanese Cyril Dabydeen, whose poetry began to appear in the late 1970s, and who has produced work continuously since then, dealing both with West Indians at home and in Canada, probably has a stronger claim to the title of the first genuinely Indo-Caribbean Canadian writer. Dabydeen's output has been prolific, with eight collections of poems, two volumes of stories, two novels, and two literary anthologies which he has edited.

Since the classification of Caribbean Canadian writing into ethnic categories may need justification, it is probably best, right at the start, to notice thematic and other differences between Clarke and Dabydeen that are replicated in the writing of their countrymen from either ethnic group. Like most other immigrant writers, Clarke and Dabydeen begin their literary careers with remembered accounts of their respective homelands, before going on to consider the lives of their countrymen in Canada. In both cases there is no question that their writing is quintessentially Caribbean. But while they may consider characteristic Caribbean subjects and themes that have to do with social and cultural dependence, and lack of economic opportunity in their region, or with exile and racism in Canada, there are significant differences in their treatment. Clarke's writing about the Caribbean tends to be political in the sense that his fiction about West Indian immigrants in Canada stresses unemployment and poverty, racial discrimination, and social or cultural conflict. In Clarke's writing we see the grinding struggle of his West Indian immigrants for survival, or the victimization of these immigrants by police brutality, themes that are seldom found in the work of Dabydeen or other Indo-Caribbean Canadian writers, who tend to dwell either on the hardships of displacement from their familiar environment, or on more inward feelings of exile, homelessness, and alienation.

Some commentary already exists on earlier Indo-Caribbean Canadian writers, mainly those who made an entrance in the 1970s or 1980s, which explains why this essay will focus on the more recent arrivals. Of the established names the best known are Ladoo and Dabydeen, but there have also been short stories by Madeleine Coopsammy, a collection *Nelson John and Other Stories* (1980) by Clyde Hosein, and a novel *Black Light* (1988) by Ishmael Baksh, all of whom are from Trinidad. Dabydeen stands head and shoulders above these writers and has been highly recognized both for the volume and quality of his work. But Neil Bissooondath with his first volume of stories *Digging up the Mountains* in 1985 was later to win greater recognition. Other Indo-Caribbean Canadian voices which, like Bissoondath, were first heard the 1980s and 90s, are Arnold Itwaru, Ramabai Espinet, Sasenarine Persaud, Rabindranath Maharaj, and Shani Mootoo.

As we shall see, it may be possible to regard Bissoondath as a transitional figure in Indo-Caribbean Canadian writing because of changes that occur later in the direction of his work; but he also deserves consideration as one of the new voices in the field. *Digging up the Mountains* (1985) and his second book, the novel *A Casual Brutality* (1988), illustrate a fundamental concern with displacement, exile, despair, and the ethnic discontent that generates these themes in his West Indies. In this sense, the dominant characters, subjects, situations and concerns in Bissoondath's first two books are unmistakeably Indo-Caribbean. In his second collection of stories, however, *On the Eve of Uncertain Tomorrows* (1990), and his second novel *The Innocence of Age* (1992), although themes of displacement, exile, and despair persist, the proportion of Indo-Caribbean content is greatly reduced. Nor is this reduction accidental, since almost from the start of his career, Bisssoondath has projected himself as a Canadian rather than a Caribbean, Indo-Caribbean, or South Asian Canadian writer. He has been surprisingly strident in this projection of himself and has written a polemical work *Selling Illusions* (1994) attacking the policy of multiculturalism that serves as a basis for promoting the coexistence of individual ethnic communities within a single Canadian, political framework. To Bissoondath, multiculturalism is nothing but a mirage that will promote separate, mutually exclusive cultural ghettoes instead of a genuinely multicultural society. He therefore rejects ethnic labels being attached to his work and for this reason is unlikely to see himself as a new voice in Indo-Caribbean Canadian fiction.

But whether Bissoondath agrees to his inclusion as a new Indo-Caribbean Canadian voice or not, his early work is essential to the establishment of Indo-Caribbean Canadian writing as a separate sub genre of West Indian literature. The study of alienation in a Japanese girl that is found in Bissoondath's first book confirms a distinct effort to incorporate non-Caribbean interests in his work. This movement away from specifically Caribbean interests becomes stronger in his second collection of stories, most of which examine displacement, exile and alienation in parts of the world other than the West Indies. In *On the Eve of Uncertain Tomorrows*, even where the title story is set in Canada, its chief protagonists are an Arab, Sikh, Haitian, Sri Lankan, Latin American, and a Vietnamese couple who live in the same house waiting nervously to hear whether their applications for political asylum have been granted. The fear, tension, and terror of their predicament are unbearable. Bissoondath's technical mastery in this respect is impressive, and its effect is often deeply moving, as at the end of the story when one of the refugee claimants learns that his application is rejected. The sense of disappointment and grief is overwhelming, and one can scarcely contemplate the failed applicant's dashed hope and bleak, possibly frightening future. Similar technical skill is evident in *The Innocence of Age*, but by this stage, one has to admit, specific Indo-Caribbean features are thin indeed in a novel that captures the exact atmosphere of place, texture of society, and flavour of life that are found in the heart of Toronto. While specific themes of displacement and exile are present, they are overshadowed by a more generalized preoccupation with ageing, failure, and loss as symptoms of urban alienation in contemporary Canada.

If all this suggests that Bissoondath cannot be regarded as a new voice in Indo-Caribbean Canadian fiction, it is contradicted by two of his earlier stories, one from his first collection, called "Insecurity," and another from his second collection, called "Security." Both stories have the same protagonist Alistair Ramgoolam whose name clearly identifies him as Indo-Caribbean. The first story portrays Ramgoolam on an unnamed Caribbean island that is self-evidently Trinidad. He is a successful businessman but feels threatened by political instablity, crime, and Black Power demonstrations around him. His fear and panic are caused partly by ethnic insecurity and partly by the chaos around him; and finally he is driven to seek refuge in emigration. He reflects: "The island of his birth, on which he had grown up and where he had made his fortune was transformed by a process of mind into a kind of temporary home" (72). And by the end of the story Ramgoolam has sent his sons to Canada and is himself preparing to emigrate from his native island.

When we see him again in "Security" Ramgoolam is "securely" ensconced in an apartment in Toronto, far away from the threats and perils of his insecure home island. But security in Canada proves illusory. The city is alien to him: its materialism, secularism, the physical environment itself. He cannot practise his religion freely: there is no yard to plant the jhandi or flag indicating completion of his devotional rites; and once in celebrating divali, a Hindu festival involving the lighting of little oil lamps, the smoke that he creates brings out the fire department and puts him and his family to shame. Not even the material success of his sons is any comfort since he regards them as "Barbarians everyone of them. Stuffin themselves in restaurants with steak and hotdogs and hamburgers" (106). What is worse, Ramgoolam is seized by something like psychic desperation when he realizes that his westernized, detribalized sons will not be able to accord him proper cremation rites when he dies. In short, although his move to Canada has brought him a measure of physical security, he remains inwardly, spiritually, as insecure as ever. Stories like "Insecurity" and "Security" confirm Bissoondath's Indo-Caribbean pedigree whatever trends his future work might take.

Three genuinely new voices in Indo-Caribbean Canadian fiction are Sasenarine Persaud (Guyana), Rabindranath Maharaj (Trinidad), and Shani Mootoo (Trinidad). Until recently, apart from two small collections of poems, some further poems and stories in journals and anthologies, and nonfiction pieces in assorted publications, Persaud has been recognized mainly for two novels—*Dear Death* (1989) and *The Ghost of Bellow's Man* (1992). As a gothic novel about a Hindu family in Guyana, *Dear Death* ventures in almost virgin fictional territory. Fictional studies of Caribbean Hindu society have previously appeared, notably in the fiction of V S Naipaul, but none has considered the supernatural with quite Persaud's seriousness and commitment. Lakshmi Persaud, a Trinidadian living in England, treats the supernatural in her novel *Sastra* (1993), but she does so largely in terms of romance, whereas Sasenarine Persaud advances life after death as a serious article of faith within a Hindu theological framework of reincarnation. In this sense *Dear Death* introduces a new religious sensibility into both Caribbean and Indo-Caribbean fiction. This sensibility may not be as strong in Persaud's second novel, although it is very much present in a controversy over the introduction of chairs into a Hindu temple. Within a fictional setting based on Guyana, the novel reproduces the social confusion, political corruption, and atmosphere of repression that prevailed under the dictator Forbes Burnham. This gives *The Ghost of Bellow's Man* a much broader canvas than *Dear Death*, and although Hindu theology is again present, it appears in more practical, less esoteric terms than in the first novel.

Persaud's first two novels do not make a significant contribution to Indo-Caribbean Canadian fiction, but they contain elements—keen, social observation; the Indo-Guyanese idiom of Caribbean creole speech; and an aptitude for humour and suspense—that are seen to better advantage in his next book *Canada Geese and Apple Chatney* (1998), a collection of ten stories several of which deal with the author's signature theme—Hinduism. The epigraph to the volume, for instance, consists of a quotation from the *Chandogya Upanishad* that attempts to define memory. The quotation is apt since the volume contains many stories told by narrators who live abroad and recall memories of their native Guyana.

Persaud's strongest assertion of Hinduism comes in a story titled "Dog." There is so much in the story about Guyanese or Indo-Guyanese attitudes and customs in treating pets that its chief appeal must be to inform or surprise readers by its unusual revelations about the mysterious practices of a foreign culture. Brownie, the dog in the story, voluntarily participates in the vegetarian diet of the Brahmin family with whom he lives. Brownie fasts as well: "Brownie would know by some extraordinary way which days my mother fasted and he fasted too. He ate only when my mother broke her fast" (11). This makes the narrator wonder "which extraordinary Yogi or Brahmin had done some terrible deed to be reborn as our Brownie to be cleansed of his bad karma"(11). In other words, Brownie's extraordinary powers justify the Hindu belief in reincarnation. The narrator continues: "Today it is generally accepted that there is life before birth: and we who have known for centuries that this is part of the parcel of life after death because we have been there and back, know that in time this too will be accepted"(11). The narrator speaks apparently out of prior knowledge as if he is the member of a privileged group—Hindus—possessing ancient, esoteric wisdom that they have generously given to the world despite the world's ungrateful resistance in accepting the gift. This dogmatic tone may generally be a harmless eccentricity in Persaud's writing, but in "Dog," in one instance when we are told that Brownie could possibly be the reincarnation of an "extraordinary Yogi or Brahmin," and we are also told that Brownie "hated the sight of dark colours" and had attacked a man who was "of African descent" and "very dark skinned" (14) the author's dogmatic and didactic tone can take on disturbing racial implications.

Persaud's success in *Canada Geese* appears in stories that emphasize creole speech, particularly its rural, Indo-Guyanese variety. Undoubtedly the best example of this speech is found in the title story of his volume, which is narrated entirely in creole. Like other stories in the volume, "Canada Geese" is set in Toronto with Indo-Guyanese protagonists who discuss both the circumstances that drove them to emigrate, and their mixed experiences as immigrants after arriving in Canada. We hear of their strategies, including illegal ones, used to survive. One strategy is an exploit to kill and eat Canada geese that are public property. The episode exposes the plight of immigrants in an alien land without money, jobs, or proper immigration credentials. But the immigrants are neither pitiful victims nor dangerous, law-breaking offenders. The author's use of humour and self-mockery gives their experience a bitter-sweet flavour that enables us to see them whole, as ordinary people using their wits to survive. Interestingly, this central episode in "Canada Geese" benefits from intertextuality to the extent that it is based on an incident in Samuel Selvon's celebrated novel *The Lonely Londoners* (1956) in which a Nigerian immigrant called Cap is driven by privation and hunger to kill and eat one of the seagulls that abound in many parks in London, England. This literary source is openly acknowledged in the following passage in which two protagonists nicknamed Hermit and Writerji track down Selvon's novel: "Well Hermit still ain't believe that this thing write down so Writerji and we gone to St.Dennis library near Weston Road and Eglinton corner and he get Hermit to borrow *The Lonely Londoners* . . . As soon as we get home he find the page and start read how hunger washing Cap tail and Cap decided to ketch seagull and eat them. We laugh good" (121). Like Selvon, Persaud achieves a combination of comic zest, hilarious wit, and self-mockery that at once empathizes with the plight of the immigrants and celebrates their will to survive.

Persaud's volume of stories confirms his arrival as one of the leading new voices in Indo-Caribean Canadian fiction. The ethnicity of his characters, his preoccupation with Hindu religious practice or values, and his peculiar mastery of the rural Indo-Guyanese version of creole speech establish beyond doubt the ethnic nature of his writing and its differentiation from the fiction of Austin Clarke and younger Caribbean Canadian fiction writers like Cecil Foster, Dionne Brand or Marlene Nourbese Philip. On other aspects of immigrant experience Persaud's fiction might overlap with the stories of his Caribbean counterparts, for example, his record of the impact of contemporary feminism on the lives of Caribbean immigrants whose attitudes on marriage and sexual relations are shaped by older, more feudalistic conventions. Two of Persaud's stories have female narrators, one of whom Shaira, in "Dookie," takes women's studies courses at university and demands that her husband share the housework with her because they both have jobs. This suggests that marriage breakdown and divorce become part and parcel of the experience of immigration, and there are several instances of this in Persaud's stories.

Rabindranath Maharaj (Trinidad) has so far produced two volumes of stories, *The Interloper* (1995), and *The Writer and His Wife* (1996), and a novel *Homer in Flight* (1997). Like his predecessors Maharaj also begins with memories of his homeland—Trinidad—in his two volumes of stories. His powers of observation are formidable; he reports on all aspects of Trinidadian society; and while it is true that most of his main characters are Indian, he also includes Afro-Trinidadians in his writing. Maharaj's studies of character are perceptive, sensitive and almost tender; they reflect a strong sense of compassion for human failings and shortcomings that are invariably portrayed in a comic light. The result is that, like the characters in V S Naipaul's *Miguel Street*, Maharaj's protagonists emerge as entertaining and endearing eccentrics. In the title story of *The Writer and His Wife*, the writer is a gas attendant named Roop who talks ceaselessly about his writing and gives unwanted advice to the long suffering narrator. Roop's long-winded advice would be solemn and boring were it not for the fact that his pompous manner is deflated by his wife's dismissive attitude towards his opinions. Thus, in the end, far from being an unpleasant bore, Roop appears a rather pathetic failure, guilty of foibles rather than vices—a true eccentric. This is the mould of most of Maharaj's protagonists, whether it is Bashir Ali of "The Librarian," or Hoobnath Hingoo of "The Metalwork Technician": Bashir displays rigid efficiency and dedication in his job as a librarian, but not in individual relationships or matters that could bring him personal comfort or emotional satisfaction; and Hingoo whose name alone makes him sound ridiculous is constantly exposed to ridicule from the younger, more qualified colleagues in his workplace.

One of Maharaj's most extensive studies of eccentricity may be found in the story "John Fitzgerald Tennyson" in which the chief character—Tennyson—is Afro-Trinidadian. It is interesting that this ethnic difference scarcely distinguishes Tennyson from his Indo-Trinidadian counterparts in other stories for, like them, he proves unequal to almost every task he undertakes. Tennyson loses jobs at a Chinese restaurant, then at a hospital, and later at a bank where he serves as caddie boy, chauffeur, messenger and door opener; yet later he fails to cope with a course in computer programming. In the end, Tennyson is sent to a mental institution, though not for long. But for all his failures and faults, and the fact that, like Roop and Hingoo, he is constantly ridiculed by people and circumstances, Tennyson is never humiliated: he may be a figure of fun, but he retains essential self-respect; and if he is somewhat silly or incompetent, at least he is not harmful, malicious or dangerous. Maharaj's characters remind us of Naipaul's Mohun Biswas, classic archetype of the rootless, bumbling Indo-Caribbean who, like Don Quixote, energetically hurls himself against numerous obstacles and enemies that always confound him. Naipaul's influence on Maharaj is as strong as Selvon's on Persaud. It is seen in inadequate, Biswas-like characters, or in characters who grapple with Hindu metaphysics; it is also seen in matters of style and technique. The incident in which Tennyson is married off to Clementine, sister of his friend Stewart, has much in common with Biswas's marriage to Shama: both Tennyson and Biswas are unwitting victims in the sense that they are not even consulted when the decision is made for them to marry. And when Tennyson imagines a newspaper report with the sentence "Women screamed and fainted" he echoes the line "Women hid their faces in their hands, screamed and fainted" which is reported in one of Biswas's journalistic pieces.

If Brian Moore's *The Luck of Ginger Coffey* is the archetypal immigrant novel in modern, mainstream Canadian fiction, Maharaj's *Homer in Flight* is its Indo-Caribbean counterpart. Maharaj follows a common tradition of immigrant authors who have given similar fictional accounts of an immigrant's arrival and subsequent initiation into Canadian society; not only Clarke, Dabydeen and Bissoondath from the Caribbean, but South Asians like Bharati Mukherjee, M G Vassanji, and Rohinton Mistry. Despite his Greek sounding name, Maharaj's protagonist in his novel—Homervad Santokie—is an Indo-Trinidadian whose Canadian odyssey transforms him from a downright greenhorn, wholly dependent on fellow Trinidadian immigrants when he first arrives in Canada, to an independent, seasoned, self-sufficient individual who is both able to manage by himself at the end of the novel and contemplate a career as a writer. Yet Homer's chief appeal is less in his actual adventures trying to cope with the problems of immigrants than in his inner thoughts and reflections. This is why *Homer in Flight* does not quite reproduce the desperation of Ginger Coffey's frenzied struggle for survival in Montreal, nor the injustice and pity of racial discrimination and police brutality among Clarke's West Indians in Toronto. Not that Homer escapes racism, but he is not as victimized by it as Clarke's West Indians, or as Vassanji's hapless Nurdin Lalani who is landed with a rape charge in *No New Land* when he tries to help a young white woman whom he thought was in distress. Similarly, Homer is not exposed to the raw violence and persecution of characters in some stories of Bharati Mukherjee's volume *Darkness*. Homer escapes from much of the physical hardship which most immigrants endure, partly because he has brought some money with him from Trinidad, but also partly because of his ability to reflect on his problems even if he cannot solve them. We are attracted more by these reflections than by the hardships of his career or his struggles as an immigrant.

Homer's reflections focus principally on comparisons he makes between Trinidad and Canada. He speaks ruefully of the chaos and disorder in his homeland compared with the relative level of order and constructive stability that he sees in Canada. Frequently too he reflects on his own "sense of destiny and the belief that all his discomforts were serving a grander purpose/that/ seemed to give,meaning to his life" (26) Thoughts about destiny, fate or reincarnation recur throughout Maharaj's stories, suggesting a Hindu sensibility similar to Persaud's; but whereas Persaud can sometimes be didactic or preachy, Maharaj simply allows his characters to elicit deductions and conclusions from their life stories, which they have also shared with the reader. In this way the reader is invited rather than compelled to consider the plausibility of the characters' conclusions within the Hindu framework of their choice. But perhaps the most appealing feature of Maharaj's reflections is his gift for presenting character through caricature, exaggeration, or farce, and his skill in employing humour, irony and satire. There is a caricature of Homer's former teacher in Trinidad, Teacher Pariag, who is distinguished by his authoritative, confident (and usually inaccurate) knowledge of Canadian culture although he has never set foot in Canada. Then there are Homer's in-laws, all new Canadians, who shorten their Indo-Trinidadian names in a farcical rush to appear genuinely Canadian. Homer's wife Vashti becomes Vee, Jagabhatia— Jay, Bahutilal—Bay, Lotika—Lot, and Balliram—Balls. In the same mad and inprobable vein of absurdity, other relatives become Bund, Bick, Poo, Emms and Sloh; and Homer himself is called Ho.

Naipaul's influence on Maharaj needs to be emphasized, for it is is quite remarkable. For instance, while Bissoondath, Naipaul's nephew has inherited certain features of his uncle's stern detachment and clinical precision in dealing with his material, he does not reflect nearly as close a relationship to Naipaul as Maharaj. Characters like Teacher Pariag are obviously Naipaulian eccentrics. So also is Mr Flint, a Canadian librarian and budding writer in *Homer* who composes fifty words every night "Not a word more, not a word less" (253). Flint is a replica of B Wordsworth in *Miguel Street* who wrote one line each month. Homer's relationship with his in-laws also reproduces the vitriolic tone and imagery of Biswas's impulsive and ineffectual denunciation of Shama and her family as when he says to Vashti "What family? You mean that nest of vipers and garden snake?" (255) Even if Naipaul's influence pervades all of Indo-Caribbean literature, for instance, in the use of humour, irony and comic technique generally, or in an all-pervading sense of loss, homelessness and dereliction that is visible in Dabydeen, Bissoondath, Persaud and many others, in no writer is the echo of Naipaul so resonant as in Maharaj.

It is fitting that this brief survey of new voices in Indo-Caribbean Canadian fiction should end with Shani Mootoo, the youngest and most recent arrival in the group. Mootoo's first book *Out on Main Street and Other Stories* (1993) is a collection of nine stories which announce the arrival of a writer with original gifts, not simply superb command of creole speech, or accurate observation of both Caribbean and Canadian subjects, but a flair for sensuous evocation of landscape and flora, and bold, startling insight into hidden and previously considered shameful recesses of human sexuality. "Wake Up" is a typical story: set in the West Indies (probably Trinidad) and told from the troubled, female consciousness of Angenie, eldest child in an Indo-Caribbean family, the story portrays a philandering husband feared for possible violence, a long suffering wife and mother, vulnerable children, and a narrator whose tender feelings for her mother and sensuous dreams about the growing pains of adolescence nurture alarm and wonder over her own unfolding sexual ambiguity.

Mootoo's fiction is notable for its candid, almost confessional nature, and a relentless, truth-driven probing into the mixed quality of Caribbean identity. From Ladoo and Dabydeen onwards, identity has been a constant concern in Indo-Caribbean Canadian fiction: there is not a single Indo-Caribbean Canadian writer who does not probe the marginality of the Indo-Caribbean cultural condition as it emerges partly from the mixed consistency of Caribbean culture itself, and partly from the minority status of Indians who form about twenty percent of the population of the English-speaking Caribbean. Identified by skin colour and appearance as Indian, but separated from India by cultural displacement, Indo-Caribbeans are moved out of necessity to adopt the culture of their African-descended countrymen; but the process of adoption has been far from smooth precisely because of the dual, competing claims of their Indian cultural inheritance on one side, and their new, creole/African adoption on the other. The uncertainty or confusion of this process is probed with peculiar insight by Mootoo's fiction. As the heroine of "Sushila's Bhakti" confesses: "People like her were neither here nor there. Roots diluted, language lost. Religion held onto only by thin strips of festivals" (63). One can imagine the dilemma of someone with Sushila's cultural baggage in Canada! As Clarke's fiction analyzes the parallel dilemma of Afro-Caribbean Canadians in terms of racial prejudice, economic exploitation, and cultural conflict, Mootoo's stories evoke the tortured confusion that pervades the Indo-Caribbean soul in Canada. Sushila is described as "floating rootlessly in the Canadian landscape, not properly Trinidadian (she could not sing one calypso, or shake down her hips with abandon when one was sung—the diligence of the good Brahmin girl), not Indian except in skin colour, ...certainly not White and hardly Canadian either" (60). The image of Sushila is haunting and may seem extreme, but it is as truthful a picture of the Indo-Caribbean Canadian predicament as we have seen so far.

Mootoo's masterpiece in *Main Street* is the title story which is written entirely in a lilting, slightly anglicized version of Trinidad speech that is in subtle contrast to the rustic, Hindi-inflected, rural, Guyanese variety of Persaud's creole. The contrast illustrates the great variety in Caribbean speech patterns, Mootoo's and Persaud's versions each being true to its historical context in reflecting differences between Indians in Trinidad and Guyana, for Indo-Trinidadians are indeed more cosmopolitan and creolized than Indo-Guyanese and therefore less prone to extremes of ethnic disharmony that have plagued Guyana for generations. "Main Street" is set in Vancouver and describes a visit by the narrator and her friend Janet to a Sikh restaurant. The cultural conflict that ensues stems partly from the direct confrontation between white and black, and partly from alienation between two types of Indo Canadians—Sikhs, and Indo-Trinidadians. The narrator tells Janet: "Another reason why we shy to frequent dere/ the Indian quarter of Vancouver/ is dat we is watered down Indians—we ain't good grade A Indians. We skin brown, is true, but we doh even think 'bout India unless something happen over dere" (45). Few writers have been as successful as Mootoo in capturing the fundamental marginality of Indo-Caribbean experience: of being Indian but not wholly so, and of being Caribbean yet without being fully creole in the dominant, African/Caribbean sense.

Mootoo's novel *Cereus Blooms at Night* (1996) was nominated for the Giller prize, and although it did not win, it achieved higher national recognition than any previous Indo-Caribbean Canadian work. *Cereus* shows that its author has as complete a grasp of her Caribbean setting, in this case the fictional island of Lantanacamara (Trinidad), as any of her predecessors, and that she exhibits both their power in observing the local landscape and their skill in recording the local speech. Yet she achieves a narrative more shocking and horrific than anything in previous Indo-Caribbean Canadian works. Within a brilliantly realized tropical setting of brightly variegated colours, irrepressible natural sounds, and teeming life, Mootoo unfolds a torrid tale of incest, lesbianism, homosexuality, drunkenness, violence and murder. The novel opens with the heroine Mala Ramchandin in a nursing home where she is cared by a male, homosexual nurse Tyler, and it is through Tyler as a guide that the reader is led into a series of flashbacks that reveal the scandalous past of the heroine's family in which Mala is raped by her father who declines into drunkenness and violence until she finally murders him. The complexity of the psychological drama and inner traumas in *Cereus* show how far Indo-Caribbean Canadian fiction has come.

If Ladoo presents a realistic evocation of actual Trinidad in his novels, Mootoo offers an equally realistic evocation of the island in fictional terms but within a more sophisticated narrative framework that employs frequent time shifts and changes in point of view that produce more powerful, dramatic action. In *Cereus* we can see themes of displacement, exile and homelessness being transformed into an exploration that plumbs the depths of the Indo-Caribbean psyche and reveals traumas of a far worse kind than the pain or privation caused by cultural displacement, exile, or immigration. But any brief survey of this type is bound to be selective, and more can undoubtedly be said about *Cereus* as about the later fiction of Dabydeen and Itwaru or the children's stories of Espinet. Still, despite its omissions, this survey clearly confirms the literary partnership heralded by the *Tamarack* West Indian issue in October 1960 and the firm roots that it has since established in Canadian soil.

WORKS CITED

Baksh, Ishmael. 1988. *Black Light*. St Johns, Newfoundland: Jesperson Press.

Bissoondath, Neil. 1985. *Digging up the Mountains*. Toronto: Macmillan.

———. 1988. *A Casual Brutality*. Toronto: Macmillan.

———. 1990. *On the Eve of Uncertain Tomorrows*. Toronto: Penguin.

———. 1992. *The Innocence of Age*. Toronto: Knopf.

Clarke, Austin. 1967. *The Meeting Point*. London: Heinemann.

———. 1973. *Storm of Fortune*. Boston: Little, Brown.

———. 1975. *The Bigger Light*. Boston: Little, Brown.

Hosein, Clyde. 1980. *Nelson John and Other Stories*. London: London Magazine Editions.

Ladoo, Sonny. 1972. *No Pain Like This Body*. Toronto: Anansi.

———. 1974. *Yesterdays*. Toronto: Anansi.

Maharaj, Rabindranath. 1995. *The Interloper*. Fredericton, New Brunswick: Goose Lane Editions.

———. 1996. *The Writer and His Wife and Other Stories*. Leeds: Peepal Tree Press.

———. 1997. *Homer in Flight*. Fredericton: New Brunswick, Goose Lane Editions.

Moore, Brian. 1972. *The Luck of Ginger Coffey*. Toronto: McClelland & Stewart.

Mootoo, Shani. 1993. *Out on Main Street and Other Stories.* Vancouver: Press Gang .

——. 1996. *Cereus Blooms at Night.* Vancouver: Press Gang.

Mukherjee, Bharati. 1985. *Darkness.* New York: Penguin.

Naipaul, V S. 1961. *A House for Mr Biswas.* London: Andre Deutsch.

Persaud, Sasenarine. 1989. *Dear Death.* Leeds: Peepal Tree.

——. 1992. *The Ghost of Bellow's Man.* Leeds: Peepal Tree.

——. 1998. *Canada Geese and Apple Chatney.* Toronto: TSAR.

Persaud, Lakshmi. 1993. *Sastra,* Leeds: Peepal Tree.

Selvon, Samuel. 1991. *The Lonely Londoners.* Toronto: TSAR. Canadian edition. First edition 1956.

Vassanji, M G. 1991. *No New Land.* Toronto: McClelland & Stewart.

Canadian Nationalism, Canadian Literature and Racial Minority Women

ARUN PRABHA MUKHERJEE

As a person whose life trajectory coincides with India's independence and coming into being as a nation state, I do not share the currently fashionable view propagated by scholars such as Eric Hobsbawm, Tom Nairn and Homi Bhabha that regards nationalism as a "pathology" or "dementia." (Nairn, 359) The postindependence India I grew up in was high on nationalism. They were euphoric times when India was poor but proud. India and Indians had dreams of a brilliant future when poverty and inequality would become things of the past. Jawaharlal Nehru's stirring speeches, delivered from the ramparts of the Red Fort in Delhi on Independence Day mornings, performed a national ritual that touched young schoolgirls like me as we listened to his emotion-packed words on blaring radios while marching in the Independence Day school rallies as they wound through the bazaar of our small town. And the words he spoke in India's Constituent Assembly on the midnight of August 14, 1947 still retain their magic for me:

> Long years ago we made a tryst with destiny, and now the time comes when we shall redeem our pledge, not wholly or in full measure, but very substantially. At the stroke of the midnight hour, when the world sleeps, India will awake to life and freedom. A moment comes, which comes but rarely in history, when we step out from the old to the new, when an age ends, and when the soul of a nation, long suppressed, finds utterance. It is fitting that at this solemn moment we take the pledge of dedication to

the service of India and her people and to the still larger cause of humanity. (quoted in Spear, 237)

These words, whose rhetorical nature is now clear to me, still manage to touch me somehow, despite the ironic resonances that have gathered around them due to later tragedies and disappointments that have dimmed the lustre of India's democracy. They are words charged with emotion and mystery, not just the arbitrary signifiers deconstructionists say words are.

That dream of postindependence Indian nationalism which was inscribed on my consciousness through various ritualistic acts, images, and cultural productions, is for me the empowering side of nationalism. Postindependence Indian nationalism was inclusionary and empowering. Free India's constitution heroically resolved to right the wrongs of the past, towards untouchables, towards the poor, towards women, towards minorities. India, as our first prime minister never tired of telling us, in those voluble speeches he never tired of giving, was going to be a model community.

I am afraid that western Marxists' and postmodernists' condescending disavowals of nationalism and nationalists overlook, as Benedict Anderson reminds us, that nations inspire love and sacrifice. (7) Such theorists are rightly reprimanded by James M Blaut for their universalist ethnocentrism which has prevented them from seeing that not all nationalisms are fascist or Nazi, that nationalisms can imagine nations that are secular, progressive, international in outlook, and culturally and ethnically diverse. (Chapters 1-4) Such versions of nationalism have been totally ignored in the western Marxist and postmodernist theorizing on nationalism. It has thoroughly overlooked the third world experience and theorizing which claims that the nation can be an "enabling idea." (Sangari, 183)

When I come to discuss Canadian nationalism, then, I do not want to begin with the universalist premise that a priori condemns and ridicules nationalism. I agree with Blaut that we must evaluate each nationalism in terms of its aspirations and achievements rather than universalize about an abstraction which has really been derived from the European historical experience of ethnic nationalisms. (33)

When I respond to Canadian nationalism, I cannot help comparing it to my first-hand experience of Indian nationalism. For many of us

South Asian Canadians, Trudeau came to represent Canada as Nehru had represented India. A majority of the South Asian immigrants who emigrated to Canada in the late sixties and early seventies, the first batch of immigrants from South Asia who entered Canada under the post-1967 nonracist immigration policy, have felt a personal gratitude to Trudeau and continue to vote for the Liberal Party because of that bond. Those of us who entered Canada at the height of Trudeaumania felt that Canada was on a cusp of change. It was hard not to be thrilled by Trudeau's message of a "just society" and "cultural pluralism." This attitude to Trudeau is alluded to touchingly in M G Vassanji's *The Gunny Sack* where East African Asian immigrants begin to compare him to a "pir," that is, a holy man with miraculous powers. (248)

Although Canadian nationalism of the sixties and the seventies is remembered for Expo '67 which commemorated the nation's centennial, for the surge in anti-American feeling and the desire for Canada's economic and political independence, and for the institutionalization of Canadian literature in schools and universities, it was the opening up of Canada to nonwhite immigration that registered most strongly with Canadians of colour. The striking down of racist immigration policies of the past was experienced by us as the most promising manifestation of the vision of a "just society."

So why is it that racial minority women have expressed such negative views about Canada? If nations are experienced as "imagined communities" and evoke discourses of kinship and home (Anderson, 143-44), why does the narrator in Dionne Brand's short story, "At the Lisbon Plate," describe herself as "[a] woman in enemy territory"? (1988, 97) Himani Bannerji's tropes of "prison" in her long prose poem "Doing Time" similarly challenge the notion of Canada as an "imagined community" and the work as a whole depicts Canada as a prison house for those who are "not white, and also women." (9) And in *Chronicles of the Hostile Sun*, Brand uses the trope of homelessness to describe her relationship with Canada:

I am not a refugee,
I have my papers,
I was born in the Caribbean,
practically in the sea,
fifteen degrees above the equator,

I have a canadian passport,
I have lived here all my adult life,
I am stateless anyway. (1984, 70)

Such alienation from a national entity called "Canada" is quite commonplace in the writings of Aboriginal and racial minority Canadian women. If Canada is "enemy territory" for Brand's black female narrator and "prison" for Bannerji's poetic persona, it is occupied territory in the writings of Aboriginal women. For Mary Panegoosho Cousins, an Inuk, Canada is a totally arbitrary colonial construction:

I am concerned that Inuit, who have an amazing history of Arctic living, have been nationalized under the flags of the USA, Canada, Denmark, and whatever country is across the Bering Sea from Alaska. We Canadian Inuit are then sub-divided by the borders of Labrador, Québéc, and the Northwest Territories.

The "outsiders" seem obsessed with drawing lines on maps, and they really believe these lines appear on the earth. What strange thinking! . . . These boundaries are the first signs that the "outsiders" decided to dominate, operate, control, and generally run people called Inuit.

.

I am concerned that these well-meaning but misguided "outsiders" did more than mess up the land. They also occupied much of the land in all these artificial communities they created. Once again, they drew lines on townsite plans telling us where to live and where not to trespass. (52-3)

Cousins and other Inuit women writing in *Sharing Our Experience*, an anthology of epistolary writing by Aboriginal women and women of colour, identified themselves as Inuit first. Similarly, Patricia A Monture-OKanee sees herself as a member of the Mohawk nation:

I am a Mohawk woman. I am a citizen of the Haudenosaunee Confederacy (the Six Nations Iroquois Confederacy). . . . My woman's identity comes from the fact that I am a member of that Confederacy, that I am a member of the Mohawk nation. You cannot ask me to speak as a woman because I cannot speak as just a woman. This is not the voice that I have been given. Gender does not transcend race. The voice that I have been given is the voice of a Mohawk woman and if you must talk to me about women, somewhere along the line you must talk about race. . . . I cannot and will not separate the two. (194)

Ever since I heard Monture-OKanee say these words at a feminist conference in 1989, I have thought of Virginia Woolf's famous statement differently. Woolf's "As a woman I have no country" adorned Women's Day posters in Toronto a couple of years ago. Perhaps, our white sisters thought they were denouncing nationalistic jingoism and promoting sisterhood by disclaiming their Canadian citizenship. However, Monture-OKanee's words help me understand the "white privilege" hidden in such gestures of denunciation. White women remain British or Canadian or American and enjoy the privileges of that status, howsoever much they claim they are just women. Women like Brand or Cousins or Monture-OKanee, on the other hand, cannot be unproblematically Canadian—or "just Canadian," as those with privileged ethnicities claim to be—because their other identities put them at a disadvantage in a racist nation-state. I, similarly, cannot speak of gender and nationalism when I speak of these women's response to the nation-state, because it is their race that sets them apart in this country and denies them the status and privileges that white Canadians enjoy. It was because of these considerations that Jeannette Armstrong chose a male protagonist for her nationalist novel, *Slash*, a choice many white feminists criticized.

Racial minority Canadian women's and Aboriginal Canadian women's discontents with the Canadian nation-state are based on different grounds, and I would not like to lump them together. Both Cousins and Monture-OKanee belong to First Nations whose borders do not match those of Canada. In their eyes, the Canadian border and Canadian culture are exercises in genocidal domination. The following words of Monture-OKanee eloquently express the First Nations' point of view:

What needs to be understood is who has done the defining. It has not been First Nations. Many of us do not accept this great lie any longer. We understand the solution lies in our inalienable right to define ourselves, our nations, our governments, and in protecting the natural laws the Creator gave us. Nor has the restructuring of law and government on Turtle Island to conform to European norms been achieved with the expressed or implied consent and/or assistance of First Nations. (196)

While 125 years of Canadian nationalist discourses have proposed a distinct Canadian identity, their explanations ranging from the pure Viking blood of northern races and the salutary effect on the same pure Viking blood of Canada's harsh winters, from Canada's cultural duality to Canada's geography (see Berger), the words of First Nations women point out how exclusionary and racist these nationalist agendas have been. The Aboriginal peoples' coinage of the term "First Nations" to describe themselves is a brilliant rhetorical intervention to counteract the racist nationalist discourse of "two founding races" which undergirds the Canadian state and all its social and cultural hierarchies. It exposes the glaring omissions in the legitimizing fictions of white-settler Canada.

The texts of Aboriginal women disturb the normalcy of Canadian literary and cultural understandings. The canonical works of Canadian literature, barring a few exceptions where Native characters are present as ghosts provoked by guilt (Fee, 1987), are oblivious to the Native presence in Canada. According to Marjorie Fee, "both general books and survey courses on Canadian literature . . . promote master narratives of the nation that ignore regional, ethnic, Native, and female difference." (1992-93, 33) These master narratives are framed in terms of Canada's two founding races, refigured as two founding peoples to suit these politically correct times. English Canadian literature courses, therefore, begin with Susanna Moodie's *Roughing It in the Bush* and not with Native orature.

Canadian literature, created, published, taught and critiqued under the aegis of Canadian nationalism promotes the settler-colonial view of Canada. Nationalist critics like Northrop Frye, Margaret Atwood, D G Jones and John Moss produced an essentialized Canadian character that, according to them, was discoverable in the literary texts of canonical Canadian writers. Canadians, these revered critics have told us, suffered from a garrison mentality because of their intimidating physical environment. They developed a victim complex, aiming only for survival rather than grandiose achievements unlike their neighbours to the south.

Although these environmentalist explanations of a Canadian identity, as well as the very obsession with a Canadian identity, have been challenged often enough, they have not been replaced yet by more inclusive theories of Canada and Canadian literature. Now we hear talk about postmodernist irony and dominants and marginals, but we do not hear any concerted responses to what Aboriginal and racial minority writers tell us about Canada and Canadian literature. Like our political leaders, who virtually ignored Aboriginal and racial minority Canadians' concerns when they came up with their Meech Lake and Charlottetown accords, much critical theory continues to be churned out in Canada that is premised on notions of Canada's duality and remains profoundly oblivious to Aboriginal and racial minority voices.

A stunning example of this exclusionary critical work is Sylvia Söderlind's *Margin/Alias* where the terms "colonized" and "postcolonial" are unproblematically appropriated for Canadian (read "white") and Québécois literature, and vast generalizations are made about nation and national identity based on the work of five white male Canadian and Québécois writers.

The enormous gap that exists between white and Aboriginal Canadians can be gauged by the white cultural establishment's response to Aboriginal spokespersons' demand that white writers and artists stop telling Aboriginal stories. These demands were immediately branded as censorship. All the old nostrums about the freedom of the artistic imagination were trotted out and replayed over and over again. While to the eurocentric mindset, the freedom of imagination may seem a universal, self-evident truth that has nothing to do with white-skin privilege, Aboriginal writer and story teller Lenore Keeshig-Tobias suggests that white writers' appropriation of Native stories is of the same order as white settlers taking away of Native land. (175)

The point is that seemingly universal, "purely" aesthetic ideas are not really universal but culture-specific. White Canadians, however, have employed vocabularies that claim universality, despite their exclusionary nature. Thus, what seems universalist and apolitical on the surface often turns out to be a euro-Canadian conceptualization.

What I would call the nationalist-universalist tradition ensures that it is white-anglo writing or angloconformist writing that gets the lion's share of attention. It is they who speak as Canadians. It is their experience, their version of history, their notions of literature, their vision of Canada that dominates. As Brand says, "Canadian national identity is necessarily predicated on whiteness. . . ." (1993, 18) Many Aboriginal and racial minority women writers have spoken eloquently about how their writing has been turned down time and again because it was not deemed "Canadian," but "ethnic," that is, emerging from, and speaking to, a minority group. When published by small, usually "ethnic" presses, the establishment—reviewers and academics—othered it in multiple ways: it was exotic; it was "black," or "Native," or "South Asian"; it was about "immigrant" experience. The category "Canadian" has been denied to these writers, and their work is seldom seen as contributing to "Canadian" life.

The canon of Canadian literature in English, formed according to the commonsense notions of Canadian nation-state and Canadian identity, is, not surprisingly, devoid of "regional, ethnic, Native, and female difference," as Fee has argued. This canon, according to Robert Lecker, who did not seem to notice its whiteness or its angloness, valorizes works that are "ordered, orderable, safe." He suggests that these texts have been read and promoted as "an expression of national self-consciousness." (1990a, 658) The preferred texts of the canon-makers, he says, are those that are "set in Canada" and focus on Canadian events and issues. (1990b, 687)

Although Aboriginal writers' works have not entered the canon even though they are set in Canada and focus on Canadian events and issues, such nationalist criteria have had an extremely negative effect on the production and reception of writings by writers of colour. The following words of David Staines are quite representative of the evaluative criteria that have been applied to devalue the work of racial minority writers:

Resonances are the intangible traces of a country and its people that haunt, unconsciously and unobtrusively, the pages of the country's literature. Resonances can be heard only by those from wherever here is, or by those exceptional artists, such as Michael Ondaatje, who seem to sense instinctively and naturally the meaning of here even though they are not from here. But the Ondaatje sensibility is rare. Too common are those transplanted writers, however gifted their writing, who try to show their Canadianness by placing scenes on Sherbrooke Street (West, of course) or Bay and Bloor, who introduce obtrusive references to Marshall McLuhan or the Canada Council, who struggle to impose references that are unnatural in their context. The truly Canadian writer writes out of his or her own world, making resonances without ever knowing it. (66)

Bharati Mukherjee was told by an eminent Canadian critic that she could not be a Canadian writer because she "didn't grow up playing in snow." (quoted in Parameswaran 86) Similarly, Margaret Atwood, explaining why she had excluded some writers in her discussion of Canadian literature, said: "It seems to me dangerous to talk about 'Canadian' patterns of sensibility in the work of people who entered and/or entered-and-left the country at a developmentally late stage of their lives." (quoted in Metcalf, 11) According to nationalist critics, in order to be considered a Canadian writer, one does not just need Canadian content in one's work; only "birthright Canadians" can be considered Canadian writers.

Such criteria have meant that non-Canadian-born writers' work has been slotted as "immigrant writing." Immigrant writing supposedly comes in two kinds: if it deals with subject matter that alludes to where the writer came from, it is perceived as nostalgic; and if it has Canadian content, it is automatically considered to be about an immigrant's struggle to adjust to new realities. As Vassanji has pointed out, white immigrant writers have not had their writing branded in this way. ("Introduction," 3) Their works are judged according to universalist criteria of merit and quickly found their place in Canadian literature anthologies. The immigrant label, then, is coded racially. The danger of such labelling, according to Vassanji, is that the writing deemed "immigrant experience" begins to "seem irrelevant to the ongoing dialectic." (3)

Too many racial minority writers have had their work turned down by Canadian publishers either because, according to them, it was not Canadian, or because they felt that the Canadian readers will not identify with it. As Cecil Foster told my students during his visit to my class, a major Canadian publisher informed him that his company's criterion for accepting a work for publication was whether "the bored housewife in Mississauga" will be interested to read it or not. Minority writers who have used non-Canadian settings have been rejected on the pretext that their work was too distanced from the Canadian reader's experience.

It is not too hard to see that the Canadian reader here is presumed to be white and incapable of taking interest in the realities of places like Barbados or South Africa, let alone to have come from there. Claire Harris, in response to a comment by Brian Fawcett about the economic difficulties regarding publishing minority writers' works, says: "This is an absurdity that presupposes that Canadians are all so racist, and so provincial that they would refuse to read the books of minority groups." (1990a, 140)

Minority writers' works set in other countries have, until very recently, either been published abroad or by minority presses. Farida Karodia lived in Canada for the last twenty-four years and yet few Canadians heard of her because all three of her books are set in South Africa and, consequently, she could not interest a Canadian publisher. Karodia's work is being marketed by Heinemann in their African Writers Series, and I doubt that it will be put on Canadian literature courses or critically responded to in the near future.

There are many ways of othering racial minority writers. A hallowed critical tradition has developed in Canada around the term "regional," so we have anthologies of critical and creative writing devoted to "Prairie writing," "Maritime writing" and "West Coast writing." But looking at these volumes, one would assume that no racial minorities live and produce work there. Claire Harris has spoken in detail about her struggle to get recognized in Canada: "Since I'm writing on the prairies, it seems to me I have a place in books on Prairie writing. Whether mine is the received wisdom on the Prairies or not!" (1993, 117). To all intents and purposes, the category "regional" has been as exclusionary of Aboriginal and racial minority writers as the category "Canadian."

The construction of "Canadian Literature" by powerful professors, bureaucrats, editors, publishers and reviewers, the majority of them white males, has been carried out under the aegis of nineteenth-century European notions of nationhood which proposed that a nation was racially and culturally different from other nations and uniform at home. A nation's literature, according to such theories, has to reflect the "soul" of the nation, its history and traditions, which are also conceived in terms of a nation's unified "spirit." Canadian literature was constructed in the service of a Canadian nation conceptualized in terms of these ethnocultural theories of nationhood. These critics believed that reading Canadian writing would help Canadian readers to develop into a distinctive national type, discover the "soul" of the country, become united as Canadians. Writers like Hugh MacLennan came to believe that their job was to produce works of documentary realism wherein Canadian readers would recognize themselves and their land. These ideas about Canadian literature have a century-long history and dominated the theoretical debates in the sixties and the seventies, the time when minority voices were beginning to emerge. Such views have stood as impenetrable barriers against minority writers in getting their works published, acknowledged, and taught as part of the curriculum.

As many nonwhite men and women have said in many places, "Canadian" is a code word for white. Camille Hernández-Ramdwar, born in Winnipeg in 1965, grew up being called by every racist epithet: "nigger," "paki," "injun," "bogan," "chink," "spic." She writes:

> The experience of being labelled at so young an age has deeply affected my feelings of being a Canadian, of "belonging." My general feeling has been that I do not feel like a Canadian (despite being born and raised here) because I am not accepted as one at face value. People, upon meeting me, still open conversations with "And where are you from?" as if a person of my complexion could not possibly be born here. I blame a lot of these continued misperceptions on the media, who seem satisfied with presenting an all-white Canadian face in advertising and television shows. (61)

Dionne Brand says that "all Blacks are always suspected of being recent immigrants." (1993, 16) Such assumptions on the part of the dominant community result in our unfriendly treatment at border checkpoints, attacks and abuse on streets, and isolation in the workplace. However, complaining against such treatment, Brand says elsewhere, brings only responses like the following: "'Oh no, we're not like the United States,' be grateful for the not-as-bad-racism-here." (1990a, 45)

These minority perspectives on Canada are seldom deemed "Canadian." The hegemonic view of Canada, the view presented at home and to the outside world, is the white, middle-class Canadian's experience. A recent special issue of *Massachusetts Review*, for instance, trotted out the familiar comparisons and contrasts between Canada and America, all predicated on white experience. How removed this Canada is from the experience of racial minority and Aboriginal Canadians became evident for me when I read the following words of Ian Angus describing his experience of crossing national borders:

> If one is crossing back into one's own country, even these questions [by customs and immigration officers] are the beginning of an embrace, a belonging made richer, more palpable by absence. Inflated, so that even official inquiries seem benign since one is forearmed with all the right answers. (32)

Angus has obviously never heard of the treatment accorded to racial minority and Aboriginal Canadians at these same borders. Yet, it is his experience that is deemed "the Canadian experience," silencing—no, obliterating—other Canadian experiences.

In her article in *Brick*, Brand exposes the racist agendas of this business-as-usual attitude of the white Canadian cultural establishment, which manufactures and promotes a perfect fit between whiteness and Canadianness:

> Assumptions of white racial superiority inform the designation of formal culture in this country and the assigning of public funds. Culture is organized around whiteness through various "para-statal" bodies including the Canadian Broadcasting Corporation, the National Film Board, the Canada Council and other provincial and metropolitan arts councils and through private media and cultural and educational institutions.

In film, radio and television, all one has to do is listen to the voices, watch the faces, note choices of themes and point of view to get it. Simply, who is reflected there? This same "commonsense" racist ideology interrogates the production of any cultural work by artists of colour and that interrogation ranges from dismissal to anointment—and far more dismissal than anointment. These works are "placed" by their relationship to and relevance for the dominant cultural form. Reviewers always comment on the "anger" in my work for example (anger having been categorised as a particularly "Black" emotion), and its portrayal of "the Black experience." White work on the other hand is never interrogated for its portrayal of "the white experience." (1993, 17)

According to the commonsense racism Brand is talking about, "the white experience" equates with Canadian experience. Other experiences, if they get noticed, are dubbed "black" or "ethnic" or "immigrant" experience, depending upon the mood of the namer, who is usually white and often, though not always, male.

Canadian nationalism, for us nonwhites, is a racist ideology that has branded us "un-Canadian" by its acts of omission and commission. Its proponents determined what is Canadian culture. Only two cultures were considered officially Canadian, although the Québécois don't feel they are treated equally (equal to the Anglos, I presume). Aboriginal cultures and rights were denied and continue to be denied. Minority Canadians were treated as second-class citizens, allowed in Canada only as beasts of burden. Canadian nationalists of the sixties and seventies seldom pondered on these aspects of Canadian history. They did not produce an ideology of national liberation that would include all Canadians on an equal footing. Instead, they constructed a Canada that was being savaged by American domination and used tropes of rape and seduction to speak about it. Their Canada was an innocent victim. These Canadian and Québécois nationalists appropriated anticolonial vocabularies to speak of themselves as "the colonized" and, in the case of the Québécois, as "the white niggers of America." In positioning themselves as victims, they forgot that they, too, had victimized and needed to make amends.

In the absence of an antiracist, egalitarian ideology, Canadian nationalists of the seventies created an all-white canon of works about small towns and wilderness, about white settlers pioneering on the frontier with the RCMP maintaining law and order. This canon was taught and written about in universalist terms, thereby discounting its whiteness.

The works of Aboriginal and racial minority writers have challenged these constructions in several ways. By positioning themselves as Aboriginal or black or South Asian or Chinese or Japanese Canadian, by writing from the specificity of their community's experience, they have called into question the universalist stance adopted by white Canadian writers. As Brand says, from the nonwhite readers' perspective, white writers' works deal with "white experience" and are therefore as hyphenated as the works of nonwhite writers.

Another strategy Aboriginal writers and writers of colour have adopted is to insist on the relevance of their so-called non-Canadian experience by pointing out that Canada has participated in the spoils of imperialism and colonialism. Brand and Makeda Silvera write about Caribbean domestic workers in Toronto. They write about the children of these workers left in the Caribbean. Nonwhite writers often challenge Canadian insularity by imbuing "Canadian" signifiers with non-Canadian connections. For example, where native-born Canadians might see only a neon sign brightening the Toronto skyline, Brand sees centuries of colonial exploitation in which Canada has participated:

> When I come back to Toronto from the Playas del Este, I will pass a flashing neon sign hanging over the Gardiner Expressway. "Lloyds Bank," it will say. Lloyds, as in Lloyds of London. They got their bullshit start insuring slave cargo. (1990a, 52)

Nonwhite writers' texts challenge Canadian nationalists' claims to Canada's unique difference from the United States and Britain by exposing its participation in the networks of international capital and colonialism. They call into question the benign Canada that nationalists like Margaret Atwood and B W Powe have spoken about, a Canada that, unlike its neighbour to the south, is not supposed to have a history of violence. By writing about Aboriginal peoples' colonial experience, the Chinese Head Tax and the Chinese Exclusion

Act, the Japanese internment during World War II, the voyage of the *Komagata Maru* and slavery, these writers rewrite Canadian history, thus exposing the lie about the innocent Canada of white-Canadian writing. Because racial minorities' experience does not respect Canada's borders and because they have global links, diasporic for racial minorities and political for Aboriginal peoples, their writing necessarily brings in these other places and their histories. Diana Brydon's comment about Brand's poem, "Blues Spiritual for Mammy Prater" is generalizable to other minority writers as well. She suggests that boundary-crossings in Dionne Brand's poetry

> question the systemic pressures that shape and mis-shape our subjectivities as people defined through categories such as gender, ethnicity, class, or nation. Her poetry, whatever its explicit subject matter or setting, explores questions of crucial interest to Canadians today. Although ostensibly addressing what some might see as an American (i.e., US) topic, "Blues Spiritual for Mammy Prater" speaks directly to our Canadian obsessions with cultural continuities and identity formation, refusing simplistic embracings of "essence" in favour of more complicated explorations of subject construction. (86)

As Paul Gilroy has suggested in *The Black Atlantic*, black experience cannot be separated and discussed as specifically African, American, Caribbean or British. He claims that a black Atlantic culture has developed whose expression exceeds the categories of ethnicity and nationality. I think that a similar analytical grid can be applied to the diasporic cultures of, for example, Chinese, Japanese and South Asians.

*

I teach a third-year course on Aboriginal and racial minority Canadian writers. One of the most frequent comments my students make during the class discussions is, "Why didn't I know about this?" They are angry that their education kept hidden from them the historical realities I mentioned earlier. The texts of nonwhite writers are teaching them things about Canadian history and Canadian people that they did not learn in their Canadian literature courses.

Along with Canadian history and society, they are also learning about oral and literary traditions that are not eurocentric. Native writers, I believe, are the most challenging in this regard when they question things such as the primacy of a white-European standard as "the criteria for all writing." (Brant, 360) By speaking of the "healing" function of writing, by substituting the concept of storytelling for "literature," Native writers force us to rethink the nature of literature and the literary institution in fundamental ways. In both their literature and theoretical writing, Aboriginal women writers have thrown challenges to predominant modes of thinking that have yet to be acknowledged.

Both Aboriginal and minority women writers have rejected the notion that Canadian writing must follow "a" Canadian tradition, which, of course, has been exclusively defined in eurocentric terms. Brand, for example, has said that she does not write from the margin of the Canadian tradition but from the centre of black tradition, which she defines as African Caribbean, African American and African. (1990b, 273) Bannerji, similarly, writes about the "gaps" and "holes" a non-South Asian reader may experience while reading her texts because her allusions are not to Greek, Roman and Biblical sources but to Indian texts such as Hindu scriptures and the Bengali writers she grew up with (1990, 33). These texts, then, need to be decoded and interpreted by paying attention to their cultural contexts, a process which, according to Claire Harris, requires "education." (1990b, 307) That, at the moment, is not the case. As Minnie Aodla Freeman says, "We do not sit with each other long enough to understand each other. We do not educate each other enough to understand each other's cultures." (188)

I cannot forget an exchange that occurred in one of my classes while studying Vassanji's *No New Land*. A South Asian student addressed a group of white Canadian students and said: "I am glad that this text will make you do the kind of work I have to do when I read the Western texts and have to learn about all those allusions by doing some legwork." That the remark provoked laughter and not anger suggests to me that we may be going through an exciting transition to a new literary paradigm.

Harris suggests that her use of African and Caribbean themes and styles "interrupts and moves beyond Canadian literature as it has been defined, as in Anglo-Saxon, male. Canadian literature is not defined along the lines of the population." (1993, 121) Harris's reference to changing demographic patterns of Canada is really a call to discuss how we are going to define the Canadian reader. The writings of racial minority writers have effectively pointed out that "the bored housewife in Mississauga" stereotype needs to be retired on account of its obvious sexism and covert racism. We have certainly reached a crisis of legitimation in Canada. The old paradigms of nationalist criticism and the white-only canon no longer convince all Canadians. Nor does the master narrative of two founding races/peoples/cultures.

The old Canadian nationalism(s), founded on racial purity and cultural duality are being challenged by those who have long been excluded from the tables of dealmakers and dice rollers. Canada needs a new nationalism, a nationalism whose grounding premise will be Canada's heterogeneity. In Harris's words, we need "a new vision of Canada . . . one that includes all its people as full and legitimate citizens." (1993, 116) Whether that Canada of our dreams will come into being or whether the force of old ideologies of race- and culture-based nations will fragment the Canadian nation state remains to be seen.

WORKS CITED

Anderson, Benedict. 1991. *Imagined Communities: Reflections on the Origin and Spread of Nationalism.* London: Verso.

Angus, Ian. 1990. "Crossing the Border." *Massachusetts Review,* 31, 1-2 (Spring-Summer): 32-47.

Bannerji, Himani. 1990. "The Sound Barrier." In *Language in Her Eye: Views on Writing and Gender by Canadian Women Writing in English,* ed. Libby Scheier, Sarah Sheard and Eleanor Wachtel. Toronto: Coach House Press. 26-40.

Berger, Carl. 1966. "The True North Strong and Free." In *Nationalism in Canada,* ed. Peter Russell. Toronto: McGraw-Hill Company of Canada Limited. 3-26.

Blaut, James M. 1987. *The National Question: Decolonising the Theory of Nationalism.* London: Zed Books.

Brand, Dionne. 1984. *Chronicles of the Hostile Sun.* Toronto: Williams-Wallace.

———. 1988. "At the Lisbon Plate." In *Sans Souci and Other Stories.* Stratford: Williams-Wallace. 95-114.

———. 1990a. "Bread Out of Stone." In *Language in Her Eye: Views on Writing and Gender by Canadian Women Writing in English,* ed. Libby Scheier, Sarah

Sheard and Eleanor Wachtel. 45-53.

———. 1990b. Interview by Dagmar Novak. In *Other Solitudes: Canadian Multicultural Fictions*, ed. Linda Hutcheon and Marion Richmond. Toronto: Oxford University Press. 271-77.

———. 1993. "Who Can Speak for Whom?" *Brick*, 46 (Summer): 13-20.

Brant, Beth. 1993. "The Good Red Road: Journeys of Homecoming in Native Women's Writing." In *And Still We Rise: Feminist Political Mobilising in Contemporary Canada*, ed. Linda Carty. Toronto: Women's Press. 355-69.

Brydon, Diana. 1989. "Commonwealth or Common Poverty?: The New Literatures in English and the New Discourse of Marginality." In *After Europe: Critical Theory and Post-Colonial Writing*, ed. Stephen Slemon and Helen Tiffin. Sydney: Dangaroo Press. 1-16.

Cousins, Mary Panegoosho. 1993. "A Circumpolar Inuk Speaks." In *Sharing Our Experience*, ed. Arun Mukherjee. Ottawa: Canadian Advisory Council on the Status of Women. 52-6.

Fee, Margery. 1987. "Romantic Nationalism and the Image of Native People in Contemporary English-Canadian Literature." In *The Native in Literature*, ed. Thomas King, Cheryl Calver and Helen Hoy. Oakville, Ont.: ECW Press. 15-33.

———. 1993. "Canadian Literature and English Studies in the Canadian University." *Essays on Canadian Writing*, 48: 20-40.

Freeman, Minnie Aodla. 1993. "Dear Leaders of the World." In *Sharing Our Experience*, ed. Arun Mukherjee. Ottawa: Canadian Advisory Council on the Status of Women. 186-90.

Harris, Claire. 1990a. "Ole Talk: A Sketch." In *Language in Her Eye: Views on Writing and Gender by Canadian Women Writing in English*, ed. Libby Scheier, Sarah Sheard and Eleanor Wachtel. Toronto: Coach House Press. 131-41.

———. 1990b. "Mirror, Mirror on the Wall." In *Caribbean Women Writers: Essays from the First International Conference*, ed. Selwyn R. Cudjoe. Wellesley, Mass.: Calaloux Publications. 306-9.

———. 1993. Interview with Janice Williamson. Janice Williamson. In *Sounding Differences: Conversations with Seventeen Canadian Women Writers*. Toronto: University of Toronto Press. 115-30.

Hernández-Ramdwar, Camille. 1993. "Once I Wanted to Run Away from Canada." In *Sharing Our Experience*, ed. Arun Mukherjee. Ottawa: Canadian Advisory Council on the Status of Women. 61-3.

Keeshig-Tobias, Lenore. 1990. "The Magic of Others." In *Language in Her Eye: Views on Writing and Gender by Canadian Women Writing in English*, ed. Libby Scheier, Sarah Sheard and Eleanor Wachtel. Toronto: Coach House Press. 173-77.

Lecker, Robert. 1990a. "The Canonization of Canadian Literature: An Inquiry into Value." *Critical Inquiry*, 16 (Spring): 656-71.

———. 1990b. "Response to Frank Davey." *Critical Inquiry*, 16 (Spring): 682-89.

Metcalf, John. 1988. *What Is a Canadian Literature?* Guelph: Red Kite Press.

Monture-OKanee, Patricia A. 1992. "The Violence We Women Do: A First Nations View." In *Challenging Times: The Women's Movement in Canada and the United States*, ed. Constance Backhouse and David H Flaherty. Montreal: McGill-Queen's University Press. 193-200.

Nairn, Tom. 1977. *The Break-Up of Britain*. London: New Left Books.

Parameswaran, Uma. 1985. "Ganga in the Assiniboine." *A Meeting of Streams: South Asian Canadian Literature*, ed. M G Vassanji. Toronto: TSAR Publications. 79-93.

Sangari, Kumkum. 1987. "The Politics of the Possible." *Cultural Critique*, 7: 157-86.

Spear, Percival. 1965. *A History of India: Volume Two*. Harmondsworth, England: Penguin Books.

Staines, David. 1988. "Reviewing Practices in English Canada." In *Problems of Literary Reception/Problèmes de Réception Littéraire*, ed. E D Blodgett and A G Purdy. Edmonton: Research Institute for Comparative Literature. 61-8.

Vassanji, M G. 1985. Introduction to *A Meeting of Streams: South Asian Canadian Literature*, ed. M G Vassanji. Toronto: TSAR Publications. 1-6.

———. 1989. *The Gunny Sack*. Oxford: Heinemann.

II. First Engagements
(Book Reviews, 1981–1999)

These reviews were first published in *The Toronto South Asian Review*, now known as *The Toronto Review of Contemporary Writing Abroad*, from 1981–1999.

Frank Birbalsingh

A LIVED EXPERIENCE

Still Close to the Island
by Cyril Dabydeen.
Ottawa: Commoner's Publishing, 1980

Cyril Dabydeen's *Still Close to the Island* is a collection of sixteen short stories dealing principally with Caribbean subjects. The volume also contains a few stories set in Canada that deal predominantly with the immigrant experience. Altogether the stories treat a wide range of subjects, but whether they record the daily lives of Caribbean villagers or of Canadian city dwellers, they resonate with the ring of truth, of authentic, lived experience.

One story, "Antics of the Insane," is a childhood recollection in which a boy reveals the domestic "antics" of his uncle and aunt who live in a Caribbean village. The uncle is an attendant in the local hospital for the mentally ill. Presumably to relieve his frustration, he often gets drunk on his way home from work. He defies his nagging wife by reading from material provided by the Jehovah's Witnesses, or by lecturing her with quotations from the Bible. The wife responds to these drunken sermons by taunting him with the remark that he behaves like the mad people with whom he works. She accuses him of not helping with the family chickens that are her central preoccupation. As it happens, these chickens develop a strange sickness that seems to confirm her husband's neglect of them. But in a scene of some suspense, he takes revenge on his wife by secretly injecting the chickens with a needle, borrowed no doubt from his work place. The story ends with him gloating over his wife's rage when she discovers

173

the dead chickens.

The "antics" of the boy's uncle and aunt are, frankly, bizarre. The reader is kept guessing whether their actions are comic, tragic, or simply mysterious. Some events appear to possess hidden significance; others seem random or bizarre—the deliberate killing of the chickens, for example. Are we to conclude that the uncle is as insane as the people he works with? Or is everyone insane, including the aunt, and the boy himself, whose reliability as a narrator we are given no reason either to trust or distrust? The uncertain effect of these stories seems calculated and deliberate, implying a fundamental ambiguity in the nature of human existence, one that is so elusive that it can only be fleetingly grasped or hesitantly suggested.

In "All for Love" the Brazilian Marco, who is a visitor in Canada, marries out of motives that are wholly ambivalent. Marriage gives Marco the status of a landed immigrant, which enables him to work legally. Meanwhile, Marco is not fully convinced that he should remain in Canada and his wife is bent on returning to Brazil. Through his main characters the author captures the complex range of reactions that assail most immigrants: love/hate for their new home, nostalgia for their native land, unreal expectations of quick success, and gradual acceptance of their real situation. The pain, anxiety, hope, despair and other mixed emotions experienced by his characters are rendered with as much fidelity, sympathy as the author devotes to most of his characters in their tropical, Caribbean homelands.

Yet it is the author's objectivity and sympathy which are most adversely affected by the uncertain, or open-ended, approach taken in many stories. In "All for Love," for example, Marco seems resolved to remain in Canada when his friend Beneditor returns from Brazil; but his resolution is undermined by his previous vacillation, and by the author's concluding comment that Marco's resolve is accompanied by a smile no doubt like the one he had when he was married to his first wife in Brazil. The fragility of Marco's first marriage leads the reader to wonder about the firmness of his intention to stay in Canada and indeed about the firmness or certainty of anything else. While such skepticism represents a valid point of view it turns Marco's predicament into a generalized abstraction that is hard to grasp and hard to sympathize with.

Similarly, in "Mouthful" two black West Indian porters in a Canadian hotel appear to be tricked by a fellow West Indian who tells them he is from Nova Scotia. The trickery seems pointless and becomes no less so for being twice described as an "anansi" trick. Trivial duplicity may very well be a Caribbean social trait acknowledged by sociologists, historians and anthropologists; but its explicit presentation in art does not automatically confer artistic significance on it. Such significance will come from more specific information about the subject, deriving from the author's own attitude towards it. Thus the deliberate reticence in Dabydeen's point of view, while it contributes some objectivity, encourages a neutral authorial stance that detracts from a clear definition both of the inner motives and outward events affecting the characters. The result is that the reader may not fully identify with the characters. Blandness is not the same as objectivity, and the neutral accumulation of accurate detail is not the same as a considered presentation of ordinary events that captures the ordinariness of life for most of us.

Still, there is enough authentic local colour in these stories to make them more than interesting, especially to the non-Caribbean reader. Vivid physical descriptions of people and places combine with dialogues using pungent, idiomatic local speech patterns to confirm the author's skill in reproducing social manners. For this reason alone *Still Close to the Island* must be accounted a promising first volume, even if such a judgement seems patronizing to an established poet who has already published four successful volumes of poetry. Perhaps reticence and neutrality arouse greater suggestiveness in short, lyric poems. Even in *Still Close to the Island*, in stories as "Mammita's Garden Cove" and "Bitter Blood" where the authentic concreteness of detail is sufficient to ward off the bland effects of a neutral tone, there is a hidden suggestiveness and recurring sense of ambiguity which proves that, in addition to accurate social reproduction, Dabydeen's fiction relies on genuine psychological insight, serious philosophical reflection, and the outlines of a vision that will undoubtedly become more coherent when it becomes more clearly defined in the author's subsequent writing.

Frederick Ivor Case

FAMILIAR SHADOWS

Shattered Songs
by Arnold Itwaru.
Aya Press, 1982.

This volume could be read as a collection of separate poems; a series of thematically connected poems or simply as one long poem. For the purposes of this review we will consider *Shattered Songs* as one poem, since there is a unity of theme and aesthetics that produces a coherent poetic vision in this work.

Though the title on the cover and also on the first page is *Shattered Songs*, it appears on a later title page that the title may indeed be *Shattered Songs (a journey from somewhere to somewhere)*. It is significant that echoes of the "journey from somewhere to somewhere" are to be found explicitly and implicitly throughout the poem. For example on page 9 the words "somewhere to somewhere" are the only ones to appear on the entire page and therefore constitute a poem or a stanza as the case may be. But Itwaru is not playing sophisticated aesthetic games. On page 9 as elsewhere he demonstrates the mastery of emphasis through the use of various stylistic and graphic processes. Perhaps the most significant example of Itwaru's achievement is to be found on page 17, which I quote in its entirety:

a moan
a whimper
a torture of silence
      a moan
      a whimper
      a torture of silence

a moan, a whimper, a torture of silence

a

moan

a

whimper

a

torture of silence

amoanawhimpera torture

Simple in its construction, this stanza is, however, a fine example
of graphic and stylistic balance enhanced by various levels of meaning, which result in a heightened poetic tension and intensity
achieved in other parts of *Shattered Songs* by more conventional
means. At this point it is necessary to point out the versatility of
Itwaru's style, which ranges from the one line of page 9, already
quoted, to the most densely written poetic prose. Though Itwaru
suppresses the use of capital letters he does make use of punctuation
to serve his own purposes of rhythm and meaning. The language,
though sophisticated, is not hermetic. Occasional lapses (see below)
are neither sufficiently frequent nor important to spoil the pleasure of
grappling with the images and concepts presented to us. For this is
"intellectual poetry" in the sense that the deep structure meaning is
often far away from what is explicitly expressed, particularly if the
isolated image or concept is to be appreciated in the context of the
entire work.

The thematic context is that of individual suffering, which is consistently presented in its proper collective setting. But Itwaru's collec-
tivity appears to consist of generations past and present with firm
negations concerning those of the future. This of itself deepens suffering since there is no solace in illusion, no frantic or serene extension
of the self in the future. The padded cell and the paddy field present
identical broken horizons whose psychic effects are symbolized by
the title of the poem.

Though the poem is well worth reading for its thematic interest
and images, its philosophical and psychological depth, it also provides some ideas on the aesthetic principles motivating its production. On page 8 we read:

> . . . the poem in
> the dungheap of quivering hands writes, bleeds . . .
> tire of . . .
> not poems . . . eternal ash, chipped bone, word to ash, act
> to ash . . .

On the one hand the poem can be perceived as having its own dynamic, which uses the poet as a mere instrument intrinsically unworthy and devoid of significant meaning. In the second quotation one concludes that the poems are "eternal ash, chipped bone . . ." Such a declaration denies the living value of the poetic act since in its realization it is burnt out—thoroughly spent. Furthermore, the word, as a principle underlined in the poem, is itself negated and becomes the sterile or sterilized act incapable of further extension, inherently unproductive.

But *Shattered Songs*, even though the efficacity of the voice is denied, is not an anti-poem. It is not an attempt to undermine accepted forms or aesthetic principles. *Shattered Songs* succeeds in crystallizing socio-psychological perspectives of a suffering, tortured soul as well as aesthetic principles in appropriate structural forms. Through a careful reading of the poem we do indeed discover "the dungheap of quivering hands," and the "word to ash" is evoked in several ways in the poem though the idea needs some extra-textual elaboration if it is to be fully comprehended.

Arnold Itwaru is a poet who has already achieved a well-deserved reputation as a literary critic and sociologist. He has written many other poems as well as prose fiction. With this type of background it is legitimate for the critic of his work to scrutinize his text, savouring the tone of the expression, the apt turn of phrase and the precision of the structure. But the poem suffers particularly in three places from surprising maladdresses. On page 21 the use of four letter words is significantly gratuitous though their use in other parts of the text is most appropriate. On page 37 there is the descent into the facile jingle:

> for weeping
> breeds weepers and angry reapers.

The use of the word "causality" on pages 7 and 29 disrupts the rhythm of the lines and introduces what one can only conclude as inappropriate vocabulary in a poem otherwise purified of the language of the sociologist.

In conclusion it must be said that *Shattered Songs* has to be considered as an important contribution to the body of literature produced by Canadians and by Canadians of Caribbean origin. What is particularly important, in this work produced by an individual who is very conscious of each word as a poetic, literary and cultural act, is the fact that the poem goes far beyond the exposition of the human condition. It does lay the groundwork of interesting theories of poetic production.

Perhaps on page 18 of *Shattered Songs* we are presented with the notion that would best help us to understand the aesthetic principles discussed earlier. Itwaru writes:

behind the line the page is empty, the shadows familiar

Daniel McBride

REVISITATION OF CHILDHOOD

Sacrifices
by Ven Begamudré.
Erin, Ontario: Porcupine's Quill, 1986

Sacrifices, a novella by Ven Begamudré, has a wistful quality about it that arises, one senses, from the author's look into his own past. The parallels in dates and times between those of the author and of the main character Harishchandra are too many to avoid this conclusion. In any event there is a genuineness of vision that brings forth the emotions and intellect at odds in the revisitation of childhood. The moral that catches one unawares in this touching and unpretentious story is that one can lose one's roots while still in the homeland—conversely, one can find them a world away.

For Harishchandra the early departure of his father to America determines that he too shall leave India to find the promised better life. The series of vignettes that move from his birth towards his departure to Canada rely upon alternating sharp and soft images, a *kammerspiel* effect laden with the poignancy of retrospection. One is given the ordinariness of the little events, each piece of time—"slice of life"—evoking the depths of feeling in the child Harish mirroring the world in which he is encapsulated:

> "Paisam, Bungaru," she crooned. "Did you miss me?"
> Why did everyone ask him this strange question? Hoping Mamma would help him answer, he turned to look at her. She stood with her back to him and spoke with Devraj Uncle. Hari then looked into Amma's large, brown eyes for the answer. She hugged him with such force that the peppermint snapped be-

tween his teeth, and suddenly his vast world—two islands surrounded by a blue-green sea—tasted minty, cool and sweet.

The transitions between these moments occur naturally, as in the overlapping visual impressions one experiences in going back into memory. Begamudré displays a fine touch in allowing the simple event to exist as a synecdoche for the larger question of Indian identity:

Azad frowned. Why did Krishna speak only English when it had been obvious in the station that he understood other languages? The man was Indian was he not? Azad smirked. Yes, they were all Indians, but they still slept in their separate berths.

The simplicity of the various elements might tempt the reader to miss the ambitiousness of the work in going after the many diverse elements that make up "India"—in particular the resonance the word has in the mind of the expatriate, or one who is about to become one. What is being left behind by Harish manages to make its complex nature felt simply and forcefully through the sensuous attachments of the child; the hold over values of the departed British Raj, the complexities of Moslem and Hindu interaction, the tokenism and patronage, the excesses, the corrosive allure of Western culture and the resulting diaspora westwards, and finally the resilience and richness of India, its obsessive presence drawing some back, emotionally if not physically—somehow all these are woven into the nucleus of Harish and his family.

The failure of Western medicine to cure the severe leg rash and boils of Harish leads to a return to Tirupati, one of the most sacred hill pagodas where Harish makes a sacrifice of his hair to Lord Venkateswara. The apparent superstitiousness here (along with the other belief of Amma that Harish only gets sick when he leaves Bangalore) is overturned as Harish is in fact cured by reconnecting with his cultural heritage. This is powerfully and simply presented after the shaving of his head as he is presented to the priest: "He raised a golden bell above Hari's head but, when he lowered the bell, Hari saw the duller gleam of brass inside."

It is the vital connection with one's mythos that is at issue here, as

181

it is throughout the story. The father of Harish has been drawn abroad in pursuit of a brighter future. The sacrifices made from this initial departure (the resulting tenuousness in the link between father and son for one) begin to unravel the "Indianness" of Harish. There is a strong sense that his physical degeneration results from this pull away from his culture. The reestablishment of the bond, made through the nucleus of the fragmented family, provides Harish with the centre in himself to take India with him as it were. His family, in overcoming the obstacles to his departure, paradoxically ensure that he will never leave "inside." The connection between his anxiety and his illness, his family and absent father, the powerful details of daily events as seen through the eyes of the child versus the impending intrusion of foreignness: all find their eloquent expression, as in the ending when Harish is finally set to come to Canada.

> Moonlight had shone through the small window and the room smelled of betel and incense, camphor and cloves. Would Canada smell this wonderful?

Sacrifices is a quietly compelling story of one who, in leaving behind what he most cares about, is somehow mysteriously brought closer to it. In the almost maudlin confession of the Sikh doctor at the end of the story one senses an inability to realize that not all sacrifices are to be understood. The doctor is himself haunted by his own tragedy in the 1947 Partition, he is weighted with the futility of that which cannot be changed or understood. But he has returned to India, to being what he simply is: "I observe the five kakkars now, of course, but I was born a Sikh." His own inner contradiction comes out following this as he says to Harish that "but then, you won't be growing up an Indian, will you?" There is distance between intellect and heart that Pascal spoke of in his famous dictum: "The heart has reasons the mind knows nothing of." So it is with Harish and the doctor, their minds drawn beyond India into the West, their hearts remaining behind.

Begamudré has created an evocative picture in this short work, one that should strike a chord for many of us, as we revisit those distant times and places from whence we came. We are all, in some sense, emigrés. The work is pronouncedly retrospective in this sense, displaying little of the fire and passion of Rao's *Kanthapura* or the humour and tragedy of Khushwant Singh; rather it has the quiet simplicity of R K Narayan's more sentimental works. Yet it might be a mistake to contrast this work too closely to others with differing purposes. *Sacrifices* is a glowing return, homeland to homeland.

Uma Parameswaran

LANDMARK

Tales from Firozsha Baag
by Rohinton Mistry.
Markham: Penguin, 1987

I shall start with two points that are peripheral to the book under review but central to South Asian writing in Canada.

When a Toronto newspaper announced that a dark horse was touted to win this year's Governor General's award, many of us no doubt kept our fingers crossed in the hope that Rohinton Mistry was the nominee who would gallop first to the finish line. Though that was not to be, the nomination itself is a landmark. What Ivar Ivask, director of *World Literature Today*, recently said when announcing that Raja Rao had been awarded this year's Neustadt Prize might well be said of Mistry's nomination in the Canadian context: "We are breaking out of a purely Western hegemony because previous laureates have been from Europe, North America . . . It's a new challenge, a new literature, a new world for many of us." The new world, the new challenge is not that Mistry is a Canadian of South Asian origin (so is Michael Ondaatje) but that the book being given recognition is about Mistry's South Asian origins and the author's first book, unlike Ondaatje's *Running in the Family* which was written long after Ondaatje became a recognized Canadian writer, and was therefore acclaimed almost as a matter of course. *Tales from Firozsha Baag* is a collection of eleven stories about the tenants of an apartment complex in Bombay, such a one as Rohinton Mistry might well have grown up in. The themes—of boyhood initiations, of everyday frustrations and of nostalgia—are universal but the details are essentially Indian, indeed essentially Parsi. However, weaving in and out of their daily routine are strands that form another pattern—of Canada in India. There are references to offspring who emigrated to Canada but returned. Jamshed the snob who held everything Indian in contempt after emigrating to the US, and Kersi, Mistry's alter ego, who lives in a run-down apartment in Toronto and exasperates his father with his brief, noncommittal letters but then sends a book of his short stories which is by inference the book under review—*Tales from Firozsha Baag*.

The *Toronto South Asian Review* was the first to publish one of Mistry's short stories. This is not just a happy coincidence but consistent with a principle for which the journal was founded in 1981, namely to identify and promote the writings of South Asians in Canada. In this, *TSAR* may be likened to Writers Workshop in India that under P Lal's editorship was founded in the 1950s to affirm and promote Indo-English literature.

Having adopted the cinematographic method of setting the book against a larger background, I would like to point out one other aspect of the background before zooming in on the contents of the volume. While innovation in technique has become an indispensable prerequisite for recognition in contemporary fiction, this book shows that straight storytelling without much narrative acrobatics is still a viable form in Canadian and Commonwealth literatures if the setting is unfamiliar and authentically represented. *Tales from Firozsha Baag* very specifically and authentically depicts the life of Parsis in Bombay. The Parsis are Zoroastrian by religion and urban-Indian by culture. "There was so much to be proud of," as Kersi's father says in the last story. "Parsis came to India from Persia because of Islamic persecution in the seventh century" and established themselves in Gujerat and Bombay. There were great pioneers, "the Tatas and their contribution to the steel industry . . . Dadabhai Naoroji in the freedom movement . . . " Though Kersi does not write about Parsis as such but about the tenants of an apartment complex, by the end of the book one gets a clear idea of the Parsi way of life: their clothing—*dugli* (worn over a shirt), *pheytoe* or *pugree* (turban), *mathoobanoo* (a woman's head-kerchief), *sapaat* (shoes), *sudra* etc.; their festivals such as *Behram roje* and rites such as *dusmoo* (10th day after a death in the family); and their food—*dhandar paatya, sali boti, pupeta-noo-gose, dhansak-masala* etc.

Using foreign words has always been a problem in Commonwealth writing, and different authors have used different methods. Earlier writers listed a glossary; modern writers such as Mulk Raj Anand and Raja Rao use literal translations of Indian terms; Chinua Achebe explains the terms within the body of the sentence. Mistry, like Salman Rushdie, goes one step further and uses neither glossary nor explanations and yet the meanings come through in most cases. In addition to distinctively Parsi usages, he liberally sprinkles Hindi words such as *budmaash, seth, chappal, bunya* most of which would be found in the *Oxford English Dictionary*. But there are certain other words that are so local that only Bombay residents would know their meaning, words like matka which is a form of gambling. By casually and confidently using such a plethora of foreign words, Mistry asserts that Canadian English should expand to include words of Indian origin.

The stories themselves are straight narratives, there are several adult protagonists and several teenage protagonists. Of the adult stories. "Paying Guests" is both funny and in the realistic mode; it depicts an all-too-familiar problem in India where tenants are impossible to get rid of. The narrator of the "The Ghost of Firozsha Baag" is Jaykaylee (Jacqueline) a Goanese live-in cook; Tehmina, of "One Sunday" is a spinster; Daulat Mirza, of "Condolence Visit" is a recently widowed woman who decides on *dusmoo* day to give away her husband's ceremonial turban to a prospective bridegroom who wants traditional attire. The gesture is both an affirmation of her past long and happy marriage and of her purposeful looking ahead to the next phase of her life.

As often happens, the stories that deal with adolescence are the most effective. Jehangir Bulsara, in "The Collectors," is a loner, a shy teenager who is befriended by his neighbour Dr Mody, a stamp collector. To increase his collection, Jehangir colludes with Eric, his classmate at St. Xavier's School, and gets stolen stamps in exchange acceding to Eric's homosexual advances. Both, teenage masturbation on one hand and Dr Mody's genuine paternal concern, are expertly delineated, and perhaps because stamps are the link between the two, when Jehangir outgrows Eric's perversions he also turns away from Dr Mody's stamp collection that Mrs Mody presents to him after the doctor's sudden death.

And then there is Kersi Boyce, the author's alter ego. His stories have the element of genuine pathos that comes with genuine nostalgia. We see his father's white hairs tugging the teenager into crying "for not being able to hug Daddy when I wanted to, and for not ever saying thank you for cricket in the morning, and pigeons and bicycles and dreams."

Kersi emigrates to Canada, and "Lend Me Your Light" (published in the *Toronto South Asian Review* in 1984) and the last story "Swimming Lessons" are about Kersi in Canada. "Lend Me Your Light" will probably be read by most as Kersi's sensitive love for his native land as opposed to Jamshed's snobbish rejection. However, there is something about the story that gets my back up; while it is quite understandable that Percy, who lives in India, should reject Jamshed, it is not entirely to Kersi's credit that he should reject Jamshed for rejecting India; one wonders just how far apart these two are; for Kersi, as indeed most of us who have immigrated to Canada, tends to magnify the mote in his neighbour's eye. I would like to study just why Bharati Mukherjee's Canadian stories in her *Darkness* (1986) and Rohinton Mistry's Canadian stories in this volume bother me, but this is not the place.

In conclusion, it should be pointed out that the cover illustration is jarringly inappropriate on several counts. The falling away of the A in the name above the entrance is a fine touch of realism and symbolism. However, the sketch does scant justice to Mistry's careful description of the apartment complex containing three blocks—A, B, C—each with three floors (though it is not clear whether this means three storeys as in Canada, or four storeys as in India as implied in "The Ghost"). The picture shows a two-storeyed block. Also, Kersi Boyce lives in C Block but in the picture, he is made to live in A Block, in an apartment that the author has described as occupied by the Rustomji's neighbours, Nariman Hansotia. The Boyces and the Hansotias and Rustomji all live on the ground floor and not on the second storey as depicted in the illustration. The cover illustration further shows Mehroo wearing her saree the wrong way. Parsis wear the saree with the pallav over the right shoulder and the edge falling in front. An unfortunate piece of carelessness that detracts from the marvelous realism of the stories, but let it pass. The stories are more important than an illustration, and the stories are good.

Colin Lowndes

LANGUAGE AND THEME

Daughters of the Twilight
by Farida Karodia.
London: Women's Press, 1986

Coming Home and Other Stories
by Farida Karodia.
London: Heinemann, 1988

In Tom Stoppard's play, *The Real Thing*, a character elaborates the "cricket bat" theory of writing:

> This thing here, which looks like a wooden club, is actually several pieces of particular wood cunningly put together in a particular way so that the whole thing is sprung, like a dance floor. It's for hitting cricket balls with. If you get it right, the cricket ball will travel two hundred yards in four seconds, and all you've done is give it a knock like knocking the top off a bottle of stout, and it makes a noise like a trout taking a fly . . . —what we're trying to do is to write cricket bats, so that when we throw up an idea and give it a little knock, it might . . . travel— . . . Now what we've got here is a lump of wood roughly the same shape trying to be a cricket bat, and if you hit a ball with it, the ball will travel about ten feet and you will drop the bat and dance about shouting "Ouch!" with your hands stuck into your armpits. (Indicating the cricket bat.) This isn't better because someone says it's better, or because there's a conspiracy by the MCC to keep cudgels out of Lord's. It's better because it's better.

This analogy is appropriate for the work of Farida Karodia because of the dilemma out of which it arises in the play. The character who uses it is a well-educated and technically proficient writer, capable of creating finely crafted "cricket bats," but he has nothing to say. Indeed, at the time he expresses his theory, he is writing sci-fi pop for TV. The character whose work he is attacking is politically engaged and may have a great deal to say, but is hobbled by his clumsiness with language. Breyton Breytenbach, whose work has provided the epigraph to *Coming Home* has also written, in agreement with Stoppard: "Aesthetics flow into ethics which leads to action. An act of beauty is a political statement." In literature matters of aesthetics are fundamental, and must be, or the idea will not "travel."

Ms Karodia, an Indian writer from South Africa who has lived in Canada since 1969, has a great deal to say. In her novel, *Daughters of the Twilight*, published in 1986, and especially in *Coming Home*, her collection of short stories published last year on which I will focus, she portrays the consequences of simply living in contemporary South Africa on characters drawn from every spectrum of that country's society: Blacks, Coloureds, Indians and Whites. None of her characters is politically engaged at the outset (though some become politicized through the events of the story); they are simply trying to live reasonable lives, an ambition not always deliberately discouraged by the system, but always rendered futile nonetheless. The cumulative impression is that the system in South Africa is fundamentally antilife, crippling even those seemingly most privileged by it. This is an ambitious and laudable project—but it makes some stringent demands on the writer.

One obvious demand is to write convincingly from the divergent points of view of a wide range of characters. Three stories are in first person. The opening novella that lends its title to the collection is told from the point of view of a black man who has escaped the grinding poverty in the valley where he was raised to become a teacher. His coming home parallels the return of his father, a violent man who routinely brutalized his family, from eighteen years in prison for assaulting a white man. The resulting events cause the narrator to confront his own hatred for his father, his mother's willingness to forgive, and the motivations for his father's violence. The character's movement and the agony at the end brought on by his understanding is convincing. Similarly successful is "Seeds of Discontent," told from the point of the view of a middle-class white woman whose growing awareness is realistically rendered. The remaining story told in first person, "The Woman in Green," is less effective. The incident seems contrived and the narrator remains too neutral and remote from the events. The story is also marred by other more basic problems to which I will return. Several other stories lapse into an anonymous, generalized mode of third person narration that does not serve them well, and perhaps implies a failure of sympathy on the part of the author.

Moreover, Ms Karodia has not been well served by her editor at Heinemann. Indeed, the collection shows no signs of editorial assistance at all: there are several typographical errors and persistent annoying problems with punctuation. More seriously, there are problems with inconsistencies in important details. The story "Something in the Air" deals with the dilemma faced by Elsie, a young girl who overhears a conversation between her father, a police officer, and one of his men, who are planning to capture a man wanted for urban terrorism: Daan Bezuidenhuit. Accompanying this man when the police spring their trap will be a young Indian who was a childhood friend of Elsie's. Her dilemma lies in the conflict between her loyalty to her father and her affection for her friend. Finally, she decides to warn her friend's parents. She thinks, "Since the trap was set for Wednesday, there would still be enough time to warn their son." However, as the story opens, it is Sunday evening, and she overhears her father say that "Bezuidenhuit will be crossing the border this Friday." "We only have five days then," the other policeman replies. This confusion of days seriously and needlessly damages the narrative.

For another example, I will return to "The Woman in Green," mentioned earlier. To make the point it is necessary to quote at length from the beginning of the story:

> I was awakened from a deep sleep by a confusion of sounds. For a while I listened to the noise and the chatter of passengers hurrying by my window, then I sat up and drowsily peered at my watch. It was a few minutes before midnight. I rolled over in my bunk to squint through the slit between the shutters. The

sign at the railway station read "Bloemfontein."

The hissing and clanking of couplings, the screeching of wheels, the shrilling of a whistle and the mist-shrouded lights on the platform lent an air of eeriness to the scene outside.

I remained by the darkened window caught up in the atmosphere but then the whistled [sic] shrilled, rudely jolting me back to reality. The train jerked forward and just as I thought we were on our way, it abruptly screeched to a halt again. I noticed a commotion at the far end of the platform and inquisitively lowered the blind a few inches, craning my neck to see. A couple hurried into view . . . Ensconced in the comfort of my bed, I felt a twinge of sympathy for the latecomers.

Later the next morning, I saw the woman again, for the second time . . .

There are a variety of difficulties here apart from the typographical error. First is the obvious confusion between wooden shutters and blinds in the railway car. Perhaps some trains have both varieties of window coverings, but that specialized knowledge of South African rolling stock does nothing to alleviate the confusion inherent in the writing. Second, the actions of the narrator are illogically conceived: she awakens, sits up, rolls over, remains by the window, then is ensconced in her bed. Third is the threadbare cliché of the second paragraph, in particular, the expression "lent an air" which makes one wince. My final objection is to the glaring redundancy in the last line quoted. Further, I suspect that the examples I have presented imply a failure to imagine completely the scene in question; that the scenes do not adequately exist for the reader because in the first place they were not vividly conceived in the writer's mind.

Ms Karodia has been better served by The Women's Press, publishers of her novel *Daughters of the Twilight,* than by Heinemann. The novel deals with an Indian family who owns a general store in a small South African town, and with the gradual erosion of their dreams and hopes as they encounter, as a family and individually, the increasingly severe restrictions imposed by South African society. It is free of the technical problems plaguing the short stories, but still suffers from a pedestrian style and an awkwardness in the development of the narrative. Ms Karodia's attempts at enlivening devices too often result in clichés as when the narrator's beautiful sister attempts to reassure her: "Don't worry, Meena, some day you'll emerge from your chrysalis . . . you'll unfold just like a butterfly," or when the mother comments on the misfortune of a relative: "It's no use crying over spilt milk," or in a description of the beautiful sister, Yasmin, with "eyes large and luminous like those of a young doe." Or they are simply inappropriate, as when the narrator relates: "I had long ago made the startling discovery that Ma, like Yasmin, had a soft underbelly of vulnerability which was rarely exposed." These stylistic shortcomings continue through the short stories.

I trust that these criticisms will not be discounted as petty carping. Such neglect for narrative detail and for right language prevents the reader from imaginatively entering the world of the story. My complaints grow out of genuine frustration that a writer with so much to say has been so sloppy, has not been able to bring the requisite discipline to bear; and that latterly she has not received the help that she needs and deserves from her publisher. And frustration because there are things to enjoy in these stories: a precision of emotional response in certain characters that carries the authority of felt experience, an occasionally vivid sense of place, and most importantly, the growing awareness of the power of Ms Karodia's larger theme that embraces the tragedy of South Africa for all its people. But such ideas remain largely inert without the art necessary to animate them.

In *Praises and Dispraises: Poetry and Politics*, Terrence des Pres writes: "right language can help us, as it always helps in hard moments, with our private struggles to keep whole, can be a stay against confusion, can start the healing fountains. And whatever helps us repossess our humanity, be able again to take our place and speak forth, frees us to work in the world. This is imagination's special task . . . " Des Pres makes clear what these stories might have been, what they might have accomplished. It is to be hoped that Ms Karodia in working on her second novel, can make progress to find the "right language' " for all that she has to say.

G D Killam

TO FIGHT, TO HOPE, TO DREAM

The Gunny Sack
by M G Vassanji.
Oxford, UK and Portsmouth, New Hampshire:
Heinemann International, 1989

Cape Town Coolie
by Réshard Gool.
Toronto: TSAR, 1989

[These books were reviewed in the original essay together with *Matigari* by the Kenyan writer Ngugi wa Thiongo. The discussion of Ngugi's novel has been excluded here.]

These [two] novels deal with Africa: *The Gunny Sack* is set in East Africa and mostly in Tanganyika-Zanzibar-Tanzania; *Cape Town Coolie* in South Africa, Cape Town District Six. The first spans four generations and describes Indian settlement, entrenchment on and eventual withdrawal from various parts of the Coast; the [second] evokes sensations among the Cape Town District Six community and that epiphanic moment, in 1984, when District Six was to be bulldozed into oblivion in the interests of the growing apartheid state and of white exclusivity. Each book, in its way has a remedial purpose and is written from within each author's own and intimately witnessed experience.

The framing context of Gool's novel is well described by the publisher's blurbs which read:

It is 1948.

The Afrikaaner Nationalists are poised to introduce the racist policy of *apartheid* into South Africa. Their plans include the conversion of District Six in Cape Town into an exclusively white residential district, and the removal of its current residents. As profiteers and politicians converge upon this slum area, its residents valiantly put up a fight. Into it is drawn Henry Naidoo, the highly principled but gentle Indian lawyer, who realizes tragically that the struggle against *apartheid* is no ordinary fight for justice. It calls for a brutality he is not equipped with.

Gool is interested in more than the struggle of a Tenant's Association to save District Six. Naidoo's story is his principal concern but he is also almost equally interested in the lives and predilections of characters—a wide range of them—associated with Naidoo. And, because he was a political theorist, Gool is interested in political motivations and how theory—there is a good deal of miscellaneous reference to political theory and theorists in the book—is made to apply to a heightened politically tense situation.

We learn of Naidoo's life from his diaries and from the people who knew him—Adrian Van der Merve, a university lecturer and his closest friend to whom Naidoo entrusts his papers and diaries who reconstructs Naidoo's life. But the authorial point of view shifts: Gool often has Henry tell his own story; an author omniscient is also employed to flesh out the life. And Gool adopts a shifting time frame moving from past to present with considerable skill, engaging interest often when it seems about to flag. For narrative pace is almost lacking here. This is an introspective and intellectual book, posing and probing into intellectual questions as these are represented by various spokesmen-characters. It is not that the characters lack vitality—too much human experience is accorded them for that claim to be put; but they are at the same time vehicles for intellectual speculation, almost too neatly arranged and arraigned to put human flesh on abstractions.

The circle with which Naidoo is intimate contains a Communist/Bolshevik from a family which, after dubious beginnings in the slave trade off Madagascar, has achieved social and educational respectability. This man, Yussouf Rycliffe, hobnobs with the hoi polloi, eventually abandons his revolutionary stance with reference to saving District Six and sells out for crass gain. There is Shaik-Moosa, a shady financier and real-estate developer, who first seeks through complicated and crooked legal procedures to gain control of the land development scheme for District Six—but who then fades out of the picture and the book. Naidoo acts as the Shaik's lawyer and we expect that some tension in the plot may develop from this. Such is not the case.

There is Gordon Stewart, son of a canny Scot who hated the British, joined the Boer Independence Fight (more usually called The Boer War), married an Afrikaans woman and brought up his son in a radical political philosophy. Such is Stewart's rage against an unjust and hopeless world that he becomes an underground anarchist and bomber.

There is Katherine Holmes, the beautiful younger daughter of a distinguished Cape Coloured family, with whom Naidoo falls in love and with whom he has a complex and unhappy though ultimately happy relationship. There is a good deal of reference to political thinkers—Nietzche, Hegel, Marx, Kropotkin, Bakunin and others without anything much being made of it—perhaps the author attributes to his readers familiarity with the opinions of these people; perhaps he is enjoining them, by holding out on them, to go to the works and read them. But there is only a simplistic application of theory in the creation and actions of the characters who are meant, one supposes, to be exemplary. The characters are stereotyped—Naidoo is a Ghandian pacifist (although it costs him his life and is a stance he repudiates in his final posthumously delivered letter to Katherine). Rycliffe is an ideologue, a Bolshevist playboy for whom people "were mere vehicles for the inevitable play of social forces." Stewart stands for violent revolution to alleviate social problems of the kind typified by the denizens of District Six. This the stance that Naidoo—reluctantly—adopts at the end of his life: "You will see that I have lost faith in pacifist answers. There is no morality left but that of the tiger: brute force. That is why Stewart is our obscene and tragic solution." It is a passage which presages the horror of the developing apartheid state: "If I die, choose him, choose blood and violence and pain. What a horrible future for our country! . . ."

This is a complex, at times satisfying, at times unsatisfactory book.

It raises questions to which it often provides no answers; it stuns, often, with an elegance of language devoted to the landscape, to nature and it almost offends with its deliberate archaisms which seem to proceed from authorial whimsy rather than to render accurately a variety of voices. Its prose at times has a Conradian eloquence and loftiness; " . . . faces, names, dates, instructions spun endlessly in and out, recurring at different levels of certainty and unsureness, circulating like tags or emblems or even more material manifestations of uncertain natural forces which were winding with fury to a preordained climax."

More than once in the novel the word "ineffable" is used, in different contexts—Adrian, as he tells Naidoo's story, says it is "like trying to unfold the ineffable." That seems what Gool himself is trying to do in this novel—it is of course the task of all serious writers. As a depiction, begun *in medias res* and told with the virtue of hindsight, it provides an historical record of the complex of forces which informed the beginnings of the apartheid state. More than this it examines complex human relations, as these proceed from questions of race and commitment to various forms of social / political ideologies. In this regard it displays a range of human activity from the most blatantly cynical and opportunistic to the most lofty (and impractical). It displays a situation without hope and, where it ends, without the possibility of redemption.

. . .

Vassanji's novel is of a different order altogether than Gool's and Ngugi's [*Matigari*]. Whereas they live within the historical moment of the here and now, whereas the one seeks to display the historical causes and the political ambiguities in the subjective political moment, and the other, to show the abnegation and enormous self-interest of postcolonial betrayal for the purposes of reforming it through militant revolution, Vassanji displays with candour, completeness and complexity, the story of Asian experience in East Africa over four generations. The story effectively begins in 1885 when Dhanji Govindji arrives at (the imaginary village of) Matamu in the Kilwa region of present-day Tanzania. He has travelled from Junapur via Porbander in north west India (with a two-month break in Muscat and a period as clerk in Zanzibar). At Matamu he establishes himself through contact with the local Mukhi, and founds a family, the experiences of which are traced by his great grandson, the heir of Dhanji and an African slave / mother.

The narrator—Huseni (he proudly takes the name of his African grandfather) Salim Juma—is inspired to tell the story of his family when he comes into possession on the death of his favourite grand aunt, Ji Bai, of The Gunny Sack of the title of the book, named "Shehru," and described by the publishers as a "drab dusty Shehrazade of the Indian and African settlements," an icon of family history, a Pandora's Box of mementos and memories. The Gunny Sack is the organizing metaphor for the novel. The memorabilia which Salim draws from it as he proceeds with the telling of his tale refresh his memories of the oral history of his people as these were told to him, or provoke research into the cause and effect of events with which various of the items are associated.

It is moot point as to whether the device assists the novel or not: certainly it does not impede its narrative. But without the Gunny Sack—to which the author returns from time to time to apostrophise it—the narrative stands well on its own and offers a realistic accounting in compelling fictional form—probably, as the publishers claim, the first of its kind—of Indian / Asian association with the East Coast of Africa, beginning in Matamu, moving about East Africa—to parts of the Tanganyikan territory, witnessing German colonization and encroachments on indigenes (African and Asian alike), the abortive Maji Maji rebellion, the First World War, the process of the movement toward Independence of East African colonies assisted by the Kenyan Independence Movement, the coming of TANU, Nyerere and the Ujamaa period, the political pact with Zanzibar and the creation of Tanzania, to the final alienation of the Asian community first through Amin's appropriations in Uganda and later with its spill-over effect in Tanzania.

These are the historical points in time which frame the narrative. The complexity of family life, of enterprises directed toward the accumulation of substance, of upward mobility are recorded—as are the family's need over the generations to live with the shame of the founder, Govindji's theft of communal wealth in his obsessive, fruitless search for his "African son" until reputation is reclaimed through the death in a car accident, of Gulam, who becomes a missionary martyr, thus saving the family name and after which it prospers.

The author provides us with a genealogical table of the families whose stories he tells. From Govindji's liaison with Bibi Taratibu, the African slave woman, a family of some 30 people are mentioned in the book; from his marriage to Fatima, daughter of the Zanzibari Widow, an equal number. What this novel shows—and why it ought to be read and considered—is that the Asian community in East Africa was in every essential way, East African—that is to say, African. Their history, as evoked through *The Gunny Sack*, becomes a recognition of and tribute to the ancestors, people whose lives and stories must be told and to whom attention must be paid: here is the authors apologia:

> There are those who go to their graves not knowing where they came from . . . who hurtled into the future even as the present was not yet over . . . for whom history was a contemptible record of a shameful past. In short, those who closed their ears when the old men and women spoke. But the future will demand a reckoning. We will not forgive those who forgot, the new generation of the Sabrinas and the Fairuzes and the Farahs . . .
>
> Ji Bai opened a small window into that dark past for me. She took me past the overgrowth into the other jungle. And the whole world flew in, a world of my great-grandfather who left India and my great-grandmother who was African, the world of Matamu where India and Africa met and the mixture exploded in the person of my half-caste grandfather Huseni who disappeared into the forest one day and never returned, the world of changing Africa where Europe and Africa also met and the result was even more explosive, not only in the lives of men but also in the life of the continent.

While there is a quality of celebration in the novel through its consummate telling, in intimate detail, of the lives of the many characters who people it, there is also a quality of objectivity, a disinterestedness which may reflect the way in which the Asian communities situated themselves in what in some respects remained an alien land. These are people who willy-nilly were placed in entrepreneurial roles under the British raj in East Africa and were made to pay a heavy price for it in the postcolonial period. They are witness to earth-shaking events in terms of what happens in the communities, even in some instances made to participate in them (the narrator for example spends a period of time as a conscript in the army). Yet they seem somehow to remain aloof from even the most devastating of these happenings and remain more observers than participants, even avoiding the most devastating forms of victimization. Perhaps this quality is summed up in a statement by Salim when he says, with reference to the purging of alternate political programmes that are proposed by a young radical group in Dar es Salaam that "I did not belong to that inner circle of hard-core theoreticians. Like most, I came for the atmosphere." And as if to secure the point he notes that the group of dissidents that was rounded up included "one Asian."

In a sense the book advocates just such a disinterested stance: the attempt of the dissidents to make or remake society through their political beliefs and actions is, for Salim (and for the author?) "a student exercise run wild."

And then the exodus from the homeland. And the Gunny Sack of history and memory which cause speculation that "destiny is ironical, or is it the ironical in us, a predisposition that makes us go after a certain fate, a certain pattern—poetry being more real than reality . . . . Something of both I suspect." The book concludes: ". . . we are thankful, for to have dreamed was enough."

Gool's Henry Naidoo advocated violence, repugnant as that was to him, as a way of achieving the just society: it didn't work (and it hasn't yet); *Matigari's* masses are still by and large faceless (even though certain individuals among them in the novel stand out clearly). Ngugi writes: he "seemed to hear the worker's voices, the voices of the peasants, the voices of the students and of other patriots of all nationalities of the land singing in harmony." But so far it is *seems* and not *is*.

Salim says that in the illusive quixotic dream may lie redemption, "a faith in the future, even if it means for now to embrace the banal present, to pick up the pieces of our wounded selves . . . because from our wounded selves flowers still grow."

Perhaps here is the real history of human effort.

Chelva Kanaganayakam

DON MILLS AND DAR ES SALAAM

No New Land
by M G Vassanji.
Toronto: McClelland and Stewart, 1991

In an essay that draws attention to the multiple fictional spaces of
writers like V S Naipaul, Sam Selvon, Cyril Dabydeen, Sonny Ladoo
and Clyde Hosein, M G Vassanji, himself a writer who occupies a
space not altogether different from those he discusses, comments on
the role of the writer:

> They complement each other in time and space, and together
> they span the literary record of a collective experience. As such
> they are like no other records. A future historian of that culture
> will have no recourse but to walk those imaginative landscapes.
> (*A Meeting of Streams*, 63)

The writer as myth maker and historian, as one who is entrusted
with the task of reclaiming and validating a past through fictive
constructs finds expression in Vassanji's first novel, *The Gunny Sack*
(1989), which traces the history of four generations of Asians in East
Africa. The reconstruction of the past now gives way, in Vassanji's
second novel, *No New Land*, to a preoccupation with the present, with
the tenants of Sixty-nine Rosecliffe Park Drive in Don Mills, whose
lives illustrate the ironies, the pathos and the hardships of having to
live between two worlds, neither of which provides the harmony of
a life that the mind imagines and craves for. On the one hand is the
memory of "home" which Haji Lalani and Missionary fondly recall
as they sit on a bench in Dar and gaze at the Indian Ocean. On the

other is the pervasive sense of futility captured in the epigraph, a quote from "The City" by C P Cavafy:

There's no new land, my friend, no
New sea; for the city will follow you,
In the same streets you'll wander endlessly

If one were to speak of what the novel is "about," it is about the immigrant population in Toronto, forced to begin a new life in a strange and often unwelcoming land, confronted with obstacles, prejudices and disillusionment. As the narrator comments, "you try different accents, practice idioms, buy shoes to raise your height. Deodorize yourself silly." For many of the characters, and certainly for Nurdin, all these prove futile. The central figure of the novel is Nurdin Lalani, a former shoe salesman in Dar es Salaam, who is forced by changing political realities to emigrate to Canada with his family. He is appalled by the lack of recognition, disillusioned by the lack of opportunity, and tormented by temptations and repeated failures. The episodic structure of the novel provides for the inclusion of a wide range of characters, the scholar Nanji, the ambitious and opportunistic lawyer Jamal, the widow Sushila, the pragmatic Romesh, the religious Zera, and so forth. Most of the characters live in the hi-rises in Don Mills, where the security of numbers provides the illusion of "home" and shelter from an alien society.

The sense of verisimilitude is one of the more striking aspects of the novel. The narrative voice, ironic and detached, provides the right balance, as the novel records a wide range of incidents, many of which drive home the reality of racism, prejudice and marginalization. And yet the referentiality is simply one aspect of the novel which often moves beyond documentary, beyond a preoccupation with the quotidian. In a memorable scene, one that intertextually recalls *The Great Gatsby*, Nurdin, responding to a question by Missionary that the plastic goddess in the lobby of the hi-rise draws attention to the absence of the male god, leads him to the window, points to the CN Tower and says: "There is our god. But he is a deep one. Mysterious." The Tower is a pervasive presence in the novel, often described in mock-religious terms that foreground its function as a symbol of "Amarapur," the promise of paradise, which always remains elusive.

The juxtaposition of the Tower and the plaster goddess points not merely to a dichotomy between the religious and the secular but also to dualities that threaten one's identity, and to values that refuse to thrive on alien soil. The flashbacks that deal with life in Dar are an early reminder that the novel is as concerned with the past as with the present. Patterns of repetition, such as Haji Lalani being slapped for looking intently at a German woman in Dar and his son later being accused of raping a woman in Toronto connect the past and the present, the private and the public. The coincidence of Nurdin's puritanical father whipping Akber for writing a letter to Sushila and years later Nurdin being tempted by Sushila (who, significantly, lives in the same neighbourhood as the girl who accuses Nurdin of molesting her) points to a deliberate undermining of the realism of the novel. The synchronic structure steers the novel away from the present to the past, to areas of experience that lie beyond the immediate referential context.

Early in the novel, the narrator points out:

We are but creatures of our origins, and however stalwartly we march, paving new roads, seeking new worlds, the ghosts from our past stand not far behind and are not easily shaken off.

The past finds expression in the puritanical Haji Lalani, whose religious fanaticism and blind adherence to a discipline instilled by the colonizers terrify the children, causing them either to leave home or internalize a sense of guilt. Nurdin, in particular, is tormented by his repressed desires, and his marginalization in Toronto is at least in part a consequence of his past. It is only when Missionary, in a wonderful gesture of transformation, exorcises the past that Nurdin becomes psychologically capable of coming to terms with the present.

Missionary remains one of the more interesting and enigmatic characters in the novel, a multiple person who combines the religious zeal of a fanatic with the pragmatism of businessman. His emigration to Canada is deliberately delayed, for when he arrives he makes it abundantly clear that the past cannot be recaptured, only moulded to suit the present.

The novel is hardly metafictional, but in the episodes that involve

Esmail the novel gets close to self-reflexivity. The metamorphosis of Esmail from baker to painter soon after he is attacked in a subway station by a teenage gang, his rejection by local critics and his subsequent decision to return to Dar and his eventual success symbolized by admiring Americans flocking to his artist's colony are obviously metonymic in intent. In some ways, Esmail is one of the few characters who succeeds, and the fabulosity that surrounds his story underscores its symbolic function.

Notions of art, audience and nation converge in the episodes that involve Esmail, and by extension they point to issues of relevance, commitment, responsibility and canonicity that relate to postcolonial writing in Canada. *No New Land* is an important work, one that foregrounds the voice of the margins,without apology or rancour. Its thematic preoccupations problematize our perception of nation and identity. In the final analysis, it compels a reassessment of the standards that govern our vision of what constitutes the canon.

WORKS CITED

Vassanji, M G. 1985. In *A Meeting of Streams*. M G Vassanji, ed. Toronto: TSAR.

Uma Parameswaran

TALKING LOUDLY

Many-Mouthed Birds:
Contemporary Writing by Chinese Canadians
edited by Bennett Lee and Jim Wong-Chu.
Vancouver: Douglas & McIntyre, 1991

This is an overdue anthology in that Chinese Canadians have lived in Canada for over a century and as a race have undergone some traumatic experiences that need to be authentically recorded. This volume contains the work of twenty Chinese Canadians whose age ranges from under ten to over fifty. Twelve of the twenty were born in Canada, three were born in Hong Kong and only two were born in mainland China. The others came to Canada via other countries. Fred Wah and Evelyn Lau are the best known of the twenty. Bennett Lee's Introduction provides a very informative background of the history and literature of the Chinese diaspora in Canada. The historical similarities between the experience and the South Asian experience are many. But this is a statement that is relevant form any immigrant groups in Canada other than those from western Europe, be they from Asia and Africa or from regions of the old Soviet Union. Settlement problems linked to language and religious differences, to racism directed form the government and from neighbours, and intergenerational gaps within the community, are parameters shared by all but the so-called founding nations; however, the cultural specifics are different for each ethnocultural group. This volume gives an overview of the specifics as experienced by Chinese Canadians, especially the racist Canadian immigration policies to curb "the yellow peril" and the Japanese takeover of Chinese provinces in the Second World War. It also shows the chasms between the first generation and second and third generations of Chinese Canadians. The new generation's reaction is extreme, either with idealized love as in Wayson Choy's "The Jade Peony" or with irreverent rebellion as in Anne Jews's "Everyone Talked Loudly in Chinatown."

Bennett Lee points out that the reason why much was not written until the last few decades is that they were, "for a long time denied full participation in Canadian society by discriminatory legislation, beginning in 1875 with disenfranchisement . . . and culminating with the exclusionary provisions of the Chinese Immigration of 1923 which in effect banned entry to Canada to all but a few Chinese." South Asian Canadian immigration and literature have followed a similar pattern.

"Many-mouthed bird" is a Chinese idiom for one who readily and indiscreetly broadcasts information that might be true but is definitely embarrassing. It takes courage for writers and editors to bring these stories into a larger market. Just as the editors have initiated a forum for identity, critics need to enunciate a critical approach to Canada's multicultural literature.

There are two aspects to the reading of writings by minority Canadians. One is the perception of the immigrant sensibility within each work, and the other is the recognition of the work as a piece of literature in which ethnoculture plays only as much part as in a white Anglo-Saxon writer's work. Please note that I am not talking of writing here but "reading." The way a minority writer is read seems to be different from the way a mainstream writer is read; in the former there is a focus on the immigrant element, sometimes to the unfair exclusion of the literary and universal elements; also, and even more unjust, some writers are labelled as "minority" and some as "mainstream" even though they might all be immigrants. Rienzi Crusz is an example of one who has had the short end of the stick on both counts. As a craftsman and artist, his poetics and poetry fall squarely into traditional "mainstream" literature but he is primarily, and often patronizingly, seen only as a minority poet speaking about immigrant themes. Michael Ondaatje, on the other hand, who like Crusz is from Sri Lanka, has been consistently seen as a mainstream writer dealing with mainstream themes. Critical reading needs to take both aspects into account—the literary/universal and the immigrant/cultur-specific.

The latter is certainly important, especially since we are in an introductory phase when different hyphenated groups are collecting their own literary records. Thus, the many-mouthed birds of these stories record simple stories about the life of the early Chinese Canadians—about Paul Yee's character, Gordon, living in the Canadian prairies in 1939, dreaming about his estate in Gum May and then realizing that "it would take more courage to return than to stay;" about Denise Chong who traces the story of her grandfather who left China in 1922 and whose daughter "left the brown coat with the velvet collar behind in Chang Gar Bin. It seemed it still belonged in China . . ."; about running restaurants and laundries—themes that in this day of controversies over cultural appropriation, no one but Chinese Canadians can write about for fear of being accused of stereotyping. This gives me pause. Do I as a non-Chinese critic have any right to say anything about this volume? I could play safe, give bland summaries, praise what is praiseworthy and omit all else, and still risk being labelled patronizing and/or ignorant.

I shall concentrate on a few of the literary/universal aspects of this volume not just to avoid the thorny issue of cultural appropriation but because I think minority writers' works deserve to be seen from the angle of art and craft as much as from the themes and content of the narratives. In this context, Jamila Ismail's poetry stands out in the anthology as a brilliant combination of innovative form and content. There are twelve pages from *Scared Texts*. All but the first page identify it as "From *Sacred Texts*." The transposition of letters might or might not be a typographic error. *Scared Texts* makes perfect sense in that the words run scared on the pages, sometimes chasing their own tails/tales, sometimes being many-mouthed birds squawking out secrets, and sometimes satirically commenting on the racist, sexist world around. However, they are sacred texts as well and for the same reasons; "just because you're scared doesn't mean this work isn't sacred." At all times though, there is a preeminence of word play that is often simultaneously sacred and profane. Lewis Carroll's Humpty Dumpty would be delighted with portmanteau words: "visiting a married couple, ivy got all wisteria about couples. / cypress observed . . ." Current events are satirically encapsulated, Tianenmen Square in: "cabbage said: the students were unreasonable. of course, / that's not how newspapers sell, but many folks in chinese / street think so. the gummint [government] had already been so patient . . ." and Rajiv Gandhi in: "the newspapers were full of praise about a head of state. / gee, periwinked, is he really squeaky clean as all the journalists / say, ohyes, peregrinned, rats squeak."

Two other pieces that were experimental in form are Evelyn Lau's "Glass" and Ben Soo's "The Water Story." Evelyn Lau ran to fame with her *Runaway: Diary of a Street Kid*. "Glass" is a horrific story of double entendre, where the narrator sees "her" after she has put her fist through the window of her apartment. "You see now why I worry about her," says the narrator of her double, over whom she has no control. "The Water Story" is a panorama of Canadian landscape, as masculine in its imagery as "Glass" is feminine.

In conclusion, *Many-Mouthed Birds* is a powerful and moving collection of Chinese Canadian writings that should be on every library shelf.

Ramabai Espinet

THE OLD AND THE NEW

The Innocence of Age
by Neil Bissoondath.
Toronto: Knopf, 1992

The title is intriguingly postmodern but that is probably the only thing postmodern about this curiously wooden account of what the publisher's blurb acclaims as a "gallery of vivid, unforgettable characters—the immigrants, the cops, the streetwalkers . . . the skinheads who roam the parks."

Vivid and unforgettable this no-name parade of characters in an equally generic late twentieth-century city are not. The mention of the Sky Dome, street names such as Yonge, Dundas and Broadview, and the Don river locate the novel in Toronto. But whatever fictive geometry lends authenticity to characterization, to locus, and involves readers (and authors, maybe) in the life of the page is singularly absent from this 308-page novel. The long arm of coincidence, however, is disconcertingly present.

In fact, after the first few pages it occurred to me that it was not a novel at all. This may be an attempt at a screenplay utilizing the sitcom technique of hanging an instantly recognizable label on a character. How else, indeed, can one distinguish these flat subjects except by raising them into relief by means of name-tags?

So, the opening gambit finds us in the Starting Gate with Pasco and his friends. We are introduced to Pushpull, the "wanker" or "jerk-off artist;" Marcus who wades through the novel trying to convince one of his buddies to accompany him and his wife on a shopping trip to Buffalo (Gimme a break, for God's sake); Montgomery the black postman; Cruise, the aging hippie; and Pasco himself, the greasy-spoon proprietor whose relationship with his son Danny (Dano) is tentatively prodded and probed from a distance throughout the course of this flattened narrative.

The introduction of Cruise provides opportunity for a level of banality rarely seen in print. For example:

> He had been a Rochdale radical in the sixties: grass for the taking, sex for the asking, philosophy and politics lurking around every corner. He claimed to have particularly enjoyed arguing Kierkegaard while "banging away during group gropes." . . . And then one day a girl claimed the ultimate freedom by launching herself off the roof without a parachute . . . There was nothing sadder, he'd once told Pasco, than a handful of hippies standing around watching the broken body of one of their friends . . .

Bissoondath has been fairly vocal of late about the issue of "appropriation," arguing that to limit a writer's imagination to the experiential is nothing but censorship. The "experiential" however, defined in its broadest possible connotations, gives life to nouns and verbs on a page. The passage quoted above aptly illustrates what happens when the experience of the imagination is not equal to the task it appropriates.

There is some sort of philosophy of living which permeates not only this novel, but all of Bissoondath's work. It is expressed at length whenever there is a pause in the action, and is also summarized at the beginning of *A Casual Brutality:*

> There are times when the word *hope* is but a synonym for *illusion*: it is the most virile of perils. He who cannot discern the difference—he whose perception of reality has slipped from *him*, whose appreciation of honesty has withered within him—will face, at the end, a fine levied, with no appeal, with only regret coating the memory like ash.

V S Naipaul himself says it far more succinctly in 1979 in *A Bend in the River*:

THE WORLD is what it is; men who are nothing, who allow themselves to become nothing, have no place in it.

In fact the major concern of this novel predicates the father-son relationship as turning upon the conflicting values of the old and the new. The old signifies permanence, nostalgia and a somewhat stick-in-the-mud sense of continuity while the new embraces disruption, change, urgency—all culminating in a dubious kind of success. One of the novel's virtues may be the adroitness with which Bissoondath does manage to show how Mr Simmons, the wealthy landlord, has achieved his success by simplifying existence down to one or two symbols and codes upon which he relies absolutely. His formula for success is unwavering fidelity to that which works. This does work technically but engagement with the character is absent and the reader is left uninterested in the insight.

A more engaging interlude is the one-night stand between Danny and a young woman who attempts to continue the intimacy the morning after. The perspective is Danny's and the cringing of the male from the unwanted feminine intimacies of breakfast and small talk as well as the young woman's pain and eventual recovery in disdain are both finely accomplished. The unfolding of the relationship between Pasco and his neighbour Lorraine is also handled with some sensitivity.

In the characterization of Sita, on the other hand, an Indo-Caribbean refugee, Bissoondath is able to achieve no particularity. She wanders through the old house, Simmons's personal and sexual slave, and her act of murder is as pointless as it is incomprehensible. It is as inauthentic as the account of Montgomery's runaway daughter Nutmeg, who changes her name to Spice when she begins to work the streets alongside a white friend named? Sugar, what else ?

Perhaps the most distressing portrait, in terms of current Toronto everyday politics, is the trivializing of the shooting of Montgomery, the black postman turned loony because of his daughter's betrayal of her parents' hopes. Montgomery is shot by the police. Eventually, Montgomery's son, a Ryerson engineering student and also an unmistakable nerd, arrives at the Starting Gate to sermonize about his version of events to his late father's friends. He laments the fact that his mother and sister have fallen under the influence of activists involved in demonstrations and press conferences. The young man laments: "They see a racist under every bed. One of 'em even told my sister that having a white skin automatically means you're a racist . . If they didn't have us, I don't know what they'd do. They'd be nobodies." What is the young man's analysis of the situation? Does he think that his engineering degree will protect him and his children from all of the various consequences of having a black skin in a city such as Toronto?

The stockpiling of disparate incidents in the life of a city can work if the city itself forms the living canvas upon which these random events come together. But the absence of specificity in place, event, character, incident and language leads into a peculiar state of drift where, at the end, one is not sure what one has read. A series of unrelated headlines, maybe? Not as the blurb points out: "a vibrant novel of a city and its people," but a characterless meandering in and out of a series of words.

Uma Parameswaran

THE LANDSCAPE OF MEMORY

Lion's Granddaughter and Other Short Stories
by Yasmin Ladha.
Edmonton, Alberta: NeWest Press, 1992

Yasmin's Ladha's collection of short stories draws in the reader in several ways. The author's Tanzanian background addresses an important aspect and asset of contemporary Canadian literature in that it expands our horizons to include a geographical landscape that is other than a geographical Canada. As I have said in one of my essays, though the landscape around me is spruce and maple, the landscape of memory is treed with mangoes and banyan, and the contribution of South Asian Canadians is that we bring Ganga to the Assiniboine not only for ourselves but for our fellow Canadian. Stories such as "Aisha" and "Lion's Granddaughter" bring East African landscapes and lifestyles to life.

Especially in the title story, we hear again the tunes and tones that spanned the world through the mission-school education that was the legacy of the Raj, taught by authoritarian white Anglo schoolteachers that we have seen in the works of Achebe, in the African stories of Margaret Laurence, in *Midnight's Children*. The Rushdie connection is established through the author-reading dialogue in the first story "Beena." The British nineteenth-century apostrophe "Dear Reader" is replaced with "Readerji" and "Yaar Reader." I see three phases in the way non-Western writers have handled words and phrases from their native cultures. These phases are chronological in the total picture but contemporary writers fit into different phases dependng on where they are at or from in their art. In the first phase, every book had a glossary. In the second phase, there was no glossary but the author explicated the word or phrase within the context. Achebe's *Arrow of God* is a good example of this strategy. Rohinton Mistry uses this strategy in his volume of short stories and in his recent novel, *Such a Long Journey.* In the third phase, there is neither glossary nor explication; the author assumes it is the reader's responsibility to work at the meanings. Rushdie does this, and his only allowance is to italicize the borrowed words. Ladha follows the Rushdie approach, combining it in the later stories with well placed explications within the context. The first story works, and makes the reader work, a little too hard at these reader-author interaction and coinages, but I suppose it is necessary in order to set up the rest of the volume in context.

Ladha's voice is that of a feminist, "my *shakti* power" as she call it. "Giving up the Company of Women" is a fine example of Ladha's shakti power. I choose it over others because I am at a phase where I am drawn to Canadian connections, where I focus only on those facets of a work that address our Canadian linkages. This is a conscious reaction to the average Canadian reviewer's tendency to focus on the exoticism of South Asian Canadians' writing to the exclusion of our Canadianness.

Yasmin Ladha is obviously versed in current crit-lit jargon, and plays it to advantage in this story to make her woman-voice poweful. She herself invokes Rushdie on the first page of the story. "When Rushdie Saab comes home. I will knead flour with flying fingers . . ." for as she says later in the story after narrating episodes of women shamed and abused, "Out of her looms Rushdie's Sufiya Zinobia . . . Such stories of woman shape/shame." The narrator of this story is an Indo-Canadian and she makes a broadside attack on various aspects of the experiences and emerging philosophies of women's lives and women's voices in Canada. To end with the only negative comment I have, Ladha is all too student-Canadian in some of her idioms and usages; for example, the use of "I" for "me" in "Egg-shell virginity / between you and I / mosaic hymen."

Frank Birbalsingh

THE WRITE IMMIGRANT

Jogging in Havana
by Cyril Dabydeen.
Oakville: Mosaic Press, 1992

The Ghost of Bellow's Man
by Sasenarine Persaud.
Leeds: Peepal Tree Press, 1992

These two books come from the two most productive Indo-Caribbean writers now living in Canada. Cyril Dabydeen is better established, the author of eight volumes of poetry and two novels. *Jogging in Havana* is his third collection of stories, and he has edited two anthologies of ethnic Canadian writing as well. By comparison Sasenarine Persaud may be regarded as a beginner, even if a promising one: *The Ghost of Bellow's Man* is his second novel, and he also has a volume of poems to his credit.

Jogging in Havana contains some of Dabydeen's best fiction so far, despite the fact that stories in the volume employ many themes, situations and linguistic strategies found in his previous work. The dominant theme remains Canadianization or the process of cultural adaptation and mixing that ethnic immigrants to Canada must undergo before achieving nationality in a more complex cultural rather than a simply political sense.

One of the more successful stories "The Rink" is about a black West Indian immigrant, George, who makes strenuous efforts learning to ice skate, while his wife Ida and his friends constantly mock him and suggest, sneeringly, that he might do better to stick to the popular

West Indian sport of cricket. As Ida puts it, "But George, you can't blasted well able to skate! You, a black man trying to do a white thing. It isn't the sport fo' you" (p. 123). In inimitably succinct and pungent creole idiom, Ida neatly sums up the dilemma of cultural adaptation faced by all immigrants to Canada and especially by those who are ethnic or non-white. But at the end of the story, when George's daughter is "skating, pirouetting, as if she was born with skates on" (125), it is clear that George's Canadianization has taken an inevitable step - his integration into Canadian culture through his children who are effortlessly Canadian in a way that he can never be.

Themes of displacement and exile, and racial and cultural integration are found in most stories in this volume whether they apply specifically to Canada or not. "Relations" and "God Save the Queen" are set in Guyana and deal with rural scenes of great tropical beauty that are disfigured by poverty, deprivation and family violence. In other stories, immigrant narrators who live in Canada reflect on the fate of their relations or friends in the Caribbean or elsewhere. In "Ain't Got No Cash" the Guyanese narrator who has immigrated to Canada visits a fellow Guyanese in New York where they discuss interethnic, crosscultural relations that evolve out of colonialism, migration and exile.

In perhaps the best story in the volume, "A Plan is a Plan," black Caribbean immigrants discuss life for immigrants in Canada, especially sexual relations between blacks and whites. But the story's distinction relies less on Fanonesque revelations about interracial sexual relations than on the vigour of its creole language. On the whole, the stories in *Jogging in Havana* tend to support the view that Dabydeen's writing could benefit from more frequent and more enthusiastic use of creole speech and narrative.

Dabydeen is adept at condensed characterization, pithy description and palatable dialogue, standard skills of a short-story writer. Often he injects elements of humour or mystery chiefly with the aim to entertain rather than expose or criticize. In the title story, for instance, we get excellent sketches of people, places and issues, as foreign academics travel to Cuba and sample Castro's socialism at first hand. Yet there is little passion in the story, which is content to evoke, without judging, the mixed reactions and varied, often contradictory impressions that come out of academic discussions and tourism in a milieu universally known for its socialist rhetoric.

Such objectivity insinuates a distinct documentary flavour to Dabydeen's writing, one in which the external features of situations are faithfully reproduced without any real desire to investigate too deeply. This suggests that in its treatment of displacement, cultural mixing, and the integration of immigrants into Canada, Dabydeen's writing itself appears to undergo a process of integration by moving gradually away from its lively, variegated Caribbean sources in terms of characters, settings and language, towards situations in a mainly Canadian environment that is less lively, more subdued and noncommittal in tone. Because of this movement, *Jogging in Havana*, and Dabydeen's writing as a whole might carry as a subtitle "The Writer as Immigrant."

*

Dabydeen was born in Guyana and migrated to Canada in 1970. Sasenarine Persaud, also born in Guyana, came to Canada more than fifteen years later. Not surprisingly therefore, Persaud's two novels *The Ghost of Bellow's Man* and *Dear Death* (1989) show less overt interest in the theme of Canadianization. Instead, both novels are studiously devoted to the Indo-Caribbean community in Guyana, where the author steadfastly explores Hindu religious and social issues that seem to preoccupy him deeply.

The action of *The Ghost of Bellow's Man* takes place largely in Turnerville, a fictional name no doubt for Georgetown the actual capital city of Guyana. The novel is partly a roman à clef with not only places but also its characters carrying the thinly disguised names of recognizable places and people in Guyana. The time is 1982 when the rule or dictatorship of Fox Burton—alias Forbes Burnham, the real-life ruler of Guyana from 1964 to 1985—is marked by social chaos, food shortages, and personal, political and religious rivalries. Everything is presented through the eyes of Raj, the young, Hindu narrator who teaches at a secondary school named South City High. The school's name is again a thinly veiled alias for an actual Guyanese high school, most probably Indian Educational Trust, and Raj's portrait of his obsequious, unprincipled and cunning headmaster Salim Sheik is one of the best things in the novel.

The social and political background of confusion and corruption in *The Ghost of Bellow's Man* is combined with the narrator's reflections on his writing career, and his involvement in a dispute over the introduction of chairs into the Hindu temple where he worships.

This makes for a somewhat self-regarding narrative in which the narrator's personal opinions and preoccupations are heard in a persistent monotone that reports, analyses and pre-digests the entire action of the novel. Consequently the narrator's point of view emerges as unquestioned, olympian, irrefutable.

One problem of this point of view is that it makes the novel less accessible to readers who are non-Guyanese or non-Hindu or both. The central issue, for instance, between those who support the introduction of chairs into the temple and those, like the narrator and his friends, who do not, seriously divides the Hindu community; but its significance is not fully explained, and the reader does not feel the sense of violation and desecration that the issue evidently causes to some Hindus. The reader is thus likely to lose interest in a central episode of the novel unless he or she shares in the unquestioned, implicit assumption of Hindu universalism that the narrative appears to expect.

It should be emphasized that the failure noted here is one of technique, not of the treatment of the religious issue. R K Narayan has written superb novels about Hinduism and Graham Greene about Roman Catholicism. V S Naipaul too, who is mentioned dismissively in the book, also deals with Hindu themes in his fiction. In Naipaul's celebrated novel *A House for Mr Biswas*, for example, when the young Biswas befouls pundit Jaram's oleander tree with human refuse so that the leaves can no longer be used in religious devotions, the reader does not fail to understand the sense of pollution and violation caused by young Biswas. But such is the intricate subtlety and extraordinary skill of Naipaul's writing that without resorting to any obvious indelicacy like using the word "shit," he is able to convey humour, irony, tragedy and comedy all at once, and absolutely without any pseudomystification or jiggery-pokery. Perhaps it is unfair to contrast *The Ghost of Bellow's Man* with one of the finest novels of the twentieth century. But Persaud's dismissive references to Naipaul in *The Ghost of Bellow's Man* should not go unanswered, even though they contradict his publisher's claim of Naipaul's "complexity of vision" in his book.

Persaud's first novel, which considers Hindu notions of transcendentalism, suffers from a similar poverty of narrative interest as found in *The Ghost of Bellow's Man*. In a review of *Dear Death*, Florence Ramdin has said, "The pressure of carrying through the author's theme falls chiefly on the prologue and epilogue . . . Each incident is self-contained, not dependent on following events for added depth or clarity. This detracts from the author's theme which the   reader tends to lose for lengths of time during the course of the novel."

These comments imply the same indulgent, authorial assertiveness which has already been noted and which tends to convert Persaud's two narratives into virtual monologues on the arcane mysteries and apparently inviolable truths of his idiosyncratic brand of Hindu belief.

To his credit Persaud shows some evidence of self-examination in his narrator's reflections on his writing career. The following passage is revealing:

> In the depths of this night I ask myself why do I write all this? A record for posterity? Because I feel that, as a writer, one day this will come in useful somewhere along the line as material for a novel? Enough. I can't wait for Friday, having time to dangle on my delusions of self-importance, "all for justice and justice for all." The war cannot be won until I'm there to win it! Seize the Day! (112)

Such confessional incertitude is winning, but it would be more effective were it not diluted with too obvious references to the writing of Saul Bellow. "Dangle" recalls the title of Bellow's first novel *Dangling Man*, and *Seize the Day* is the title of his fourth novel. Apart from that, Persaud's title contains Bellow's name, and in the second to last paragraph of *The Ghost of Bellow's Man*, his narrator feels like a "ghost" presumably of Bellow's "Dangling Man." The same paragraph also mentions that Henderson was "making rain in Africa" a reference to Bellow's fifth novel *Henderson the Rain King*. Another reference, "Raju, the corrupt tourist guide in India," is to R K Narayan's novel *The Guide*. Such excessive name-dropping invites suspicion of parasitism which has a cancelling effect on the merits of his book. For there is no connection between *The Ghost of Bellow's Man* and Bellow's perceptive, compassionate and humane study of the fragile and attenuated consciousness of people in the second half of the twentieth century. Nor is there any resemblance between Persaud's book and the loving celebration of enduring Hindu values for which Narayan's fiction is justly famous.

Despite these strictures against *The Ghost of Bellow's Man*, the novel shows signs of improved technique over *Dear Death*. Its social and political background is more vivid, and there is an occasional note of lyricism in some descriptions. Persaud's excellent control of creole idiom and expression is a wonderful resource which, like Dabydeen, he mysteriously underuses. Perhaps he too is becoming victim to the writer-as-immigrant syndrome in Canada.

Sumana Sen-Bagchee

BEING AND BECOMING

Her Mother's Ashes and Other Stories
by South Asian Women in Canada and the United States
edited by Nurjehan Aziz.
Toronto: TSAR, 1994

In recent years TSAR has brought out several well-focussed anthologies, *Shakti's Words* (1990), *The Geography of Voice* (1992) and *Domains of Fear and Desire* (1992), which have all demonstrated the ability to satisfy both the general reader and the academic. *Her Mother's Ashes and Other Stories*, edited by Nurjehan Aziz, maintains standards that more than meet our expectations. It is a delightful collection of short fiction by South Asian women in North America, with stories that explore marvelously different depths and heights of feminine experience. Also, in this volume TSAR has come up with a collection that changes certain givens about the practice of anthologizing in Canada. First, *Her Mother's Ashes* erases the usually retained boundaries between Canada and the United States. The twenty contributors featured here are somewhat too neatly and equally chosen: ten of them live and work in America. This erasure of boundary is a decidedly healthy decision by the editor, particularly at a time when "zoning" in anthologies often becomes an excuse for narrow, and sometimes needless, privileging of particular groups. In an age of cross-border shopping, a volume like *Her Mother's Ashes* defines its space rather appropriately by juxtaposing stories by South Asian women writers from various contexts in North America. It ably demonstrate the commendable range and variety of the writers' talents. The stories in this volume will certainly alert the reader to the fact that the term "South Asian" is rather broad and certainly does not imply any sort of cosy homogeneity; they will also counter the conventional Western tendency to overlook the many subtle and even some not-so-subtle differences among South Asians.

This anthology demonstrates yet another disregard for convention, and in doing so exhibits laudable editorial discretion, as it excludes some near-canonical names in South Asian women's writing, notably Bharati Mukherjee and Anita Desai. Instead, it makes room for seldom-anthologized but promising writers like Hema Nair and Tahira Naqvi. This exclusion further accentuates the notion of "difference," because it also breaks the pattern of predictability in anthologies such as this. The sheer range of writers here is noteworthy, and the informed reader will find that nearly every possible category of that umbrella group, "South Asian women," has been represented. I say "informed reader" because there is much in these stories that bear upon what Arun Mukherjee in her Introduction calls the "specificities" of the South Asian identity. For instance, a story like "AIDSwallah" by Feroza Jussawalla revolves around Zoroastrian concerns about purity and cleanliness, which are quite distinct, say, from the usual Hindu strictures on untouchability. The volume will also offer many interesting and surprising nuances of South Asian lives as reflected in stories by immensely diverse writers with origins in Pakistan, the Philippines, East and South Africa, Trinidad and India.

Readers of "immigrant Indian literature" will be relieved to see that this editor has steered clear of the usual "nostalgia and regret" mode, and there is, instead, a refreshing variety. Even in the piece by Himani Bannerji, whose work is usually characterized by an insistent agenda of race and gender issues, one is pleasantly surprised to find the anguish of lonely women in an alien surrounding being foregrounded over the racial, or even exclusively gender, implication of the situation. When Debi Bardhan of Calcutta loses herself in the near anonymity of Debbie Barton, she still does not quite realize what she has relinquished. But the corpse of another Indian girl who commits suicide suddenly alerts her to her namelessness as she begins to identify with the girl and her loneliness. And even if there are incidents in which Debi is called a "fucking Paki" and moments when she feels "invisible," the pivotal moments are those in which she can recover her identity through the dead woman's. Here is a powerfully evocative story in which the images of the corpse, and of the zombielike protagonist, both give startling significance to the solitude of immigrant women.

The predicament of the single or lonely girl in North America, a recurring motif in several pieces, however, takes some interesting shapes in this collection. For example, the opening story, "Why Am I Doing This?" by Hema Nair, is about Vijaya, "thirty-two years old, working in a bustling small town in the United States and living in her two-bedroom apartment, paid for by her earnings as a physical therapist." But Vijaya's life of near-perfect adjustment to the North American mode hides two deep scars: her "tortuous divorce" in India from a philandering husband, and her recently developed habit of "spending her evenings stealing from the mall." Vijaya's deviant behaviour, we realize, is a result of her loneliness. She misses the "huge umbrella of relatives" that protects her Chinese friend Nina Wang and, unlike Margy, she has no boyfriend to fill her empty hours. Vijaya, in spite of her "condo" and career, still is a misfit in the West. She is laughed at when she mispronounces UPS as "ups" and she thinks being called "Mowgli girl" by her patient, Mr Kerr, is a compliment.

But then again, in this collection with its rich variety of themes and styles, not all stories about the single girl are similar. In Nazneen Sheikh's "American Date," the seventeen-year-old Pakistani protagonist discovers to her chagrin that her all-American date, Blond Burt, captain of the football team at Sunset High, "really like[s] boys, but asked [her] for a date to look good." This must be one of the most sparkling pieces in this collection; the wit in the surprising ending is balanced by the narrator's voice as she posits herself between the culturally innocent Pakistani girl and the normally excitable teenager slipping off her girdle in anticipation of the high point of a first date. A skillful blend of the comic and the tender makes this a highly enjoyable story.

Similarly, Tahira Naqvi's "Love in an Election Year" is remarkable for its ironic yet humorous depiction of the dulling of a daring, romantic young woman into a "fat and dour" matron. Or there is Bapsi Sidhwa's satiric-comic narrative about the new-immigrant wife discovering the actual naivete hidden behind her Americanized husband's know-it-all facade. The editor's fine sense of balance and judgement is evident from the generous mix of these humorous stories and others which, I think, reflect the more sombre mood of the anthology's title. That is, while there is a decidedly healthy departure from the "immigrant's lament" tone of far too much diaspora literature, this is still an anthology based in memory, and more particularly, in a preoccupation with the issue of "who we are"(xiv).

But defining "who we are" is more intricate for some as Uma Parameswarn suggests in "Freeze Frame." In that story a group of Canadian- and Indian-born women meet to "celebrate" the impending divorce of a friend. The unanimity of their feminism and of their other liberal ideas is abruptly fractured when a younger woman in the group admits that she is saddened by the news. Her admission draws out the same emotions from Maru, an older member of the party. Although she is not yet ready to admit the fact, what Maru discovers in her thoughts is a seepage from her past, a culturally authentic notion of love and marriage that her current social perspective too easily regards as "outdated." I found Parameswaran's story to provide an interesting variation on the theme of marriage and the immigrant woman in North America.

There is a wide range of stories here about marriage, the breakdown of marriage or of women strengthening their marriages through their sensitivity and wit. But the reader will be satisfied to find that whatever the context, the question of a woman's self-knowledge or her empowerment cannot always be answered in terms of pat Western feminist theories. Indeed, there are intriguingly different treatments of the theme in some of these stories which testify that the formulaic hardly works for all women, even when they are ethnically related.

I cannot end this review without mentioning some of the pieces in this collection which are remarkable for their style and their artistic excellence, and the widely acclaimed novelist Meena Alexander's "No Name Woman" easily comes to mind. This reads, in parts, like a prose poem and has a richly woven texture made up of a woman's memories of several countries and continents. Another very well-crafted story is Roshni Rustomji-Kerns's "A Memory of Names," also based on a woman's life of migrations and cross-migrations between India, France, England, Mexico, America, and Guatemala. She has stories from all these places but has no memories of either a birthplace or a birth mother.

Finally, I must say, *Her Mother's Ashes and Other Stories* will capture the reader's attention with its eclecticism and its unconventionality.

Krisantha Sri Bhaggiyadatta

HEARTS AND MINDS

Funny Boy
by Shyam Selvadurai.
Toronto: McClelland & Stewart, 1994

Shyam Selvadurai's *Funny Boy*, a novel written in six stories, is an honest and riveting retelling of a boy's growing up during the last two decades of turmoil in Sri Lanka. The book comes out at a time when that country is trying to come to grips with the legacy of violence and authoritarianism. Selvadurai's openhearted rendering of the scarring events, their reverberations, the *small choices* made among a particular set of people, seems especially poignant, as the country attempts the process of healing and rebuilding.

The strength of *Funny Boy* comes out of the author's skillful capacity to take the reader through the boy Arjie Chelvaratnam's gradual uncovering of an adult world beset with violence, betrayal and sacrifice, thus compelling us to look at realities in horrific yet almost ordinary detail.

While recounting a child's awakening, *Funny Boy* also subtly and unobtrusively touches the more traumatic political moments in the island's recent past: the production and dissemination of racism among children and through the schools, the state-organized pogroms from 1977-83, disappearance, torture and the Prevention of Terrorism Act, the 1982 Jayawardene referendum to thwart elections, and the dispersal of thousands of people across the globe.

The power in the writing of Selvadurai, now based in Toronto, comes not simply from his ability to simply recollect memories, but to select particular words, nuances, gestures, characters and events that point to an organic coherence. And while the stories don't follow exact history, the organization of the stories seems almost to follow a curriculum for sociology: gender, compulsory heterosexuality, racism, the national security state and terrorism.

Despite these heavy topics, critics have called *Funny Boy*, nominated for the 1994 Giller Prize, seamless and easy to read, which is a tribute to the author's craft; but, particularly if you're Sri Lankan, the events which are written about are most difficult and painful, and many was the time I closed the book to weep.

Even for someone given to tears only on windy, wintery days or in darkened movie theatres or out of overwhelming powerless rage, the book's reading tended to be punctuated with weeping, weeping for a beautiful land and weeping for a people blighted by imperialism and war. At the same time the novel evokes common experience—oh how painfully familiar—children sculpted and disfigured, and yes, supported, by extended families and friends, the pedagogy of a still colonized school system, and how the world, the state particularly, breaks in, burns, mauls and molds—or certainly tries to.

While much is yet to be written in a novel way of the incredible violence unleashed, *Funny Boy* joins a spate of novels and short-story collections about Sri Lanka/ns published internationally recently— Yasmine Gooneratne's novel on Sri Lankans in Australia, *A Change of Skies* (Penguin); Carl Muller's boy's clubby paean to the Burghers of Sri Lanka, *The Jam Fruit Tree* (Penguin); Gamini Salgado's posthumously published *True Paradise* (Carcanet/Rupa); Romesh Gunasekera's justly acclaimed collection *Monkfish Moon* (Granta); and the Booker-nominated *Reef* (Penguin)—I believe *Funny Boy* is the first novel published abroad and in English that focuses on the "ethnic conflict" in Sri Lanka. Too bad the book is available to English readers only

Sri Lankans, Tamil and Sinhala, and Sri Lanka, hit the world news in a big way in 1983, and perhaps for the first time dented Canadian consciousness through the usual "third-worldese" reportage of shops and bodies burning in uncountable collectivities; "Tamils, terrorism and Tigers" joined the old key words for Sri Lanka: tea, tourism and trinkets. Invariably, news items from the corporate wire services (e.g. Reuter, AP) since then have carried in their "origins paragraph," the so-called history of the problem: that the majority Sinhalese, Aryan and Buddhist, have been fighting the minority Tamils, Dravidian and

Hindu, interminably for centuries. (The effect of such simplicities reappear in the reviews of Selvadurai's book)

Canadian conscience was presumably challenged further when, in August 1985, two boats of refugees were abandoned off the coast of Newfoundland, and the Canadian corporate media switched into full gear, disgracing itself further by blurring the distinction of immigrant and refugee, portraying refugees from Sri Lanka as aliens, liars, economic migrants and the like.

Funny Boy gently yet surely gives the lie to the name-calling with its account of July 1983, in "A Riot Journal: An Epilogue." While the characterization of the pogroms as a riot is controversial (to Selvadurai's credit, the account mentions that thugs were provided voting lists), I would certainly recommend this book to the immigration department and the refugee hunters. I also liked the fact that the story showed that some people were aware that leaving Sri Lanka was not a passage to freedom or anything like the West is usually portrayed as or likes to portray itself as.

The stories show people confused and torn, forced to deal with identities so recently constructed that we've never had to examine them before in such a searing light. By speaking to our common humanity, *Funny Boy* joins the canon of literature written about communalism, that time-bomb legacy of European colonialism. And considering the terrible problems of coming up with a "balanced" portrayal, given the preponderance of armed critics, Selvadurai has managed to treat all Sri Lankans, sometimes even the villains, in a decent and loving way.

Funny Boy also shows nuance and complexity in how it portrays both communities, as in "Radha Aunty," which depicts the contradictions of essentializing ethnicities, ultimately portraying real people caught in horrible matrices. Lovers from different communities are torn apart by the rising tensions. In this story, it is Janaki, the Sinhalese domestic, who reminds Radha, who is Tamil, about the reasons behind the family's objections to Radha being friendly with a Sinhalese man.

> Janaki sighed and said, "You were too young to remember when they brought the body home . . . It was as if someone had taken the lid of a tin can and cut pieces out of him."

226

I stared at Janaki in shock.
"I know, I know," Radha Aunty said, brushing aside Janaki's remarks. "But is that a reason to hate all Sinhalese?" (59)

At the same time, in "Small Choices," a young man from Jaffna realizes it's too dangerous to remain in Colombo. Without glorifying the LTTE, the story shows why people have had to choose armed resistance.

In "Pigs Can't Fly," Arjie Chelvaratnam discovers the word "funny" has a third, non dictionary definition, a new meaning. He is thus isolated out of the playful world of siblings and cousins, fingered as a "faggot," interestingly enough by a young cousin just returned from England, full of the essentializing verbiage educated Westerners are capable of. In the ensuing attempt to straighten him out, the mother is blamed (as the latest silly report from the Clarke Institute of Psychiatry in Toronto will concur): "You're the one who lets him come in here while you're dressing and play with the jewellery" (15). In what is surely the most brilliant scene in the story, perhaps the book, the boy is banished from the mother's bedroom, as from a womb, from the realm of innocence and childhood.

Arjie, after describing with mystery and awe his occasional ritual of watching the making up, through cloth and paint, jewel and aromatic, is confronted with a closed door. A door he cannot enter, and a door his mother cannot open:

> "I waited patiently, thinking . . . Amma had forgotten, I knocked timidly on the door. She did not answer, but I could hear her moving around inside . . . I crept away . . . It was clear to me I had done something wrong, but what it was I couldn't comprehend. Later . . . as I listened to the sound of her voice, I realised that something had changed forever between us." (16-17)

Banished from a world he loves, he flees to the edges of the island, to the possibilities, the ocean nearby and the beautiful earth; sky and waves take on a menacing mien: the turquoise blue sea of the early evening becomes, under the midday sun, "a hard silver, so bright it hurt my eyes." (38)

In interviews, Selvadurai has had to point out that he is not only gay, he is also an upper-middle-class Tamil male from a certain part of Colombo. In the few published interviews I saw the tired binaries of "Are you a writer who is black or a black writer"—in this case "gay"—were posited and denied. In one review much copy was spent on how he was discovered, and by whom, much of the review, along with its gay Sri Lankan titling, taking on a Livingstonian (or is it Columbian) tenor of dark discovery. The book cover doesn't help with its North Indian typography and its references to "haunting" "passages," "discovery" and "dangerous and unfamiliar territory."

Still, characterized within the canon of *The Empire Writes Back*, writers in English who write in the West and for the West are still bridled by the need of marketeers to provide a stable of entertainers, interpreters, informers and assuagers, not to mention the mimics and the bewilderers.

While *Funny Boy* does entertain and explain (there's a glossary for the Lankanisms), the problem of criticizing the book is that it is written through the eyes of a young boy and well, when the narrator sticks to his immediate experience, one can only say he saw what he saw. He offers a glimpse of the repression of the majority of the people—not so much Sinhala or Tamil but rural—as in "See No Evil Hear No Evil," when his mother and he go to a village in search of a witness. But generally, while his narrative traverses important moments, other underpinnings to the conflict, like economic and class issues, are less apparent. Stories spawned by the imposition of market economy in the 1980s, with mass firings of workers and the accelerated uprootment of rural people, await another book. (Considering the Booker (Sugar) Corporation's collusion in rural displacement, such a book probably won't be published internationally, let alone get their literary prize.)

Still, *Funny Boy* excels in its focus on the ethnic conflict, by writing a very detailed personal, yet not so atomized and individualized, account of growing up amidst turbulent political changes. Beyond that, it neatly writes our own dark desiring bodies into the story of what is called politics, history, etc.

In graduation from "The Best School of All," Arjie pays tribute to his Sinhalese pal and lover's courage, when he wonders at all the gay kids, imprisoned in silence, who had passed through the hallowed walls of his school. To that end Arjie speaks of writing for his life. "All

I can do is write," he says, record the horror, the kind that passes for everyday ordinariness, and crescendoes into the apocalypse that unfolds and tears people apart.

Sri Lankans, as the rest of the world, disinformed and deceived by international and internal information systems, yearn for a/the truth to be told, for one strong narrative that would bind our terrible sadnesses and stalwart strivings into a contestatory testament for liberation that would not make our suffering useless, and at the same time make them of the past.

In the meantime, however, not always to our liking, the narratives continue to arrive ruptured, unbound and in fragments, but surprisingly, sometimes, in subtle yet impassioned evocation of what we witness. *Funny Boy*, through its candour and integrity, leads the way in putting together hearts and minds, the soul, and yes, the body.

Diana Brydon

WHAT MATTERS

Oppositional Aesthetics: Readings From a Hyphenated Space
by Arun Mukherjee.
Toronto: TSAR, 1994

Arun Mukherjee is one of the most exciting critics working in Canada today. What a pleasure, then, to discover that her important book, *Towards an Aesthetic of Opposition: Essays on Literature, Criticism and Cultural Imperialism* (Williams-Wallace 1988), has been reissued in an attractive new format that includes some of her more recent articles as well. Readers interested in exploring alternative readings of Canadian culture and in understanding the politics implicit in the universalist canon have long been frustrated to discover that *Towards an Aesthetic of Opposition* was out of print. As one of the fortunate owners of a copy, I can attest to how often I find myself turning back to it to remind myself of what really matters, of why I choose to teach literature in a university, and why it is important to keep insisting on the political interestedness of what the dominant media present as "common sense" or "human nature." Countless students have borrowed this book and subsequently cited it in their efforts to expand its insights into new directions of inquiry. They too will welcome its reissue within an expanded and altered format.

Mukherjee was among the first in Canada to raise the questions now associated with the more progressive tendencies of postcolonial theory: questions about power, value, and the discursive strategies of cultural imperialism. Essays such as "The Vocabulary of the 'Universal'," "Ideology in the Classroom," and "The Third World in the Dominant Western Cinema" are classic investigations of crucial issues still underexamined in Canadian literary and cultural studies.

These essays are essential starting points for further work in these interconnected fields. Mukherjee crosses the boundaries between popular and elitist culture, showing the ideological links that bind them, and that form the unexamined ground for classroom discussion. She argues for a more activist and engaged form of critical practice that goes beyond formalism to connect writing and the world.

As she put it in her original introduction:

> The stance of these essays is confrontational, not out of choice but out of necessity. I have tried to point out how the dominant discourse in North America dehistoricizes and depoliticizes everything so that non-white, non-male, working-class ways of apprehending reality seldom get a hearing. (6)

This clear, no-nonsense approach is typical of her style. Her writing is energetic and incisive. She displays a devastating ability to home in on the heart of an issue, identifying what is really at stake in a debate or in a work of fiction and refusing to be positioned by the assumptions of those whom she opposes. She is at her best in bringing a fresh perspective to works that Canadian specialists may have thought we knew inside out, as in her reading of Earle Birney's "Bear on the Delhi Road" from her position as an Indian-born reader returning the tourist's gaze, or her reassessment of the bases of Michael Ondaatje's reputation in "The Sri Lankan Poets in Canada: An Alternative View." Her reading of *Coming Through Slaughter*, for example, introduces the historical and racialized specificity of Buddy Bolden's background that the novel and its critics have ignored.

Oppositional Aesthetics: Readings from a Hyphenated Space is divided into two parts, with sections of the earlier book interleaved between new chapters on related themes, chiefly focusing on South Asian Canadian literature and Canadian culture. Part One, entitled "The Colour of Theory—A Non-White Reader Reads," includes chapters exploring the reading and teaching practices of the author, self-identified (in the title of Chapter 2) as a "South Asian (Canadian, of course) Academic." Part Two, entitled "Minority Canadian Writing," includes articles and book reviews on writers such as Rienzi Crusz, Michael Ondaatje, Neil

Bissoondath, Ven Begamudre, and M G Vassanji.

The newer essays develop the same concerns that gave the earlier book its power but they sound more confident, more comfortably grounded in claiming the space of an "oppositional aesthetics" that the author need no longer posit only as a goal. The tentative pointing of the earlier title (Towards an Aesthetic) has been replaced by the confident occupation of the "hyphenated space" in *Oppositional Aesthetics*. Mukherjee is even comfortable moving beyond opposition into fuller explorations of the ambiguities of living with colonial legacies and their representation within literary works. In these more recent essays, she makes greater use of her personal experience and her insider's knowledge of Hindu culture and the Hindi language. "On Reading Renu," for example, adds translation to criticism as another possible site for the decontextualizing erasures of cultural imperialism. "Narrating India" locates Mistry's award-winning novel, *Such a Long Journey*, within the circulating narratives of contemporary Indian history and politics, and the specifics of the Parsi experience, elements ignored by most Canadian reviewers.

The final two essays on the fiction of M G Vassanji are perhaps my favourites. Here Mukherjee is writing about work she respects and admires, work, as she puts it, that "asks tough questions about history, colonialism, and the ambiguous role of Indians as a comprador group whose dual role as the colonized and as collaborators makes it hard to portray their situation in the binary opposition of colonizer/colonized prevalent in postcolonial criticism" (167). In response to such honest and accomplished writing, Mukherjee develops a nuanced and thoughtful reading of Vassanji's work that stresses its implications for many communities of readers, including Africans, Indians, and Canadians. To her, Vassanji's stories help us confront the hardest questions, such as: "But how does one write if one belongs among the oppressors rather than the oppressed? What does one write about if one cannot point a finger at someone else?" (173); and, "Can settlers and colonizers live down their past?" (176).

This is a challenging and sometimes controversial book: it is tough, intelligent, personal, and political in the very best senses of these words. "Moral passion" and "social consciousness" are the values that engage Mukherjee "most deeply in literary texts" (viii); and these are the values she makes matter most for her readers also. In identifying such problems as "how wide the gulf of misunderstanding is between those who find racism and colonialism in women's writing objectionable and those who do not notice it" (xi), her concern is always to bridge that gulf and "to bring the day closer when universities will consider all cultures as equal and valuable and all human beings as equal and valuable" (15-16). This book should advance that cause. I recommend it.

John Clement Ball

TAKING THE MEASURE OF INDIA'S EMERGENCY

A Fine Balance
by Rohinton Mistry.
Toronto: McClelland and Stewart, 1995

A Fine Balance is Rohinton Mistry's entry into that most risky of literary sweepstakes: the longer, more ambitious second novel that follows a spectacular first success. Overextended talent, editorial knives too confidently put away, reviewers circling like sharks—the perils of the genre are legion. Just ask Nino Ricci. Mistry, however, has proved himself to be both brilliant and blessed. Not only is this novel stunningly good, it has also been seen to be good. With its Giller Prize swiftly bestowed (at a point when few besides jurors and journalists had read the book) it has already received commendations that will only enhance Mistry's stature. His career appears charmed in a way many authors—not to mention his own beleaguered characters—can only dream about.

Not that Mistry has been without his critics. Arun Mukherjee's mostly favourable review of *Such a Long Journey,* recently reprinted in *Oppositional Aesthetics,* ends by registering objections to the novel's "sexist" sexual humour and "stereotyped and unidimensional" portrayals of women characters (150)—a line of critique recently fleshed out in an article by Gordon Ekelund. Mukherjee's final words exhort Mistry henceforth to "convey a more equitable balancing of the male and female aspects of our humanity"(151). *A Fine Balance* will probably not convince everyone that its representational politics are flawlessly balanced—nor may it care to—but in its careful exploration of diverse gender, class and religious subject positions, it is a much more inclusive work than its predecessor.

The primary setting is a Bombay-like "great city" under the Emergency Rule of 1975-77, with flashbacks to faraway villages and towns before, during and after Partition. The focus on the Parsi community that characterized Mistry's previous work is widened considerably: *A Fine Balance* is healthily infected with what Saleem Sinai, in that other great novel of the Emergency, calls "an Indian disease, this urge to encapsulate the whole of reality" (Rushdie, 84). The four major characters are two middle-class Parsis and two Hindu Untouchables, while the scores of minor and middling characters comprise a superabundant social spectrum of Muslim rent-collectors and tailors, Sikh cabbies, wily beggars, disillusioned lawyers, murderous strongmen, corrupt slumlords, profiteering police, radical students, and—in a cameo no less unflattering than her appearances in *Midnight's Children* and *Such a Long Journey*—Indira Gandhi herself.

The big city performs its time-honoured literary role as locus of such diverse and contradictory realities. To a modernizing post-independence India, Bombay becomes what London, according to Raymond Williams, became to industrial-age Britain: a multiplicitous magnet for people from all over the country, a future-oriented place increasingly "producing and reproducing . . . the social reality of the nation as a whole" (Williams, 148). One of the novel's characters (the tailor Om) calls the city "a story factory . . . a spinning mill" (467), and in his ability to weave unlikely narrative bedfellows into a tightly plotted web of interconnections, Mistry exploits the urban landscape's labyrinthine overlappings of lives as cleverly as Dickens at his best—in *Little Dorrit*, for instance. As two of Mistry's new arrivals experience it, the city that at first seems "a universe of frightening chaos" eventually reveals "that it was not all madness and noise, there was a pattern in things" (138). In a novel much given to occupational metaphors, the "pattern" is not just a street pattern, but a pattern of interweaving itineraries and narrative threads.

The narrative hub within this urban fabric is a domestic space of occupation: a home the Parsi widow Dina Dalal has fiercely protected from a rapacious landlord. When failing eyesight threatens to end her tailoring career and the independence it provides, she refashions herself as entrepreneurial middle person, hiring two slum-dwelling tailors (the low-caste Ishvar Darji and his nephew Om) for commercial piece-work in her back room, and taking in a student (Maneck Kohlah) as a paying boarder. Initially relations among this foursome are tense and guarded; class-conscious Dina is strict and exploitative, the tailors suspicious, and Maneck divided in his allegiances. But just as *Such a Long Journey*'s Gustad had to shed his stern patriarchal shell, Dina gradually becomes less rigid, more accommodating; over time her new household becomes a moderately happy and prosperous "family." She emerges as a woman of rich complexity and strength. Easily Mistry's most fully developed female character, Dina is a person of dynamic agency, possessive of a sophisticated and believable interior life. She is a woman whose successes are of her own making, whose failures stem, with one prime-ministerial exception, from the blinkered oppressions and cruelties of men.

So, a desirable tipping of the gender scales may have been achieved. But then, this is a novel that makes much of "balance." In fact, it becomes something of a mantra in the novel, and takes on ever deeper shades of meaning and association. Some usages are conventional: Maneck noting that "good and bad" are interlinked (378), Vasantrao Valmik advocating a life-philosophy that maintains "a fine balance between hope and despair" (279). "Balance" is not always so benignly commonsensical, however. For a village thug enforcing caste discipline, an Untouchable's transgression of his prescribed profession "distort[s] society's timeless balance" and must be punished by a hideous death (177). The street performer Monkey-man, whose feat of balancing children atop tall poles provides the book's cover image, enacts a different kind of balance in his retributive, tit-for-tat killings. At times, the invocations of balance here are as gruesomely ironic as in Shakespeare's *Measure for Measure*.

Inversion is a kind of balance. And according to another of the novel's recurring sayings, "With the Emergency, everything is upside-down. Black can be made white, day turned into night" (362). Guilt and innocence, justice and injustice, victims and oppressors: the lines of exchange across these binary divisions are well travelled. Mistry is unblinking in his satiric staring-down of those who supported, legitimated and performed Emergency's horrors. "Balance" and "satire" aren't usually compatible concepts (although Chinua Achebe's work notably gets celebrated under both banners), and Mistry often departs from his commitment to full-bodied characterizations to offer scathing portraits of both the street-level perpetrators (goondas, police, Family Planning enforcers) and the smug bourgeoisie for whom the top-down suspension of human rights means improved labour relations and trains running on time. Even Dina's brother, Nusswan, the most fully portrayed member of this oppressor group, calmly advocates "eliminating" 200 million "surplus" people, pleased that Emergency allows those who think like him "to freely speak their minds" (454). Sometimes, however—as with Sergeant Kesar—Mistry will grant a redeeming humanity to figures whose actions make them monstrous. Indira Gandhi may make her most visible impact as an 80-foot cardboard cutout that topples over and kills people at a rally, but not all of her enforcers are so two-dimensional.

Mistry, like most good writers, is deeply concerned with the moral dimensions of his characters' lives.[1] And what galvanizes this novel is not only the urgency behind its rogues' gallery of moral grotesques, but also the way the intersection of the political and the personal is given such compelling moral resonance. Dina's development (as a person and as a character) goes hand-in-hand with her movement from a belief that Emergency "doesn't affect ordinary people like us" (88) through an experience of immediate impact on her "family" members, and correspondingly from a sheltered isolation from her city world to a network of community involvements that transcends religious and class divisions. She struggles into a politicized sense of mutual responsibility. By contrast, Maneck's tragic limitation (as a person, though not as a character) is his refusal to shed his apolitical detachment beyond a certain point—to embrace his entangledness with the messy injustices of the world and take a stand.

Of course, in the upside-down world of Emergency, easy moral categories become irrelevant. When an influential strongman named Beggarmaster—a man who customizes children's bodies to make them profitable beggars, and whose retribution against enemies is swift and horrible—when such a brute becomes a protecting saviour to Dina and her family, are they morally compromised by their dependence on him? Can they (or readers rooting for their success) do anything but cheer him on? Moreover, is Mistry's later revelation of Beggarmaster's soft-hearted, family-oriented side a recourse to cheap sentiment in order to make a bitter pill easier to swallow? Or does it simply drive home the outrageous moral contortions required of anyone—participant characters or observing readers—trying to come to terms with Emergency?

It is Mistry's ability to draw the reader into this time of crisis—to allow us to feel its horrors and develop vicarious stakes in the lives affected by it—that distinguishes his treatment of the period from Rushdie's in *Midnight's Children*. To be sure, the novels have many interesting parallels (as literary critics will undoubtedly be demonstrating for years to come): their social and historical comprehensiveness, their inclusion of specific events like the Bombay language marches and the stealing of the prophet's hair. Both novels pay extensive and unflinching attention to the bodily inscriptions of history; Mistry's use of motifs of mutilation and severance (of limbs, of hair) as both literal effects and grotesque symbols of Partition and Emergency is often reminiscent of Rushdie. But as brilliant as Rushdie's achievement is, his novel is less directly involving than Mistry's. His Emergency (like his Partition and his India-Pakistan wars) is distanced by its translation into spectacle. As a reader, I sometimes feel I am watching a series of dazzling performances rather than inhabiting a collection of lives. The two books are equally accomplished at their very different projects, so comparing them becomes an apples-and-oranges proposition. *Midnight's Children* is mesmerizing, sensational, politically explosive. *A Fine Balance* may not be as innovative or daring, but in its quieter way it is just as skilled and no less politically charged. It is also as engrossing and moving as anything I have ever read.

NOTES

1. In her essay on *Such a Long Journey*, originally published in the *Toronto South Asian Review* and reprinted in *Oppositional Aesthetics*, Arun Mukherjee criticizes my review of that novel (in *Paragraph* 13.3) for discussing moral aspects at the expense of political specificity. I have immense respect for Mukherjee's work, and while some of her points are well taken, I have not hesitated to invoke a moral perspective again. As I have recently written elsewhere (see *Descant* 91), I too dislike universalizing critical frameworks that cast third-world novels free of their local moorings into the sea of a

generalized "human condition." If my comments on Gustad's "moral growth" and the novel's engagement with "important moral problems" were sins of omission, this was more a function of the two paragraphs I was able to devote to the novel—and of my desire to find common ground among three different books in that most superficial of genres, the omnibus review —than it was of any intent to elide the political. As my comments on *A Fine Balance* suggest (though again, a review can only say so much), I see the political and the moral as inseparably linked. Political positions are inevitably moral ones, and engagement with the political dimensions of life may lead to a strengthening and clarifying or to a weakening and corrupting of moral views. Mistry is not moralistic, but his work has moral dimensions, just as the political criticism of Arun Mukherjee addresses such moral issues as fair versus unfair representation.

To briefly address Mukherjee's other criticisms: I continue to see the Victorian novel as a significant precursor of Mistry's work (though of course not the only or even the main precursor); I still think realism is as good a label as any to describe his mode of representation. And as for the "inane" remark she attributes to me regarding Mistry's theme being "the impermanence of all things" it does not appear anywhere in my review, and must have come from one of the other critics she targets. Still, I'm surprised that an idea so central to Indian philosophy would be scorned as so irrelevant to an Indian novel.

WORKS CITED

Ekelund, Gordon. 1995. "Left at the Station: The Portrayal of Women in Mistry's *Such a Long Journey.*" *The Toronto Review of Contemporary Writing Abroad* 14, 1: 6-14.

Mistry, Rohinton. *Such a Long Journey.* Toronto: McClelland and Stewart, 1991.

Mukherjee, Arun. 1994. "Narrating India: Rohinton Mistry's Such a Long Journey." In *Oppositional Aesthetics: Readings from a Hyphenated Space,* by Arun Mukherjee. Toronto: TSAR.

Rushdie, Salman. 1991. *Midnight's Children.* New York: Penguin. Originally published 1980.

Williams, Raymond. 1993. *The Country and the City.* London: Hogarth. Originally published 1973.

Amritjit Singh

NO LONGER FAR AWAY

No More Watno Dur
by Sadhu Binning.
Toronto: TSAR, 1994

This is a bilingual collection of poems written and published between 1973 and 1993 by the Vancouver poet Sadhu Binning, who explains in a prefatory note that "while many of these poems were written in Punjabi, a significant number were conceived originally in English." All the poems appear here in both languages on facing pages and this is a notable aspect of this volume's significance for Canadian literature—it suggests rightly that the poet, a new Canadian, is free to write in Punjabi or English as he pleases and yet it is important for the rest of us to hear his voice. Binning is one of the several Vancouver writers of South Asian background who have since their arrival in the 1960s and 70s written mostly in their native Punjabi. The group includes writers such as Gurcharan Rampuri, Ajmer Rode, Darshan Gill, Ravinder Ravi, Surjeet Kalsey, Giani Kesar Singh, Sukhwant Hundal, Surinder Dhanjal, and many others who have been productive in many genres. There are Punjabi writers such as Iqbal Ramuwalia and Sukhinder in other Canadian cities, especially Toronto. By one estimate provided by Binning himself, there are over a hundred such writers in Canada, including fifty-five who have published at least one book and nearly twenty with more than three books to their credit. The total number of books produced so far by these Punjabi Canadian writers is close to two hundred. Hence Punjabi Canadian literature is a significant part of Canadian writing that remains seriously neglected in literary circles. (A 1980 bibliography of Ethnic and Native Canadian Literatures prepared by John Miska lists more than

2200 titles in forty languages; the number is surely much higher by now.)

In an unpublished essay, entitled "Punjabi-Canadian Literature: Reflections of the Changing Community," Binning discusses how Punjabi writing in Canada, like Punjabi writing in the United Kingdom and the United States, continues to receive considerable attention as an extension of Punjabi writing in India and Pakistan. He makes a strong case for examining this vital literary phenomenon as an integral part of Canadian literature, especially in view of the changing attitudes within the South Asian community towards issues of home, nation, migration, and exile. In the last decade or so, a fair quantity of Punjabi Canadian writing has appeared in English translation in anthologies and journals, but most Canadian writing in South Asian languages remains invisible and inaccessible to North American readers. Only two Punjabi Canadian poets have published volumes of their own poems in English—Ajmer Rode (*Blue Meditations* and *Poems at My Doorstep*); and Surjeet Kalsey (*Footprints of Silence* and *Speaking to the Winds*). *No More Watno Dur* is the first substantive volume of poems by one poet to appear in a bilingual edition and TSAR deserves praise for bringing it out. Readers in Punjabi are familiar with Binning's work from his two earlier volumes of short stories (*Kis Da Kasur; Lihon Lathe*) and two volumes of poetry (*Sone Rangi Sarak; Rishte Dariawan De*). A volume such as *No More Watno Dur* opens up the real possibility for other Canadian writers and readers to discover what a Punjabi Canadian poet such as Binning is experiencing, thinking, and expressing without his being forced to sacrifice his medium or his message for some dubious reward or recognition.

Binning's poems chart out the journey, suggested by the title (meaning, "no longer far from the homeland"), from *watno dur* to *watan*, coincidentally the titles of the two Punjabi journals with whose editing Binning was associated in the late 1970s and the early 1990s respectively. (Unfortunately, both magazines had short life spans because of poor reader support.) The two poems about the death in Vancouver of his father—"River Relations" and "No More Watno Dur"—sit at the centre of this volume both literally and figuratively. These two poems invoke the ritual immersion of his father's ashes not in the Ganga, the Yamuna, or the Sutluj, but in the icy cold waters of the Squamish river. The ritual itself and the letter the poet writes to his family in India about the death represent his new link to Canada. As Binning sees it, the letter "is written / from my country to another country," as "one rupturing relationship" gives "birth to a new one." Unlike the poet's early twentieth-century ancestors whose strained faces at a cremation are captured in a photograph that forms part of the cover design for this beautiful volume, the poet views the river ritual as signalling a shift in his immigrant life. As he immerses the remains of his dead father in the Canadian river,

> The strangeness of the place melted
> a personal image now flows in memory
> perhaps that's what my father meant
> by relations of rivers to men.

While most of the poems are about "becoming Canadian," they portray a relationship to the new homeland that continues to be scarred by the same alienation and fear that the earlier South Asian migrants had experienced. And yet these poems represent a new power, derived from the poet's keen observation of life and people, a modulating voice that narrates and describes his varied experiences, and an implicit determination to face the challenges of racism and discrimination—sometimes with humour and compassion, but more often through a global understanding of race, gender, and class in Canada.

The emotions and experiences that find expression in these poems are mediated through the consciousness of a complex individual who will not settle for any confining view of nation or identity, race or class. The poet is ready to condemn or document the consequences for people of colour of systemic racism or exclusion in North America. At the same time, he does not hesitate to expose class exploitation or religious hypocrisy in India (as, for example, in "Chameleons," and "Peace and Religion in India"), or to suggest how these patterns relate to neocolonial tendencies throughout the world (consider, for instance, his provocative view, in "To Mother Teresa," that the Nobel Laureate is being used by the ruling elite for their own ends), or to examine the sadness or diversity behind the apparent ethnocentric sameness of white Canadians (as he does by unearthing "their hidden humanity" in "The Seventy-fourth Avenue").

Nearly every poem in the volume unravels the contradictions of human behaviour and the ironies that characterize global migration. For example, in "Revenge," a non-white male driver observing a white woman "behind the white thumb / on the edge of the road" considers the seductive possibilities of reprisal to appease his "torturing memories / three hundred years / of butchery and robbery." But in modulating the persona's controlled anger in a fashion that is typical of Binning's many poems on racism and colonial exploitation, "that spell of momentary madness is broken" as other questions arise:

> What kind of thought is this?
> when do you ever find
> real criminals
> on the edge of the road like this?

The unspoken thought that this white woman looking for a ride is most likely not a perpetrator but maybe a victim too of class and gender exploitation is brought home to us in another poem, "And You Know It," where in contrast to the reaction of the round-bellied, foul-smelling boss, the unsmiling secretary stares at the big bundle of mail the postman brings,

> and always with a deep sigh she says
> "is that whole thing for us?"

Silence and understatement are as much a part of the poet's aesthetic as open protest over past acts of blatant racism or present episodes of subtle discrimination (as in "The First Encounter"). The volume, dedicated to the passengers of the *Komagata Maru*, opens with two poems about that "heart-breaking incident" in 1914 when a group of over 300 Punjabi men, women and children were not permitted to land in Vancouver after two months or more of legal battles and police harassment. The responsibility of the "walking stones" in the first poem who laugh and turn away at the persona's questions gains a resonance from their absence in the second poem among the leaves, the birds, the snow and the rain, the rivers and the winds, which the poet imagines must have welcomed the *Komagata Maru* passengers to the shore. Nature does not love or despise people on the basis of skin colour or national origin, it is the humans who create and live by such ideologies. And yet, many other poems in the volume reinforce the message of the cover picture of an early twentieth-century cremation of a Punjabi worker. Gathered in the picture are not only the dead man's compatriots but also white fellow workers, who watch the unfamiliar ceremony with sad and curious eyes. In Binning's layered understanding of neocolonial economics and racial politics, the need not to demonize ordinary humans of any background is an essential part of the struggle against exploitative power structures.

The poet's ability to create memorable portraits of working-class individuals and to cross gender lines in the process is well-illustrated in many poems, including "My Mirror" and the four "postman" poems (68-89) based on his own experiences as a mail carrier for several years in the Vancouver area. In "My Mirror," the poet successfully captures the voice of an illiterate woman who works "the graveyard shift" as a cleaner at an airport and forms a special affection for a mirror in one of the bathrooms she cleans daily. This mirror becomes her means of relieving her loneliness in a strange and hostile world. It becomes a companion, a listening but uncomplaining friend, a surrogate notebook, for the persona to share her secrets, her worries and anxieties, her dreams and hopes, her "bitter sweet memories" of childhood in a Punjabi village. Her desire to "possess" the mirror in an exclusive relationship is interrogated by her own thought that "after all a mirror is only a reflection of humans" and cannot possibly belong to any one person. The persona in "The Postman" imagines himself, not unlike "a tall and proud tree somewhere / piece by piece delivered to a garbage heap" in the form of junk mail he brings daily to people's doors. Other poems that reflect a strong feminist consciousness include "Rebellious Sita," "That Woman," and "Washing Dishes," where a husband's participation in household chores is seen as "part of the / new social reality."

I have been impressed by Binning's handling of a variety of poetic forms in this book, especially by his ability to sustain long poems that is evident not only in "My Mirror" and "The Seventy-fourth Avenue," but also in "My Thirteenth Year in Canada" and "Reply"—both of which use a kind of Wordsworthian apostrophe to explore the contradictory and inhuman demands made upon new immigrants of colour in North America by citizens of European descent. The following lines from "Reply" are reminiscent of Richard Wright's view of African American life in *Twelve Million Black Voices* (1941):

> you say we can't change
> but the changes we make
> coming from our villages to Vancouver
> you haven't changed that much
> in three hundred years

One can certainly find in these poems a few examples of awkward expression in English and encounter resonant Punjabi phrases or images that are nearly impossible to translate. It is understandable too that some of the more personal and lyrical poems (such as "Parents" and "A Tale") do not work as well in English translation as the poems dealing with the contradictions of racial politics as it affects diasporic lives. Yet the humour of "The Grass and I" comes through well in the last line. Again, the situation in "Neighbour" is likely to ring a familiar note for many immigrants of colour in North America, as are the cultural clashes that shape the dilemma of the middle generation in "Father and Son."

It is hoped that *No More Watno Dur* is the first in a series of books from TSAR that will showcase the best work by many Canadian writers of South Asian background who choose to write in Punjabi, Gujarati, Hindi, Tamil, and other languages. If that is the case, TSAR is sure to earn the gratitude of many readers, South Asians and others alike, who cannot enjoy such writing in the original. The bilingual format of *No More Watno Dur* opens up Binning's writing to a broader set of readers without excluding those who would rather enjoy his poems in Punjabi, and could also serve the classroom needs of young readers engaged in learning Punjabi in academic and nonacademic settings. Certainly, the publication of *No More Watno Dur* represents an important idea, that of bringing into focus the works of writers who have chosen not to surrender to the demands of false or facile definitions of Canadian writing in their diasporic search for "imaginary homelands."

Lien Chao

SEXUAL OBSESSION AND VIOLENCE

Other Women
by Evelyn Lau.
Toronto: Vintage Canada, 1995

Evelyn Lau's name is well known to Canadian readers. Born in 1971 to a Chinese immigrant family in Vancouver, Lau published her first book, *Runaway: Diary of a Street Kid* (1989) at age eighteen. *Runaway* immediately became a national bestseller and brought its author enormous media attention. The book was translated into German, French and Spanish; CBC Television even made a TV movie of it. Lau is also a productive poet; she has published three collections of poetry: *You Are Not Who You Claim* (1990), *Oedipal Dreams* (first published in 1992; republished in 1994), and *In the House of Slaves* (1994). When *Oedipal Dreams* was nominated for the Governor General's Literary Award in 1990, Lau became the youngest writer ever nominated for the highest literary award in Canada. Her first short story collection, *Fresh Girls and Other Stories* (1993), was also published in the United States and the United Kingdom in the fall of 1994. Because of her youthful achievements, the Canadian Author's Association voted Lau the most promising writer in 1988.

The publication of *Other Women* (1995) is supposed to be the turning point of Lau's writing in terms of its subject matter. Previously, her poetry and short stories almost unanimously depict prostitution and sadomasochism. This depiction inevitably draws the reader's attention to the writer's past, framing her writing in an unwanted way. When *Fresh Girls* was published, one of her interviewers expressed his concern about Lau's depiction of the same topic; Lau told him that "I promise this is the last thing I write about

S&M." Two years later, Lau's first novel, *Other Women*, was published, so, is it a turning point regarding her subject matter?

Other Women is a dramatic monologue narrated by its heroine,
Fiona, an established visual artist, about her sexual obsession with an
older and married businessman, Raymond. After a casual meeting,
the two start to meet in hotels and restaurants for mutual interest.
However, this mutual sexual attraction quickly cools off to an unreturned love for Fiona when Raymond makes it clear to her in a verbal
statement, "you know how important my marriage is to me. You
know I love my wife" (3). If a traditional plot of a love triangle is not
quite completed here, it is developed virtually in Fiona's imagination.
While part of the story contains some reminiscence of her meetings
with Raymond, the rest of the novel dramatizes her sexual desire for
him and her ever deepening pain and loneliness without him.

Lau develops Fiona's unquenchable sexual desire for Raymond,
which can only be soothed through an imagined, sexual violence
imposed on Raymond's wife, Helen. The vengeance is presented as a
direct physical action conducted by Fiona on Helen: "I wanted to
strip Helen naked, . . . put my face against her chest and listen to her
heartbeat climb towards orgasm, ... I wanted to examine between
her thighs with the probing interest of a physician . . . " (184). Fiona's
hatred of her rival is further intensified as any violence against
women could be: she wants to see Helen being violently raped at a
knife point in a parking lot:

> I imagined myself watching unflinchingly as the white, faintly
> circled skin of Helen's throat met the mirroring flash of a
> stranger's knife. He would shove his hand swiftly under her
> skirt, fumble past the silky layers of lingerie for her hole. He
> would leave forever an impression of his identity inside her—
> her vagina would remember forever the whorl of his thumb-
> print, and the bladed edges of his nails. And then his penis,
> rough and blunt as a bat. The sounds she would make, twisting
> in his arms, would sound from where I stood like sex, like the
> sounds I imagined she sometimes still made with you. (185)

The choice of words in this paragraph captures the vicious plot of
a male rapist who attacks a physically unguarded woman. However,
since the raping is an imagined rape and mouthed by a female

247

character in a monologue, one wonders why the author needs to borrow this kind of male sexual violence and crime to satisfy the unfulfilled sexual desire of a female character.

Furthermore, the episode of sexual violation is made the climax of the novel. Structurally, it suggests that the rest of the story be simply a foreplay leading to the climax; "like sex," as the narrator says cruelly and crudely. As a result, this scene not only sends cold sweats and goose bumps to the reader's back, but also makes the reader, especially a female reader, feel being personally violated. The climax is then followed by an imagined divorce imposed by Raymond on his wife, and the novel moves quickly to its denouement. The structure of the novel gradually reveals the heroine's psychological and physical need to conduct a sexual crime against another woman.

Regarding the narrative mode, *Other Women* is a monologue or confession. In order to defuse the otherwise monotonous tone of such a narrative, Lau skilfully changes the point of view from first-person peripheral to third-person omniscient in every other chapter. This switching is also paired with the relevant change of the addressees. To be more specific, when Fiona speaks in her first person voice as "I," she speaks directly to "you," who are simultaneously Raymond and the reader. This pairing, directly and psychologically, involves the reader in Fiona's love affairs and sexual fantasies to experience the author's sexual politics. The switch of the point of view does offset the intensity of the relationship between the narrator and the reader deriving from the "I-speaking-to-you" situations; however, it only partially distances the reader from Fiona's unreturned love and imagined violence.

So, is *Other Women* different from Lau's previous writings in terms of its subject matter? The answer is yes or no. If genitals, breasts, nipples, sexual scenes are like commas and periods in Lau's previous writings, they are more economically dotted in *Other Women*. It seems that the author has put a strict control over the relationship between Fiona and Raymond that sexual intercourse is not allowed except in Fiona's imagination. This is one difference that Lau has managed to maintain in this book. In that sense, she has probably fulfilled her earlier promise: *Other Women*, her first novel, is not about prostitution or S&M. However, comparing it with her earlier writings, it does not lack sexual violence against women.

Arun Prabha Mukherjee

NO EASY SOLUTIONS

In Another Place, Not Here
by Dionne Brand.
Toronto: Knopf, 1996

At the outset, let me admit that *In Another Place, Not Here* is one of the toughest novels I ever sunk my teeth into. It is a novel told in many voices, in many places, in many times, all neatly jumbled together, as these things are usually jumbled up in people's heads. The challenge for the reader is to keep it all sorted out as she navigates through Brand's richly textured language. One has to be fully alert to catch on to the syntax, the voice, the chronology, and the place that together make meaning in a narrative. During my first reading, I floundered rather than navigated. I had to keep going back, reread again and again in order to keep myself on course.

In Another Place, Not Here withholds and tantalizes right to the last page. Then, if you are a serious reader, you have to go back to page one and reread the whole novel again. And this time, because you know the basic plot, you have a compass to chart your course. You now know when a character is in the Caribbean and when in Toronto, when in a dream and when recalling real events.

Now that I have done my home work, I know the basic plot: Verlia is a thirty-year-old Black woman who came to Toronto in the early seventies at the age of seventeen. Rejecting the narrow bourgeois life of her aunts and uncles, she joins the sisters and the brothers in the Black Power Movement. Her heroes are Fanon, Marx, Gandhi, Castro, Che Guevara, Lumumba, Samora Machel, Angela Davis and George Jackson. She wants a revolution in her lifetime and works nonstop organizing rallies, putting up posters on lampposts in the dead of night, teaching Black children how to avoid arrest, and educating herself by reading the stalwarts of the left. When arrested after a demonstration, when a policeman twists her arm out of its socket, she keeps her sanity by repeating Che's words like a mantra: "At the risk of seeming ridiculous, let me say that the true revolutionary is guided by great feelings of love" (165).

At the age of thirty years and one month, Verlia reaches the end of her rope and goes to the Caribbean to join the Revolution, leaving her lover Abena because "she needed a mission outside of herself . . . She could not be swallowed by any comfort, she could not take that as all. It may be enough for Abena but not for her" (97).

On the island, she is assigned the job of organizing cane cutters on the Oliviere plantation. She falls in love with Elizete, one of the cane cutters:

> Had anyone told her she would not have believed that she would wake up in this room. This morning is shedded in light and dust. That wooden window will open. The hand opening the wooden window will be the hand of the woman I sleep with in this room . . . It is a room where I will open my eyes and the woman opening the window will be the woman I will live with for ever. I will not look at her, I know her face, it is melting into the soft sun she lets in with her hand on the window. I do not need to look at her face, it is the face melting into the sun at the window . . . That she would envy hardship, that she would envy the arc of a cutlass in a woman's hand. That she would fall in love with the arc of a woman's arm, long and one with a cutlass, slicing a cane stalk and not stopping but arcing and slicing again, splitting the armour of cane, the sweet juice rushing to the wound of the stem. That the woman would look up and catch her looking and she would hate herself for interrupting such avenging grace. (201-3)

But the Revolution goes awry. Clive, the leader, is shot dead. And soon after, the Americans, with help from other island governments, invade. Verlia, along with other members of the militia gathered in the cemetery, hears and watches the Yankee planes:

The planes circling, in sounds those mornings had never heard before, yet all the water smelled like any other day, any other morning. She'd thought the sound of bombers would poison the water, make the river boil like hell surging in its belly . . . Not even the earth sided with them and that in the end was unbearable. What did they think they were taking? Only her heart. And take it then, not even that was hers anyway. "We can't own nothing," Tante Emilia used to say, shrugging. "Nothing. Black people can't own nothing. They take it away so till we don't know how to own it."

Well, let them take her heart too. If it was so important to some white man thousands of miles away, so important that all these planes were coming for it and all these bombs were going to kill it, let them have it. (116-7)

The last glimpse we have of Verlia is jumping off a cliff into the sea. The last sentence of the novel discloses the meaning of the title: "She's in some other place already, less tortuous, less fleshy." "In Another Place," then, means the place where people go after they die. "Here," by the same token, is the world of the mortals.

After the reader has put together this jigsaw puzzle of a story line, fragmented in a thousand odd shapes, the next hermeneutic step begins. Is this yet another revisitation of Grenada after its appearance in Brand's poetry collections *Chronicles of the Hostile Sun* and *No Language is Neutral* and the short-story collection *Sans Souci*? If so, how important is it for the reader to situate the novel in a real time and a real place? For this reader, the invasion of Grenada on October 25, 1983 by 1900 American troops, with the nominal help of forces from half a dozen Caribbean countries, is the "cataclysmic hell" (108) that leads to Verlia jumping off the cliff. It seems to me that Brand is linking Verlia's jump to her death with the defiant suicide in 1650 by forty Caribs, men, women, and children, the original inhabitants of this island, when they lost to the colonial invaders.

But since Grenada is nowhere mentioned by name, is Brand generalizing about the Caribbean as a whole? The loss of specificity, from my point of view, is troubling. It leaves open the possibility of depoliticized readings that will focus on the complexities of Brand's fragmented narrative and bypass its political passion.

I wish that the narrative was a little less opaque. I wish a helping hand had been extended to me as I stumbled through my first reading. The story line I have charted above does not do justice to the first part of the novel, which is focused on Elizete. It is about Elizete remembering Verlia as she first saw her in the canefield. The first hundred pages of the novel switch back and forth between the voices of Elizete, the omniscient narrator, Adela, and the woman Elizete was given to. The second time around, the reader knows that Elizete is mourning Verlia. One knows how to read "Verlia left me" or "after Verlia went away." But during my first reading, I could only be puzzled about why Verlia had left her and where she had gone. Had she left Elizete because she "couldn't just live in a personal thing . . . Not enough" (103)? If the reader figures that to be the most probable reason, then Elizete's coming to Toronto is mistakenly interpreted by her as the chasing of a reluctant lover.

The result of not knowing a vital piece of information resulted in a misreading on my part the first time around. I obviously could not respond adequately to Elizete's grief and, therefore, to her tone and mood. Moreover, even if I had twigged on to Verlia's death, I still would not have known the cause of it until the last few pages when I decided (since the diary does not use place names, it is up to the reader to decide the locale) that it was Grenada that Verlia's diary was about.

Anyhow, the next question to ponder is why the novel is written as an elegy, a lamentation, a dirge. Elizete is the archetypal wanderer, arrived in Toronto like a piece of flotsam. Verlia is presented to us as refracted through her consciousness: a woman who was "burning bright" (9) like Blake's tiger. But it is Elizete, the earth-bound woman, who must live on to the end of her days in a world that is uniformly bleak. The island, though beautiful, is not a paradise. Adela, the slave-woman ancestor of Elizete, called it Nowhere. The spirits of hanged slaves still roam the island. Contrary to the tourist posters, for Elizete the island is nothing but scarred and wounded legs earned by working in the canefields. So when Abena, the Toronto social worker, tells her, "Go home, it's not a place for us," she replies: "Lady, look at my foot. I can't take the field no more and is only field waiting for me" (110).

Verlia had asked the revolutionary's question: "What is to be

252

done?" She had looked for recipes for revolution in books and in the deeds of revolutionary heroes. But she is dead and the narrative voice bleakly informs: "Call this living. This ain't no living. This is where you do that Black woman trick. Squeeze water from a stone, steel your Black woman self to bear the street, hope for another century, make something that can last another age, something that can wait, for some light" (83).

Verlia has escaped to "another place, less tortuous, less fleshy." But Elizete and the countless other Black women whose suffering is recounted in the novel must go on, survive on hope, wait for another century. In the meanwhile, they must suffer the brutalities inflicted by the police, the immigration, the exploitative sweatshop employers and men. And often they have no recourse. Elizete is raped by the man whose house she cleans:

> She knows that in the house she's just left the man has not moved. He is sitting on the velveteen sofa or perhaps looking at sand out his window. He does not fear her, he knows that she will not tell anyone. He knows that the fingers of her left hand will be numb for some time to come. They are swollen. Her eyes are bloody, almost closed. There is a bruise near her waist, under a rib. He knows that she will not go to a hospital. He knows that she will not go to a police station. She knows that she cannot go back to the sewing factory. She won't tell anyone. (93)

No, Black women have not come a long way, baby. The novel suggests that the world is still being run by slavers and slave drivers. One can still hear the harsh music of chain and coffle on the Jane Street bus:

> And you thought that you were sloughing off skin over the Atlantic dressing in your real self. Here. Impermanence, which perhaps you felt all along. Perhaps it was built into you long before you came and coming was not so much another place but travelling, a continuation, absently, the ringing in your ears of iron bracelets on stones, the ancient wicked music of chain and the end of the world. (65)

I remember the blues song as I read about the unrelenting harshness of these Black women's lives: "No body knows the trouble I have seen." I think of the Rastas, "By the rivers of Babylon . . . " I think of Bob Marley, "No woman, no cry."

The novel offers no easy solutions, no symbolism of rebirth or arrival of a new Messiah. Black women, it seems to suggest, are on their own. If there is a ray of hope, it is in the meeting of Elizete and Abena: "Abena was dry-eyed and shining as if she'd finally understood" (237). Joined through their love for Verlia, they support each other. It is as though the last moments of Verlia's life can only be narrated after Elizete and Abena have found each other. Both of them had blocked Verlia's suicide/murder out of their consciousness. The entire novel is a preparation for facing those last hours, narrated not in Elizete's but partly in Verlia's and partly in the narrator's voice:

> Someone taking a shot of rum across the harbour saw them fall, saw the arms wide at the end of the cliff, heard the pound, pound, pound po, po, po, po, pound of the guns driving them off the cliff's side into the sea. Someone saw the steel black shank of the armoured cars crumbling the cliff top. Someone who could not stop shaking. Someone spilling rum saw them tumble, hit, break their necks, legs, spines, down the cliff side and some of them flew, leapt into the ocean. someone saw the embrace. A long and dead arc, green and black hitting turquoise. (246)

I think of Yeats's line: "A terrible beauty is born." I think of all the bombs that have fallen in my lifetime and I feel sad. I think of the thirty percent unemployment in present day Grenada. I think of the hundreds of thousands of Iraqi children who die because of lack of food and medicine while the "civilized world" enforces an embargo on their country. They are with Verlia, "in another place, not here." The question the novel throws at us, those of us who are here, in this place, is, what are we going to do about it.

John Clement Ball

NICEFOLKSVILLE

Any Known Blood
by Lawrence Hill.
Toronto: HarperCollins, 1997

Few Canadians likely think first of black history when they hear the name "Oakville, Ontario." This prosperous bedroom community outside Toronto, once said to have the highest per-capita income in Canada, has become synonymous in the public imagination with dull, white-bread prosperity, safe suburban distance, and, not too accurately, a racially and culturally homogeneous populace for whom "upper-middle-class" would be the only kind of hyphenated identity. Indeed, the contemporary narrator of Lawrence Hill's *Any Known Blood* calls Oakville "terminally pleasant," and his great-great-grandmother dubs the pre-Confederation village "Nicefolksville." But if Oakville was "nice" in the 1850s, it was so in large part because it was a major terminus for the Underground Railroad; the village accommodated many escaped American slaves. Hill's second novel gives new meaning to Oakville as "safe" retreat and buffs up its "dull" image by engaging with the fascinating past of its black community. His multigenerational narrative shuttles across a century and a half of history and border-hops between Oakville, Ontario and a better-known black city, Baltimore, Maryland.

The novel is narrated by thirty-eight-year-old Langston Cane V, the latest in a family line of intelligent but willful and restless souls. Dimly familiar with various legends surrounding his forebears' political and emotional entanglements, he finds himself with the time and yearning to investigate the lives of the Langston Canes I-IV, filling in gaps in his knowledge as one way to cover over some big holes left in his life by a recent divorce and the loss of his job. The latter he has brought on himself by an act of capricious rebellion: he used his speech-writing position to trick a provincial minister into contradicting party policy on a proposed human-rights bill. This quixotic act of resistance (which costs the minister his job too) affiliates Langston not only with the wider black community (who applaud his intervention) but also with the earlier Langstons, whose politically engaged lives exemplify important aspects of black experience in the US and Canada. The light-skinned Langston, whose mother is white, sets off for Baltimore to unlock the secrets of his black family and, as so often happens to fictional biographers, to discover new things about himself.

The novel intersperses the framing story of Langston's months in Baltimore with accounts of the most significant episodes lived by earlier Canes. Hill's deft cross-cutting keeps things moving; he gives past and present portions roughly equal time and comparable narrative interest, so the reader does not become impatient with one in anticipation of the other.

The contemporary story traces Langston's dogged and serendipitous research, his reunion with his father's estranged sister Mill, a friendship with a West African "illegal" named Yoyo, and an emergent romance. But beyond the quotidian personal, the novel shows Langston continuing to be drawn (usually by accident) towards public heroics; a good-samaritan act after a drive-by shooting earns him recognition by Baltimore blacks, and back in Oakville he helps locate neo-Nazis who have kidnapped his father, a prominent activist. Although Hill does not overly stress the intergenerational parallels, he does, through Langston V's public achievements and personal conflicts, suggest lines of continuity between him and those whose names he bears.

The earlier Langston Canes were all community builders of a kind. In addition to the activist father, two earlier Langstons were ministers in the African Methodist Episcopal Church. And Langston I, the runaway slave whose compelling story is the final destination of Langston V's probings, played a part in John Brown's idealistic but failed Harpers Ferry Raid in 1859. But as the ancestral stories unfold—told through conversations, letters, diaries and conventional novelistic prose from Langston V—the various Langstons become interesting not only for the ways their public affiliations and experiences of blackness reflect their times, but also as individuals. The dynamics of their marriages, familial tensions and careers make enjoyable reading; each Langston has a story worth telling, and each (with the exception of number II, who inexplicably gets short shrift) comes alive in context with the people, things, conditions and ideas of his time and place.

As social history, there is great value in this novel. The product of Hill's own extensive research into his family history and those of black communities in Maryland and Oakville, it offers a fictional family ("almost all invented," Hill assures us in a postscript) inspired by a real one. The fictional Canes encounter some real people—the famous John Brown and Frederick Douglass, as well as some lesser-known figures—and while the author takes liberties with the historical record, his postscript carefully details the changes. In the clarity with which it manages five generations of stories, keeps its eras authentic and its relationships intelligible despite a non-linear, unconventional structure, *Any Known Blood* wants and deserves to be taken seriously as fictionalized history. However, there is something in that very clarity that, despite Hill's storytelling gifts, makes it less satisfying as historical fiction—that diminishes its virtues as a novel.

It is a book too eager to make its characters appealing by making them articulate. Hill writes dialogue that sounds stylized in the manner of certain vintage movies; working against the strength and individuality of the characters as they have been conceived is the fact that across the centuries, borders, races and classes, they mostly sound the same when they open their mouths. Specifically, they tend to be forthright, earnest, good-naturedly chatty, occasionally witty, and intelligently responsive. Here is the concluding exchange in Langston V's first meeting with his sharp-tongued Aunt Mill:

"Good-bye son," she called out.
"Bye, Mill."
I walked down the path towards Sarah [his Volkswagon Jetta]. "That your car?" she called out. I nodded my head as I unlocked the door. "Ugly little thing. Is that what people drive in Canada?"
"We've just got this one model."

"Don't mock me, son. I'm not as dumb as I look. Where you staying?"

"Three-oh-eight Adell Street. In Charles Village."

"Good. Down here in West Baltimore, black folks would eat you up."

"There are black folks in Charles Village."

"Not the same kind," she said. "Around here, folks would use you for target practice. Well, if the police lock you up, don't call me for bail." I looked at her evenly. "I don't hold no grudge against you, boy, even if your pappy did marry a white girl. It's just that I don't want to see you, is all."

I drove away. In the rearview mirror, I saw her watching me until I turned the corner.

Aunt Mill's bark, we rightly suspect, will turn out to be worse than her bite. Something about this writing reminds me of television.

There is little of the mysterious or inexplicable about Hill's people, and what there is, we soon realize, will be revealed to Langston and to us in due course. For all its injustices and inter-personal conflicts, Hill's world is ultimately a rather cheerful, humane place that inspires optimism: that problems will be resolved, enemies reconciled and wounds healed; that order will prevail and any ornery or anti-social types will for the most part come round and do the right thing. Even the Ku Klux Klansmen and neo-Nazis, perhaps because they live in Oakville, turn out to be hapless amateurs who politely fold when confronted with authority and pose no permanent threat.

As if defused by the pleasant spirit of Nicefolksville, Hill's novel suffers from a kind of shiny polish that keeps the reader on its attractive surfaces while shying away from incomprehensible depths. However skillfully crafted, it lacks the rough edges, the darkness and danger and the brutal pain that its subject matter would seem to require. The overall effect is of black history "lite," packaged to reassure rather than challenge, explain rather than question, entertain rather than engross.

Experienced readers of contemporary historical fiction—their palates whetted by writers like Rushdie, Morrison, Vassanji and Ondaatje—will probably find themselves wishing for something richer and more provocative.

Linda Hutcheon

FRUITFUL DUALITIES: CONTEXTUALIZING CRUSZ

Dark Antonyms and Paradise: The Poetry of Rienzi Crusz
by Chelva Kanaganayakam.
Toronto: TSAR, 1997

Insurgent Rain: Selected Poems 1974–1996
by Rienzi Crusz.
Selected and Introduced by Chelva Kanaganayakam.
Toronto: TSAR, 1997

Chelva Kanaganayakam has already taught us much about South Asian writers, especially as exiles, through his earlier books, Structures of Negation: The Writings of Zulfikar Ghose and Configurations of Exile: South Asian Writers and Their World. His new and welcome work on Sri Lankan Canadian writer Rienzi Crusz continues his exploration into the creative trauma of exile and displacement in both historical and personal terms. The focus of the book is therefore both on the poet and his work (largely poetry, with some prose) and also on the larger postcolonial cultural and social context in which that work is both written and read. Kanaganayakam draws on his deep knowledge of the field of postcolonial literature and theory to enrich our understanding of Crusz's work, which he places in a broad context of writers that ranges from Christopher Okigbo to Salman Rushdie, from Rohinton Mistry to Derek Walcott. Here we get scholarly analysis presented in such an accessible and engaging manner that this study can stand as a model for academics wanting to reach a larger reading public.

Given his past work on how exile influences the work of South

Asian writers, Kanaganayakam is sensitive to differences both in reasons for exile (economic, personal, political) and in responses to it. He is also attuned to the dualities of exile as loss and gain, alienation and attachment. The writing he has studied, both earlier and here, has been writing that can be described as simultaneously rooted and cosmopolitan—in other words, as complex as any diasporic hybrid writing can possibly be. Rejecting the often too limited analyses of multicultural writing in a Canadian setting, he follows the lead of his poet in concentrating on issues of language as much as on issues of ethnicity and immigration. Scrupulously fair and even handed, Kanaganayakam presents the critical response to Crusz's work—positive and negative—in a helpful and constructive manner. He also gives the reader a fine, complicated sense of the ranges of modes and tones, as well as themes, in the poetry—from the oppositional to the celebratory, from the bitterly ironic to the yearningly elegiac.

What this study does is to place Crusz precisely and illuminatingly within a variety of cultural contexts (Sri Lankan, Canadian, but also British, European, even—briefly—South American) so that we can understand better the complexities of both his writing and its reception. It supplements this context-building with personal information, but, significantly, what we learn about the poet as man is what we need to understand the poet as writer. The family context is clearly important to the reading of this lyric poetry, but that context is handled here with admirable tact and a sensitive respect for privacy, often using the poetic utterance itself to express best the relevance of the information offered—on subjects from education to personal relations. Though he obviously had access to personal letters and had the poet's cooperation, Kanaganayakam is discreet, and his revelations are always in the service of our better understanding of the work itself.

The presentation of Crusz as a bit of an anachronistic figure—that is, more in the lyrical tradition of romanticism than modernism (or postmodernism)—rings true when one turns to the poems themselves. *Insurgent Rain* is a collection of Crusz's work from 1974 to 1996, selected and astutely organized by Kanaganayakam. It is prefaced with a brief but very effective version of the major thesis of *Dark Antonyms and Paradise*. The linguistic transformation of the everyday into the extraordinary and the constant sense of the poet's own voice do seem to place the work securely within the two-hundred-year-old romantic tradition. Since Crusz writes in English—and not Sinhala or Tamil—he unavoidably writes for multiple audiences, some of whom will not be familiar with indigenous Sri Lankan cultural contexts. Kanaganayakam has added, again tactfully, very brief explanatory notes to aid readers who may not know details of geography, fauna, or politics. For some of us, then, new meaning is added in this way to the wonderful music of lines such as "jambu, mango and mangosteen; / guava and rambuttan, the tender cadju / wrapped in green leaves, the jaggery bell / of the godambara-roti man."

Instead of being organized by date of composition, the poems are united by themes, thus making the major preoccupations of the poet the focus of the book, rather than any notion of his poetic evolution. Included here, therefore, are new poems with old, revisitations of terrain once travelled and now reconsidered. "The Raging Chaos of Love" section, for instance, offers poems that move from pain, loss, and betrayal (at the end of his first marriage) to more positive, gentle, moving articulations of love to his present wife Anne. But this is less a temporal range than an emotional one. The lines to his first wife, "Where were you in the ravaging end? / Why those strange silences / when dark prophecies / were in full bloom?" are from a new poem, even if the emotions that inform them are familiar from the early volume, *Flesh and Thorn*. The second section of the collection (and each takes its name from Crusz's own poetry), "The Marshmallow Land" is—not surprisingly—about the shock at and eventual accommodation with Canada's climate and North American consumer culture. The poems' often bitter ironies are juxtaposed at times with nostalgic memories of a warmer land and an earlier time when "winter's myths" had not yet "reached deep / into the marrow."

Facing the physical but also the social cold of his new country, Crusz is both scathingly critical and movingly forgiving. This contrast can be seen most clearly in the section that bears the same name as Kanaganayakam's book "Dark Antonyms and Paradise." There is a deliberate change from the title of Crusz's poem, which is "Dark Antonyms in Paradise," and this is done, I believe, in order to set up (paradoxically) yet another binary or antonym between Crusz's urge to see things in binary opposites (the "dark antonyms") and the transcendence of those very binaries ("paradise"). The poems support well Kanaganayakam's thesis that, in the end, Crusz does manage to go beyond those oppositions that are nevertheless so central to his work: oppositions between Canada and Sri Lanka as places to live, between his Portuguese and Sinhalese heritage, between his English language and his Sri Lankan experience, between the Sri Lanka of memory and the reality of today—itself split between capitalist prosperity and spiritual, human suffering. Ever aware of the power of nostalgia to eliminate negative memories and enshrine the positive, Crusz may yearn for "the green land / forever green, / the lost country / ever perfect" but he knows that such a place exists only in the mind—or in poetry. The complex responses to exile that Kanaganayakam outlines in his book are here most evident, as we too, as readers, experience Crusz's alternating moods of celebrating or castigating and ironizing. While living in Canada, as the poems of "The Igloo of Heaven" section show, he has come to accept that the "white marshmallow land is now mine / conquered, cussed upon, / loved." The poems of the Sun-Man, the raven and the elephant bring the Sri Lankan past its metaphors, but also its beliefs and values—into fruitful dialogue with the present. In "The Umbrella of Doting Children" section, the poet comes to terms with his familial past—in moving elegies to his parents and brother, Hilary—and present, especially in the poems to his son Michael.

By contrast, the poems in "A New Architecture" are self-reflexive poems about Crusz as poet, about the process of writing poetry, about his inspiration, aims (a "new way / of looking at the real world") and diverse influences ("from Milton and Shakespeare, / Blake, Eliot and Yeats, / the Latin boys Neruda and Paz, / the two girls Sexton and Plath; / must have heard the sure sprung rhythm of Hopkins, Dylan's Welsh rabana beat"). This poetic self-consciousness continues into the next section, "These Other Configurations," but this time the "beauty and vulgarity of words," as the poet puts it, are engaged to examine the beginnings and endings of life, in which death is "not the end / but the sweet beginning, / life's first celebration." These poems lead easily into the final section of religious or spiritual poems called "Soul of a Faltering Saint." Interestingly, though no matter what the theme, the poet's sense of irony never leaves him, even when writing about what, as a boy, he had learned to believe one could ask from God. In the poem, "Yes, in Our Father's House There Are Many Rooms," the poet ups the ante with a barbed irony aimed at several targets:

A colour TV would be nice
   (preferably a 24-inch)
would help to look in on Colombo,
Cosby and Matlock
keep track of what's happening
in *In the Heat of the Night*
I almost forgot,
I'd also like to beg
for some spaces
for my kids and my good wife, Anne.
So could you please
change the accommodation
to a small bungalow?

Throughout his work, Crusz has combined irony such as this with elegy, satire with nostalgia, bitterness at human injustice with sensual evocations of nature. The "dark antonyms" do not disappear, but, when viewed over a period of twenty years, they do indeed seem to be transcended. There are still deep ambivalences, but towards both the past and the present, towards both Sri Lanka and Canada.

In these poems and in this study of Crusz's work, we get a firm sense of the poet as craftsman and as the paradoxically private public man. It is fitting that TSAR should publish these two books (and in such handsome editions), for the success of Crusz's work in Canada and abroad owes much to its support and we, the readers, are grateful for that. Kanaganayakam's fine study will go a long way to winning Crusz the further recognition that he deserves. It will also contribute greatly—as Crusz's poetry always has—to the on-going and crucially important problematizing of the entire concept of "Canadian-ness," in part because the dualities or antonyms never totally disappear, even in their transcendence. As Kanaganayakam puts it: "the voice is Canadian in its understanding of the nation but is expressed through a sensibility that is distinctly Sri Lankan. The language system is Sri Lankan, in its registers, its phrases, it use of proper nouns, but the poetic mode is clearly western. The stanzaic patterns are western while the weltanschauung is Sri Lankan." But it is precisely such fruitful dualities—creatively fused—that make Canadian literature as rich as it is today.

Chelva Kanaganayakam

DANCING IN THE DARK

Homer in Flight
by Rabindranath Maharaj.
New Brunswick: Goose Lane, 1997

When Homerwad, the protagonist of *Homer in Flight*, is given his immigration papers in Trinidad, the official in the Canadian Embassy asks him whether he had ever been told that he looked like James Wood. Perplexed, Homerwad wonders aloud whether James Wood is a Canadian politician, and is told that he is an American actor who appears in gangster movies, often taking the role of a small-time crook. Thus begins, on an ambiguous note that anticipates future transformations, the journey of Homerwad (later abbreviated to Homer) from the Caribbean to Toronto, his experiences in a new land, his struggle to maintain an authentic identity in an atmosphere that threatens to "fix" him in a predetermined mould, and his own willingness to compromise his values in order to survive.

In a novel strongly reminiscent of V S Naipaul, M G Vassanji and Sam Selvon, Rabindranath Maharaj traces the narrative of a Biswas-like figure, ill at ease in two worlds, but unwilling to accept the role of an outsider. Vassanji's novel, *No New Land* (1991), also set in Toronto, offers a useful comparison, but the two novels work with very different perspectives. Unlike Vassanji's novel which probes the challenges of maintaining "difference" by focusing primarily on conflict between the mainstream centre and the multicultural periphery, *Homer in Flight* looks at the fragmentation of a community from within and places less importance on the hegemony of the centre. There is no attempt to withdraw from or downplay encounters that display a schematic opposition. In fact, the novel is quite candid in its evocation of racism, as in the episode involving the supervisor at a factory when the supervisor tells Becker, an immigrant from Guyana: "Maybe you all idiots over there, living in jungle with no factory. Pissing from trees, too" (76). Yet with all the instances of stereotyping that the novel records, the main source of conflict lies within the community. Constantly unsettled by the expectations of a homogenizing centre, the immigrants in the novel become willing accomplices in their own marginalization.

It is hardly surprising that both the protagonist and his wife Vashti enrol in a course on Victorian literature. For Vashti, the posturing afforded by the experience becomes a form of escape from her own identity, and the preoccupation with Victorian fiction is one of the many ways to seek assimilation. Homer is less captivated by Victorian writing, despite his own literary ambitions which lead to a book at the end. For him Victorian literature is a reminder of his own status as an outsider. The contradictory responses are significant, for the novel too recapitulates this duality, for it is in many ways a mimetic work along nineteenth-century lines, particularly in its wide range of characters, its omniscient narration and its comprehension evocation of place. The intertextual connections with Victorian authors, particularly Dickens, is a further indication of the novel's genealogy.

Notwithstanding the obvious connections with the Victorian novel, this work is hardly about consolidation; rather, it is about fragmentation, the contingency of identities and the problems of projecting the diasporic experience in relation to a binarism that sees a white, conservative centre and a coloured, multicultural periphery. The novel is not unaware that such binaries do exist, but it is more concerned with how quickly the marginalized become victims of their own biases and contribute to the perpetuation of inequalities. The immigrants learn to deny the multiplicity among themselves, thereby creating a context in which only a simplistic model of oppressor and oppressed can exist.

One of the many ways in which the novel stresses the danger of accepting given identities is by moving back and forth from Trinidad to the immigrant's world in Ontario. The parallels are striking: Homer passes off as a Catholic in Canada in order to secure a job; the mother in Trinidad willingly becomes Christian after the death of her husband. Uncle Shammy spends his days in a mental institution in

Trinidad and Homer fights desperately to stave off a threatening breakdown. The drudgery of the printery in Trinidad is matched by the boredom of working in a library in Hamilton. Such examples do not forge connections between the two countries, or lead to a naive universalism about the human condition in general. But they do emphasize continuities that in turn repudiate easy generalizations about home and exile. The past thus becomes a reminder that the notion of identity does not sit easily within a binary model.

A totalized identity, the novel repeatedly claims, can only make the immigrant's life a trauma, except for those who work within an essentialized sense of self. Those who resist such attempts at fixity may want to return "home," only to find that home is no longer the same. Some recreate the old world, as Bay does when he escapes into an agrarian fantasy and constructs a map of Guyana in his garden. For Homer, the defence is a cynicism that costs him his marriage but enables him to resist fragmentation. When, for instance, he tells his wife: "What eating me? You want to know? Every damn body want to take a little bite from me. Bite, foot gone. Bite, hand gone. Bite, belly gone. Bite, Homer gone" (182) he recognizes the total obliteration that is possible with the disintegration of his identity. In short, the novel is about the complex process by which the denial of multiplicity leads to the process of constructing simplistic identities that are themselves hegemonic and oppressive. And it is reassuring that in a novel that, despite all its humour, projects a bleak vision, the protagonist survives. Homer does not succeed—at least not in the conventional sense—in Canada, but he learns that he must jettison mimicry and forge his own path, even if it means locating himself at an angle to his own community. In its attempt to depict plurality as a necessary condition of recuperating the experience of exile, *Homer in Flight* becomes a thoughtful and intriguing novel. Maharaj is an important novelist, and one looks forward to his next work.

Joseph Pivato

IMMIGRANT DEVILS

Devils in Paradise: Writing on Post-emigrant Cultures
by Pasquale Verdicchio.
Toronto: Guernica Editions, 1997

Italian Canadian poet and critic Pasquale Verdicchio has chosen a powerful image for the title of his first collection of essays. The paradise of the title is the New World, pristine and beautiful; the devils are the unwanted immigrants who come in and corrupt it. The image captures Verdicchio's historical reconstruction of the racialization of various ethnic groups in North America. The essays collected in this volume examine a number of texts which engage the discourse on race: Italian Canadian novels, the films of Spike Lee, minority women's narratives, John Fante's novels, Italian poets, the photographs of Tina Modotti, the language of Italian immigrants and personalities from popular culture. While Italians in North America are the primary focus of these essays the discourse is taken well beyond the immigrant ghetto and European culture.

The first essay is appropriately entitled "Subalterns Abroad," an allusion to the writings of Antonio Gramsci who coined the term *subaltern*. The political philosophy of Gramsci informs many of the essays as Verdicchio explores the roots of race in North American culture. In this essay he compares Italians in the United States with those in Canada in order to discover the nature of multiculturalism. By including the United States and its history of racism, Verdicchio has the reader question Canadian assumptions about cultural differences and reconsider terms we commonly accept. For example, he finds that he must use the terms *race* and *ethnicity* together, because in the United States the two are linked in the politics of identity, whereas in Canada they are not often seen together. Are Canadians reluctant to discuss issues of race and racism, or do they simply hide the notions within the term "ethnic"? Verdicchio briefly examines the work of Antonio D'Alfonso, Marco Micone and Dore Michelut to explore how these writers question the forces of the dominant English culture in Canada.

In the essay "The Borders of Writing: Nation, Language, Migration," Verdicchio looks at the use of majority languages by minority writers as a means of resistance to cultural assimilation. He compares writers within Italy itself who challenge linguistic standardization with Italian Canadian writers who use the English language in a subversive manner. In the postcolonial context Verdicchio observes that this is a worldwide phenomenon:

> Today, the languages of colonialism are themselves being colonized by the very elements they sought to subdue . . . Nations that find themselves overwhelmed by the influx of diverse populations are hard pressed to define a national characteristic that, in turn, represents their relationship with the rest of the world. (16)

In "Tracing the Ground of Identity" Verdicchio compares popular icons like Madonna and Camille Paglia to women writers who engage the questions of race and racism. Popular culture can tell us a good deal about the racial identities of young people. In contrast to street culture we have the obscure Italian American novelist, John Fante. In "Fante's Inferno" Verdicchio explores the racism and sexual tension in *Ask the Dust*, between the character Bandini and a Mexican girl. Is Fante racist or is he in fact attacking racist notions? Do we consider this question only in the American context, or must we consider Fante's Italian background? Maybe an answer can be found in another Verdicchio essay?

There is one important essay that makes the whole collection worth reading: "If I Was Six Feet Tall, I Would Have Been Italian," an exploration of the cinema of Spike Lee. The Italian characters in *Do the Right Thing* (1989) and *Jungle Fever* (1991) illustrate Lee's understanding of the position of Italians on the margins of American society. Verdicchio's critical analysis of *Do the Right Thing* looks at

Lee's use of the history of racism against Italians, their self-hatred as immigrants in juxtaposition to racism against African Americans.

> These films use Italian immigrants as a sounding board to address issues of ethnic inclusion/exclusion, solidarity, difference, and similarity. Lee casts Italians as different, but not so different from Blacks, because in the end they too cannot achieve full acceptance. This re-establishes the Italians' ties with the typifications assigned them in their homeland and as immigrants, and thereby highlights their marginality. (78)

Verdicchio considers the shifting racial identity of Italians in Europe and in North America and shows how race is a social construct determined by political power rather than by biology. In *Jungle Fever* Lee investigates the question of sexual relationships between Italians and African Americans. By depicting a young Italian American woman having an affair with an African American man, Lee explores not only racial identity, but also the Italian American male's fragile sense of sexual potency. Deep-seated fears come out in both groups over this affair, which becomes an anatomy of a mixed -race sexual relationship.

Because of his work on Gramsci, Verdicchio brings a philosophical-political perspective into his essays not often found among Canadian writers and theorists. It remains to be seen what influence these theories will have on our reading of ethnic minority writing in Canada. It is clear from the essays in this collection that Italian Canadian writers are engaged in more than just producing novels and poems, they are consciously creating an intellectual discourse on the many aspects of ethnic minority writing and film. This intellectual enterprise is assisted in large part by Guernica Editions through its ongoing series of essay collections on questions of minority cultures.

Maria Redi

PACI'S SEVENTH

The Rooming-House
by F G Paci.
Ottawa: Oberon Press, 1996

With the publication of his best-selling first novel *The Italians* in 1978, Frank Paci became one of the founding authors of Italian Canadian literature. His importance as a writer was confirmed with the highly acclaimed second novel, *Black Madonna*, a work still popular in university literature courses because of its powerful portrait of two Italian immigrant women. The force of Paci's prose is due to his uncompromising honesty and heartfelt realism. Even if there were no body of writing that we could identify as Italian Canadian, Paci would be an important voice in Canadian writing. The publication of a seventh novel of this high quality is an achievement in itself.

Frank Paci, Pier Giorgio Di Cicco, Marco Micone, Mary di Michele, Fulvio Caccia, Mary Melfi and Antonio D'Alfonso were not the first Italian Canadian writers, since there had been several immigrant writers from Italy in the 1930s. But they were the first to realize that there was a critical mass of texts to constitute an identifiable body of writing. This was articulated by Pier Giorgio Di Cicco in the introduction to *Roman Candles* (1978). Joseph Pivato, who is familiar with the history of this Italian phenomenon, maintains that the critical year is 1978, when these writers began to publish in English and French. In 1986 they founded the Association of Italian Canadian Writers.

The Rooming-House is the fourth novel in the series which began with *Black Blood* (1991) and narrates the story of Marco Trecroci, a young man who grows up in an Italian immigrant family in Sault Ste Marie, Ontario, the setting of several Paci novels. These novels trace the development of Marco (now called Mark) from a boy to an aspiring novelist and so constitute an apprenticeship narrative about the growth of the young artist. *The Rooming-House* finds Mark in Toronto working as a proofreader for Adanac Press, a nationalist Canadian publisher, and trying to write in his spare time. The naive young novelist is having trouble with his writing and with his relationships with various women. He becomes infatuated with an older woman, Marian, an editor-writer at the press, and with Milly, a sexually active next-door neighbour in the rooming house. Paci's reconstruction of the 1960s culture of Toronto is fascinating in its details.

Mark has successfully completed university and is ready to begin his career as a writer, but is haunted by his experiences as a young man back in the Soo and at university. And while he was encouraged to write by none other than Margaret Laurence herself, he has a sense of inferiority about his abilities. This poor sense of self esteem is not helped by the senior editor at the press, Charlie Macrae, who is not willing to recommend Mark for a junior arts grant so that he can finish his novel. Macrae does not think Mark knows the English language well enough since it is not his mother tongue. This is not an unusual experience for the ethnic minority writer in Canada. We recall that W O Mitchell had Nino Ricci leave his writing class at York University, "as he would never be a writer." Ricci's first novel, *Lives of the Saints*, went on to win the Governor General's Award for Fiction some years later.

In the current Paci novel there is little evidence of Mark's Italian immigrant background. The reference to the language problem is one of the few suggestions that perhaps Mark is not a WASP. It is as if Mark, by earning an English degree from the University of Toronto, has escaped his Italian peasant background. Of course he has not transformed himself into an English Canadian since he is reminded of his ethnic roots in many subtle ways. Before Mark can become a writer he has to achieve greater maturity both as a human being and in his relationships with others. He gradually outgrows his sexual fantasies with the women in his life and finds that what they have to offer him are sad stories about their lives. Mark learns to relate to them as human beings who need love rather than as objects. Mark is eventually prepared to begin his writing and to meet Amanda, the woman he falls in love with near the end of the novel. They plan to go to Europe together, in particular Italy, a recognition that Mark must learn more about his immigrant background before he can deal with his new Canadian reality as a novelist.

Unlike the previous novel in the series, *Sex and Character*, this one is less preoccupied with abstract philosophical ideas about the meaning of life and art and focused more on real human relationships. We are reminded of *Black Madonna* as the narrative explores the motivation and behavior of its women in sensitive detail. Is it easier for an immigrant who has experienced life from the margins to understand the aspirations and fears of women? We would like to think the answer is yes.

This novel can stand on its own as an engaging story. But it only tells part of the story of Mark's life. Is it important for a reader to know where Mark has come from, and where he has been? The novel also anticipates where Mark is about to go. It is not the trip to Italy that it foreshadows, but the fact that Mark is still learning about himself and has a long way to go. Thus the novel is incomplete because its subject is an incomplete man. But then, many ethnic minority stories deal with people who are still becoming, still forming from the fragments of an uprooting and migration, and the trauma and adjustments of a new country. Paci is a master of the art of self-exploration. It is a very complex quest and we need the series of novels to examine every detail in the life of its character.

Leslie Sanders

PLENITUDE

Returning the Empties: Selected Poems 1960s-1990s
by Lakshmi Gill.
Toronto: TSAR, 1998

Returning the Empties. As the title of a volume of selected poetry, the image is particularly striking, and resolutely Canadian. It evokes a housekeeping ritual that marks the aftermath of a party, the last act of moving house, or merely a weekly routine. The gesture is ecological, tidy—and somewhat melancholy. The author's note on her title remarks, "I quaffed and I thank you for the fill of life, Canada," but without this gloss, the title seems more darkly ambiguous and ambivalent.

It is difficult not to read Lakshmi Gill's intensely personal poetry as autobiographical. If it is so, then the last decade of her life has brought her much anguish. The collection is divided into decades, and the Nineties section contains poems of retrospection made more pressing by cancer. In one poem, the poet seeks a house in which to die: "Set off by a long narrow road / deep in its five acres of woods, / the house greets me: Will you be the one?" "We have a life in the city," her son observes, drawing her back from the house and the various ends she imagines for herself ("Househunting "). Observing her sister's struggle with the same disease, the poet observes: "What it is, of course, is / she's scared to die . . . But, I say, what if the cancer / doesn't get you? / What if a falling piano splats you instead?" ("What If"). "Time Expired" contemplates a life's span as the relentless movement of the hand of a parking meter. "At the End" imagines the arrival of "The poem that will write itself at the last minute . . . " Yet there is no self-pity in these poems, rather there is a quiet curiosity about change. "I don't know when it got away from me / or if I even had a say in it, say, / a little say in its transformations . . . " ("I Turn"). Gill retains in this recent work the deadly wit that marks her earlier poems, for example in this retrospective ("The Poeteacher") of marriage: "The man / on the recliner with beer on the floor flipped / her channels, turned her off after the news at eleven / and broke her heart". After raising three children on her own, "on a half-time job in a city where all / needed jobs. The jungle was more civilized / . . . Now it is quiet . . . Gently it comes in the lovely hour/when everything shines inside her: the joystick, the ruins, / the mislaid unborn." The word *elegiac* comes to mind trying to describe the tones of the poems in this first section, yet by no means are they all introspective. The opening salvo, for example, "When the LA Cyborgs Come," rebukes Canadians and Americans alike (shades of Atwood's *Surfacing* in its tone). The apparent refuge that Canada holds for "the misfits, the drifters" is slyly compromised by the ways in which the poem depicts return to what is left of the land, thanks to the "tree-huggers." Or, more metaphysically, "In Search of New Diction" ruminates on the variety of ways humankind has imagined its relation to gods, to no avail: "What lifetime of gods in our minds / What fascination with omnipotence / Immortality, hierarchy. / What need for perfection. / Who will burn the old words?"

Four decades of writing are included here, beginning with the present and moving to Gill's earliest poetry from the Sixties. Read together, the collection is a life's chronicle, especially the chronicle of an immigrant life and consciousness. Beginning as it does in the present, read in sequence the poems reduplicate the imaginative journey and yearning of which Gill speaks in her epilogue, "Puja for Papa":

> Somewhere, maybe in Hoshiarpur
> in his village Posi,
> the ashes that flowed from Stanley Park waters
> have found a river there
> rested there in its depth in fluvial tendrils.
> A final rest
> beyond my imaginings, in that village
> I dream of on solitary nights

in this foreign city
when my heart pauses as his face forms in the dark
and his voice assures me:
Someday, you will see India,
you will come home, you will know home,
you will flow back into your beginnings.

We know from a poem in the initial section that the poet, native of the Philippines, adulthood primarily spent in Canada, (principally in New Brunswick and then Vancouver), never made that journey back to the land of her father. Yet the poems that are strung out along these years, like the flowing ashes, do reach back and mingle. She is, as she said in an interview,[1] "mongrel" herself, and her references mix and blend as in "Doxology to Grandmother" ("Glory to you, Grandma / vessel of noble children / Mahawoman, ever present / in the day of Brahma . . . "). Many poems of the earlier years rely on New Brunswick landscapes, mediating their meditations through nature, as in "Marshscapes" and the poems from "Sackville Serenata" from the Eighties, or "Marshland Wind" from the Seventies. Gill works in a variety of forms, and achieves much that is moving and memorable in each. In the early work her immigrant loneliness and uneasiness are a concern, but later she embraces her displacement in "I Tell You, Mr Biswas," concluding in her dialogue with the central character of V S Naipaul's novel of the period, "my homelessness is my freedom." "Relax, Mr Biswas," she advises him. "They, too, have their angst. It's their word. / Pluck up the roots of their language / and be free." Yet Vancouver, and by extension Canada, remains a "foreign city"—for father and daughter alike. For Gill, however, the place of beginnings stretches out over generations, and homelessness is a shared inheritance. She writes in a Seventies poem: "Countryless, orphaned, / we were sailors, / scurvy-ridden, eating rats / who had thrown away the charts / caught in the doldrum. / Land, ho was a cloud on the horizon / as we lay dying on the deck / in this ship that stood still" ("Home"). This "we" links her and her father, as in the later work, but in her poetry the homelessness of which she speaks becomes a dimension of spirit, the only way to counter and accommodate a life that by its nature affords no peace. Gill is no romantic; nature's harshness is tangible and so the object of her curious gaze;

human nature's harshness is more amorphous and disturbed and is typically implied in her meditations rather than directly confronted.

Taken together, Lakshmi Gill's poems are haunting; individually they are memorable. There is no single thematic here, but rather the lifelong reflections of a woman who sees, thinks and feels deeply, turning her estrangement and pain into understanding and insight. I began by noting the Canadianness of Gill's title, and so I will also conclude. Gill's poems cross and re-cross this country; they evoke its writers as well as its history and politics in the latter half of this century. They fully inhabit this space, and return not empties but plentitude. TSAR should be congratulated for making this collection possible.

NOTE

1. Interview with Arun Mukherjee and Leslie Sanders, August 1994 (unpublished).

Contributors

JOHN CLEMENT BALL is professor of English at the University of New Brunswick.

FRANK BIRBALSINGH is professor of English at York University, Toronto. He is the author of, among other works, *Novels and the Nation: Essays on Canadian Literature.*

DIANA BRYDON is professor of English at the University of Western Ontario.

FREDERICK IVOR CASES's review was first published in *The Toronto South Asian Review*, Volume 2, Number 1.

LIEN CHAO is the author of *Beyond Silence: Chinese Canadian Literature in English.* She lives in Toronto.

RAMABAI ESPINET is professor of English and Communications at Seneca College in Toronto.

LINDA HUTCHEON is professor of English at the University of Toronto and the author of, among other works, *The Canadian Postmodern: A Study of Contemporary English-Canadian Fiction.*

CHELVA KANAGANAYAKAM is professor of English at Trinity College, University of Toronto.

G D KILLAM's review was first published in *The Toronto South Asian Review*, Volume 8, Number 2.

COLIN LOWNDES's review was first published in *The Toronto South Asian Review*, Volume 8, Number 1.

AMIN MALAK teaches English and Third World literatures at Grant MacEwan Community College in Edmonton.

DANIEL MCBRIDE's review was first published in *The Toronto South Asian Review*, Volume 6, Number 1.

BRUCE MEYER is Director of Creative Writing Program at the University of Toronto School of Continuing Studies. His next book, *The One Story: Literature and the Great Books*, is forthcoming from Harper Collins.

ARUN PRABHA MUKHERJEE is professor of English at York University in Toronto. She is the author of numerous works, most recently *Postcolonialism: My Living.*

UMA PARAMESWARAN is professor of English at the University of Winnipeg.

JOSEPH PIVATO teaches at Athabasca University in Edmonton and is the editor of *The Anthology of Italian-Canadian Writing.*

MARIA REDI is a writer living in Saskatoon.

LESLIE SANDERS is professor in the Humanities department, York University, Toronto.

SUMANA SEN-BAGCHEE teaches in the English Department of the University of Alberta.

AMRITJIT SINGH is professor of English at Rhode Island College.

KRISANTHA SRI BHAGGIYADATTA is a writer and poet living in Toronto.

RINALDO WALCOTT is assistant professor of humanities at York University, Toronto, where he teaches African American and Black Canadian literatures. He is the author of *Black Like Who? Writing Black Canada.*

Source Acknowledgements

"Dialogue as a Discursive Strategy in Chinese Canadian Poetry" by Lien Chao was first published in *Beyond Silence: Chinese Canadian Literature in English* by Lien Chao, 1997 (TSAR).

"A Passionate Dance: The Poetry of Rienzi Crusz" by Chelva Kanaganayakam was first published as "Introduction" in *Insurgent Rain: Selected Poems 1974–1996* by Rienzi Crusz, 1997 (TSAR).

"The Singing Never Stops: Languages of Italian Canadian Writers" by Joseph Pivato was first published in *The Toronto Review of Contemporary Writing Abroad*, vol. 16, no. 3 (Summer 1998).

"The Shahrazadic Tradition: Rohinton Mistry's *Such a Long Journey* and the Art of Storytelling" by Amin Malak was first published in *Journal of Commonwealth Literature*, vol. 28, no. 2 (1993).

"Canadian Nationalism, Canadian Literature and Racial Minority Women" by Arun Prabha Mukherjee was first published in *Postcolonialism My Living* by Arun Mukherjee, 1998 (TSAR).

Reviews by various contributors were first published in *The Toronto South Asian Review* and *The Toronto Review of Contemporary Writing Abroad*, 1982–1999.

AUTHOR INDEX